For Joseph,
who deserved better.

Contents

Names   1

204824   21

164   63

17,923   133

Strike   215

20378   267

Afterwards   289

Sources   319

"I would like to express my opinion. I think it is a most improper procedure."

Hearing this, the councillor will have looked up from his papers, spread out in front of him on the high desk at which he sat. There were a great many of them and he had spent the last few minutes thumbing them into a sort of bundle.

There were too many papers, in fact, to be read in a single afternoon. A single very warm afternoon.

What the councillor said, as he heard it, seemed weak; his voice thin and far too high.

"May I say, we have nothing to do with the way of procedure. We are the members of the tribunal. It is all right for you to come here and talk like this, but we are spending our time for nought."

"Are you suggesting that I am spending my time for nought?"

There was something in the question that demanded a firm reply.

"Address your remarks to the chairman. We are spending our time for nought and we are not going to sit here and try these cases. I am not going to come wasting my time for nothing and let cases go off like this."

His collar, already stiff, felt suddenly tight and his moustache ragged. The wretched man simply would not let up.

"You talk about wasting your time, but I should like to point out that you might also consider my time, which is possibly as valuable to me as yours is to you."

His voice was rising even more and he began to think he could be heard outside, on the street. He was now aware of the windows; the open windows. They're not keeping the heat out, for God's sake, they're letting it in.

"You might perhaps be in the army."

He thought that might sting.

"I am a volunteer for the work I do, as well as you members of the tribunal are. I was somewhere else yesterday. Today I am here, and tomorrow I will be somewhere else again. By this action of yours my time is wasted perhaps more than yours, as I have to go a great deal further than you."

"It does not matter to me, Mr Chairman, what time of his is wasted. I am speaking of my own time."

"It is supposed my time is paid for, but I can assure you it is not so."

"Instead of coming here on soft jobs, you ought to be in the army."

"I?"

"Yes, you."

"If you think a man nearly fifty years of age—"

"They are volunteering up to fifty."

"I have volunteered."

"Have you?"

"Yes, I have."

"Then it is a pity they did not take you."

There was laughter, but it was more hesitant than he had expected. Then the chairman spoke.

"The meeting is closed, gentlemen."

NAMES

1

The red sails of Marsh Mill stand out from the white of the tower against which they turn. It is a seventy-foot cone whose distinctive colour comes from the wash that coats its sides. For a while, it was also smeared in animal fat to make it waterproof.

The mill was put up in 1794 at the expense of Bold Fleetwood Hesketh. He was the lord of the manor and had already drained the low-lying, waterlogged land on which it would stand and for which it would be named. He is remembered in an inscription on the lintel over the tiny door.

The tapering, shuttered wooden sails are at least half as long as the mill is tall and they hang from a huge wooden cap, which sits on top of the cone like an upturned boat. The cap could be turned into the wind and the black of the tar that coats it stands out from the red of the sails and the white of the tower.

By 1896, the wooden sails were rotten through and through and one of them had dropped into the yard below. It was then that Bold Hesketh's successor got rid of the mill. The following year, in celebration of the Diamond Jubilee, it was painted from cap to base in patriotic colours and they say the job was done without scaffolding of any kind. Bold's successor was his nephew, Peter Hesketh-Fleetwood, and he had good reason to sell. In the years that followed, the cost of repairing the mill would come close to £300.

Marsh Mill ground the grain and then the corn of local farmers for more than a century. It would go out of business in the 1920s, reopen at the very end of the decade as a café but close for good when two women fell to their deaths from the decrepit balcony that ran around the second floor. It would serve as a furniture store and then a factory where false teeth were made, but for now, because its gear was badly out of date, the mill produced nothing but animal feed.

*

Joseph Blackburn was born in 1886, in plain sight of the mill. He was the son of Thomas and Elizabeth Blackburn, who were in their forties by then. They already had eight living children and their ninth would be their last, so Joseph was closer in age to his nephews and nieces than to some of his siblings.

In common with many people of their class and time, members of the Blackburn family shared a small number of given names. In Joseph's generation and the two before it, the boys included at least nine Johns, seven Williams, six Jameses, five Thomases, three Edwards and Septimuses and one Charles, one Alfred and one Miller. Of Josephs there were two, and each of them also had the middle name Septimus. Among the girls there were five Marys, three Elizabeths, two Ellens, Janes and Mary Annes and one Ann, Nancy, Margaret, Rosamond, Roshannah, Rachel, Hilda and Emily. The Blackburns had shown a little more imagination in their naming of girls.

Although I call him Joseph, I know that won't be the only name he answered to. For much of this story he was simply 'a local man' or 'an attested man' and at the end, I imagine, he will have been just 'Private'. On official letters, of the kind that had started coming through the door more frequently of late, he might have been called 'Mr', although in many cases a simple number will have been made to suffice. At home, when he was at home, he will have been 'Joe' and 'our Joe', and also 'son' and, lately, 'Daddy'. In more cloistered moments, I dare say he might have been 'darling'.

Joseph married Jessie Bennett when he was twenty-two and together, they had two children: Elizabeth and another Joseph, born either side of the start of the Great War. Neither child would come to know its father properly, for Joseph Blackburn died in August 1918.

*

For all but the last few months of his life, Joseph, and then Jessie and then Elizabeth and Joseph Junior, lived in Thornton, at Rose Cottage on Raikes Road. The town lies at the heart of the Fylde, a peninsula in Lancashire that is bordered on three sides by water – by Morecambe Bay to the north, the Ribble Estuary to the south and the Irish Sea to the west. The Fylde has a long coastline and it is there that its largest towns can be found: Blackpool, and the other resorts of Lytham, St Annes and Cleveleys, and the port of Fleetwood.

There have been people there since ancient times and those people included the Setantii, who were part of a much larger tribe that dominated what is now northern England. The name was given to them by their Roman conquerors and it meant 'dwellers in the country of water'. The Setantii occupied large parts of present-day Lancashire and adjacent counties, from the Mersey to the Lake District. They were an ingenious people and the first, it is said, to build a port on the west coast of Britain. That port stood on land now lost to the sea close to the mouth of the Wyre, which is the broad tidal river that cuts the peninsula in two. The river is the longest in England whose end can be seen from its beginnings.

The Fylde was also known as Windmill Land, because of the large number of ancient mills that dotted the landscape, clinging stubbornly to whatever slight inclination could be found, their wooden sails stuttering in the uninterrupted gale. There were once around forty of them and even as late as the 20th century, at least fifteen remained – at Kirkham, where the mill was a lookout post during the Civil War; in Carleton and Hambleton;

5

in Freckleton, Wrea Green and Treales; and in Singleton and Staining, where, unusually, the sails had been fashioned from canvas. Lytham Windmill is the most venerable of them all, there having been one in the town for over eight hundred years; while the rickety mill at Warton had been taken there in the 1770s from the village of Rufford, which lies a few miles to the south, across the River Ribble. The mill at Clifton and Damside Mill in Pilling were each the work of a local millwright, Ralph Slater. He it was who also built Marsh Mill for Bold Hesketh.

The windmill that lies closest to Blackpool now stands on a main road into the town. Little Marton Mill was built in the 1830s to replace a smaller one that had existed for at least forty years. It, too, is built in the tower style, with white walls, a black cap and tapering sails. For the last nine decades it has been dedicated to the memory of Charles Allen Clarke, the radical, writer and publisher.

Allen Clarke was a devotee of Walt Whitman, and of his devotee, Edward Carpenter. He was also a friend of Robert Blatchford, the Manchester-based poet, journalist, campaigner and bicyclist. With Carpenter and Blatchford, Clarke shared a faith in a sort of libertarian socialism and he would make repeated attempts to put that faith into practice. At the general election of 1900, for example, he was chosen to contest the parliamentary seat of Rochdale in the Labour cause. Though his campaign was unsuccessful, it was also impressive, not least because parts of his manifesto were written in Lancashire dialect. Clarke had recently published perhaps his greatest book, *The Effects of the Factory System*, which offered an impassioned critique of the cotton industry and came to the attention of Tolstoy. The grand old Russian writer had the book translated into his own language and he would exchange letters with its author for a number of years.

In the early 20th century, Allen Clarke lived in Blackpool. There, he founded his own model settlement, the Daisy Colony, and, from premises among the oyster bars and phrenologists of the Golden Mile, produced widely-read newspapers, such as *Teddy Ashton's Northern Weekly*. And it was Clarke who first called the Fylde 'Windmill Land'. That was the title he gave to another of his books, which was inspired by bicycling trips he, like Robert Blatchford, had made. The book was a heady brew of history, folklore and plain tall tales, and it was published in January 1916, just after the Battle of Loos and just before the Battle of Verdun.

The Blackburns, and also the Bennetts, lived in places Allen Clarke wrote about – small settlements clustered together on the banks of the Wyre, to the east of Blackpool with Fleetwood more or less to the north. The village of Preesall, which sits across the river from Fleetwood, is one such place. The site of another impressive tower-type windmill since the early 19th century, it was from there that most of Joseph's grandparents came. One of his grandfathers, meanwhile, was born in the tiny but resolutely seafaring village of Skippool, which sits on the west bank of the Wyre, on a creek at the point where the river takes an emphatic rightwards turn towards the Bowland Fells.

For a while in the 18th century, and perhaps improbably, Skippool rivalled Liverpool for the size of its trade. The little port had good links with the Caribbean and ships from Barbados could often be seen there, unloading their cargoes of rum, sugar and tobacco. Skippool also received flax and cotton from Russia as well as bird guano, which came from Africa and was used locally to make fertiliser. There were stone-built warehouses along the quayside, as well as a bone mill which – ten generations of local schoolchildren have grown up knowing for certain – was haunted by the ghost of a miller who had hanged himself inside. The Skippool of the Georgian age was a place of strong ale and tottering mariners, of whores, smuggling and press gangs, and of ad hoc cockpits where illicit gambling could be done. From the mid-19th century, however, the dominance of the expanding docks at Liverpool, and also the growth of the town and port of Fleetwood, posed a challenge to which the village found itself unable to respond. Within a few years, Skippool had entered a terminal decline.

Mainly, though, Joseph and his relatives lived in Thornton, which lies immediately to the south of Fleetwood with Blackpool to the west.

2

The place where Thornton now stands has been settled since the Iron Age, and it was once crossed by a proper Roman road. It is the turn that road took, sharply to the north between modern-day Preston and Kirkham, that is said to show that Fleetwood was not the first port on the Wyre.

There has been a village of sorts there since at least Saxon times, although it is first mentioned in the Domesday Book, which calls it Toretun in the ancient 'hundred' of Amunderness. The area is described as mainly waste with few inhabitants and that was still the case on the eve of the 19th century, when, before putting up his big, white windmill, Bold Fleetwood Hesketh set about draining the marshes. It was only then that agriculture could begin in earnest.

The lands of the Hesketh family took in much of the Fylde and also large parts of surrounding areas. By the 20th century, they stretched from Heysham in the north to Southport in the south and resembled nothing so much as the old kingdom of the Setantii. For close to two hundred years, the family had been joined to the Fleetwoods, the heart of whose estate was at Rossall. That was a settlement which had once been owned by a brother of King Harold and was occupied by Cistercian monks until the Dissolution. There, on the edge of the Fylde and at the westernmost fringe of its estate, the Fleetwood family put up a great hall. A whitewashed, rambling edifice of irregular shape, with libraries, an organ room and a gazebo, it was the latest of several that had, over the years, been effaced by the sea and the constantly shifting sands.

By the 1830s, Rossall Hall was occupied by Sir Peter

Hesketh-Fleetwood, Bold Hesketh's successor, who had been High Sheriff of Lancashire and was now a Member of Parliament for Preston. A Conservative and supporter of Robert Peel who, like many such men, would come to proclaim himself a Whig, Sir Peter favoured the cause of Free Trade and opposed slavery. He also argued for the abolition of capital punishment and produced one of the first English translations of Victor Hugo's novella *The Last Day of a Condemned Man*, to which he added his own *Observations on Capital Punishment*. Sir Peter's work was dedicated to Queen Victoria, a fact which fuelled suspicions that the new monarch also took an abolitionist view.

The fourth decade of the 19th century was a wretched one for Sir Peter: his first wife succumbed to tuberculosis, he himself contracted scarlet fever and then lost an eye and Rossall Hall was badly damaged in a storm. His remarriage in 1837 brought only temporary consolation, for the following year, Sir Peter's daughter, Maria, died at the age of eleven years. She would be interred in the family vault in a casket made entirely of glass.

It was Sir Peter who built the first real defences against the Irish Sea, and in the years that followed, he could often be seen touring them in a two-wheeled pony trap. It was also Sir Peter who developed the town of Fleetwood, but the debts he incurred in doing so would devastate his life and the family estate.

Thornton began to develop at much the same time. In 1840, just before Joseph Blackburn's father was born, a direct railway line was opened up to Fleetwood, linking the port to Preston and the new and expanding national network that lay beyond. The line was in part paid for by Sir Peter Hesketh-Fleetwood, but it would be his last such investment and one he would never recoup. Within four years he had auctioned off the contents of Rossall Hall and left Lancashire for good.

For a while, train passengers hoping to travel to Scotland could do so only by alighting at Fleetwood and completing their journey by boat. In 1865, when Jessie Blackburn's mother was born, a halt was opened up at a convenient point on the Preston-to-Fleetwood line and a station was erected. It was named Thornton-for-Cleveleys and would remain in place, even after a direct route to Glasgow had been established.

The development of Thornton that had begun with the coming of the railway picked up speed in 1890, when a chemical works was opened by the newly-created United Alkali Company. The people and money the new works attracted led to significant expansion of the town and in April 1900, it was given one of the new urban district councils, replacing the parish council that had been created only six years before. Thereafter, and for much of the century, chemicals and the land would be the most significant industries in Thornton and by far the greatest employers of local men.

*

At the time of the Great War, then, Thornton was a flourishing town. It covered almost a thousand acres of land, contained nearly twelve hundred houses and had a population of five thousand people. It could also boast a brand-new sewage system, installed at a cost of over £20,000, and its station was an established feature of the national system.

Nor had the representation of the people been ignored. The council had twelve elected members, three for each of the town's North, South, East and West wards, and they convened at the offices in Four Lane Ends on the second Thursday of every month. The council's officers, meanwhile, comprised a clerk and a treasurer; a medical officer of health, who was a local doctor; a collector of taxes; and a surveyor, a gas manager and an inspector of nuisances, three jobs that were combined in a single, no doubt very busy, man.

Thornton had a police station in the charge of a sergeant,

together with seven constables, and it had a fire station with a superintendent. It also had four schools, the oldest of which had been founded two centuries before, and it could boast several places of worship, including the Anglican Christ Church and the neo-Gothic Roman Catholic Church of the Sacred Heart, which was twice as big. There were chapels for the Wesleyans, the Methodists and the Primitive Methodists, and also an iron mission church, out on the marshes by the new chemical works.

The town had two banks, each of which was open for four hours on Tuesdays and Fridays, and for those with notable events to record, a registrar visited every Tuesday morning, when he could be found at the house of a Mr Billington, near to the railway station. And through the town's three sub-post offices, the people of Thornton received six postal deliveries a day.

Alongside its plethora of farmers, market gardeners and nurserymen, the town also had builders, joiners, plumbers and an architect; a solicitor; a cabinetmaker; a cab proprietor; a cycle-repairer; grocers, greengrocers, confectioners and fried fish dealers; a beer, wine and spirits retailer; newsagents, shoemakers, hardware dealers and ironmongers; a coal merchant and a chimney sweep; several physicians; more than one insurance agent; a stationer; a bootmaker; hairdressers; a draper, a tailor and a dressmaker; millers, a milliner and a midwife; a manure manufacturer; a watchmaker; and a wholesale pianoforte dealer. In Miss Ethel Tonge and Miss Martha W. Park, LLCM, Thornton also had not one, but two teachers of music.

The town had at least one drugstore and three public houses: the Gardeners' Arms, the Burn Naze and the Bay Horse. The town also had branches of the Fleetwood Co-operative Society and the Manchester Taylor-Mills Mutual Self-Help Money Society; clubs for bowling, billiards and tennis; a section of the St John Ambulance brigade; and a lodge of the Royal Antediluvian Order of Buffaloes. It could also boast a regular meeting of the Independent Order of Rechabites, which took place on the evening of every fourth Monday, in a 'prospect tent' at the Primitive Methodist chapel.

Finally, Thornton had a Ratepayers' and Property Owners' Association, a Masonic lodge that met every fourth Saturday, and a Conservative Club and a 'habitation' of the Primrose League, each of which was named for the town's Member of Parliament, Colonel W. W. Ashley.

3

Wilfred William Ashley, after whom both the club and the habitation in Thornton were named, had an impressive lineage. He was a son of Evelyn Ashley, a lawyer and politician who had served as private secretary and biographer to Lord Palmerston. The two-time Prime Minister of the United Kingdom, who began as a Tory and ended up a Liberal, was the husband of Evelyn's grandmother. She, in turn, was the sister of another two-time Prime Minister, the resolutely Whig Lord Melbourne, who gave Evelyn his middle name.

During the second of W. E. Gladstone's own stints as Prime Minister, Evelyn Melbourne Ashley served as a junior minister, with responsibilities for trade and then for colonial affairs. He was himself a child of Anthony Ashley-Cooper, the seventh Earl of Shaftesbury – the Tory politician and social reformer, whose work brought protections for mental patients and stopped children being sent up chimneys.

Educated at Harrow School and at Magdalen College, Oxford, Wilfred Ashley had since 1906 been Member of Parliament for Blackpool, the parliamentary constituency of which Thornton was then part. In 1918, he would be returned for Fylde, the new constituency into which the town had by then been placed, but four years later, he would quit Thornton for a seat closer to home. Colonel Ashley would, like his father, serve as a minister and eventually, indeed, he would ascend to the Cabinet. He was a man of considerable means, having through his link to Lord Palmerston inherited the Broadlands estate in Hampshire, with its Palladian-style house and Capability Brown gardens, and Classiebawn Castle on the west coast of Ireland.

Colonel Ashley was also a military man. He had been such since 1886, the year of Joseph Blackburn's birth, and he had seen service in the Grenadier Guards. In the first year of the Great War, he commanded the 20th Battalion of the King's Liverpool Regiment, which was one of those that made up the so-called 'Liverpool Pals'. Like others, the 20th was based at the imposing old cavalry barracks that stood in Seaforth, near to the docks immediately to the north of the city of Liverpool.

In 1917, Colonel Ashley helped found the Comrades of the Great War, which was intended to be an overtly patriotic version of other, more radical organisations, such as the National Federation of Discharged and Demobilised Sailors and Soldiers. The principal architect of the Comrades, however, was Edward Stanley, the seventeenth Earl of Derby, who had also been a Grenadier Guardsman. His father had, like Wilfred Ashley after him, represented the town of Blackpool in the House of Commons. A candidate sponsored by the National Federation had recently been the only one to oppose Lord Stanley's son in a by-election in Liverpool. Despite that inconvenience, the younger Stanley had swept to victory, gaining almost three quarters of the vote and becoming, at twenty-two years of age, the 'baby' of the House of Commons. Although he would lose the seat the following year, when the constituency was abolished, he would return to Westminster in 1922, this time in the Fylde seat recently vacated by Wilfred Ashley.

Colonel Ashley would leave the House of Commons altogether in 1924, when he was made a peer, became Baron Mount Temple and joined the House of Lords. His daughter, Edwina, would marry Lord Louis Mountbatten, later Viscount Mountbatten of Burma and the Viceroy and Governor-General of India.

A vocal supporter of the policy of appeasement towards Nazi Germany, Lord Mount Temple would establish the Anglo-German Fellowship and the Anti-Socialist Union, serving as chairman of each organisation simultaneously. He would also call for the revision of the Treaty of Versailles and express his support for Adolf Hitler, whom he would meet several times. Indeed, in September 1936, Lord Mount Temple would share an intimate dinner with the Führer on the eve of the Nuremberg Rally and the following day, at the rally itself, he would be one of those proclaimed Ehrengäste – honoured guests.

*

Joseph Blackburn's father, Thomas, grew potatoes, oats and barley, those being the chief crops in Thornton in Edwardian times. It is likely that he also produced tomatoes and some cabbages. To grant him the dignity he claimed for himself, Thomas Blackburn was a market gardener, working from home and on his own account, and that would be his trade until the day he died. Joseph was at first his father's assistant in the garden and then he became his partner.

As they did their names, members of the Blackburn family shared the same few trades, both among themselves in the early 20th century and with their forebears. Often, and as with Joseph and Thomas, those trades had to do with the land. Joseph's grandfather, great-uncle and uncle had been farmers and at the outbreak of war, many of his other relatives were farm servants. That was true of five of Joseph's uncles and both his mother's grandfathers, and also of three of his own brothers – Edward, Robert and William – who were agricultural labourers. The farms on which these men worked lay within a few miles, and even a few hundred yards, of each other, and of Joseph's own garden, and most were in sight of the River Wyre and of Marsh Mill.

Where Joseph's relatives were not engaged on the land they often followed trades closely connected to it. Another of his grandfathers, John, for example, had been a blacksmith since the 1840s, while in the following decade, John's son, William, was a blacksmith's apprentice. In the family of Joseph's wife, Jessie, there were wheelwrights going back at least three generations, to her grandfather and her great-grandfather. Both men were engaged in that trade at the midpoint of the century and each combined it with that of carpenter, in which the elder of them had been engaged for nearly thirty years. Well before the outbreak of war, the yard beneath Marsh Mill – now free of the battered sail that had once lain there – was home to Jack Breckell's wheelwright shop. He was Jessie's uncle.

A number of Joseph's relatives worked as labourers, even if not on the land. At the turn of the century, for example, his brother, John, was an outdoor labourer while another brother, Edward, who had worked in agriculture, was now a chemical labourer. Edward Blackburn was in fact employed by the United Alkali Company at its new and expanding works at Burn Naze.

As might be expected given the times, Joseph's relatives also worked on the railway. That was at one time true of his father, for example, who was a porter from the time Thornton acquired its station. Thomas Blackburn was a railway platelayer a decade later, when Joseph's brother, John – the future outdoor labourer – was a porter as well. John Blackburn was still working on the railway ten years later, by which time Jessie's uncle, Septimus, was a railway clerk. (He too was still engaged in that office ten years later.) One of her other uncles, James, ran the gamut of railway occupations, having been a labourer, a platelayer, a gatekeeper and, in the 1880s, a porter.

One of Joseph's great-uncles, who was also then a railway porter, had previously worked on the land and would, ten years later, be described as a 'gardener-domestic'. His brother, Robert, meanwhile, had also been a domestic servant, while at the turn of the century, another brother, Thomas, was a footman, if only of the non-domestic kind.

Among other occupations of those in Joseph's circle, his

wife's uncle, Charles, worked in the port at Fleetwood, while his own great-uncle, William, had been engaged on the sea, or maybe on the Wyre, as master of a steam dredger. In 1891, Joseph's two sisters, Mary Anne and Jane, were apprentice dressmakers, while in the two decades that followed, his wife's uncle, Robert, worked in a public house in Blackpool. It is, in fact, in the licensed trade that the earliest occupation for one of Joseph's ancestors can be found. As early as 1762, his great-great-grandfather, John, had been the keeper of a Fylde coast inn.

In Jessie Blackburn's family, farming, though it went back at least to her great-great-grandfather, was much less common. Since the 1850s, and maybe long beforehand, many of her ancestors had been butchers. That was true of her great-grandfather, her grandfather and two of her uncles, and it was also true of her father, William. In 1896, however, when he was thirty-four years old, William Bennett was merely a butcher's assistant. The reason for his change of career is obscure, but it might have had something to do with his personal circumstances. It was in that same year that William's wife, Mary Bennett, died. She was Jessie's mother and her daughter was only nine years old at the time.

*

As war approached, then, Joseph Blackburn was in his late twenties and living with Jessie and their children, and also with his parents, at Rose Cottage in Thornton. His brother, Thomas, was also there. The one-time non-domestic footman was older than Joseph and was now working as a chauffeur. Joseph and Thomas were the only children of Thomas and Elizabeth Blackburn still living with their parents. Although most of their siblings remained on the Fylde, at least two of them – their brothers, Robert and William – did not.

Robert Blackburn had moved from Thornton with his wife at the very end of the 19th century. An agricultural labourer on the Fylde, he had now became the operator of a stationary engine. That occupation was one he shared with William, who had joined his brother subsequently, and it would later be taken up by two of Robert's sons.

The place where the two brothers lived was Seaforth, which lies at the mouth of the River Mersey, close to what, at the time, was the edge of the Liverpool docks. That vast maritime complex had been expanding inexorably northwards since the beginning of the century and drawing in men from towns and villages, and from farms, for many miles around. The docks at Liverpool had quickly gained much of the shipping trade that was to be had on the west coast of England, and had established particularly strong links with the Baltic and also, in succession to Skippool, with the islands of the Caribbean.

For much of the 19th century, Seaforth was the site of Seaforth House, a modest mansion about four miles outside Liverpool, which was built by Sir John Gladstone on marshland he had drained for the purpose. A Scottish merchant and later a Member of Parliament, Sir John was a Whig who later became a Tory and he had considerable business interests, not least in Russia and Scandinavia, but also in Demerara and on the island of Jamaica. A trader in corn and cotton, but primarily in sugar, he would in time be the master of a number of plantations and more than a thousand slaves. He was also the father of W. E. Gladstone, who would be Prime Minister of the United Kingdom on no less than four separate occasions and under whom Evelyn Ashley would one day serve.

In Seaforth, Robert and William Blackburn lived in Rossini Street, which consisted of two modest terraces of a couple of dozen houses. That street, along with Balfe and Verdi Streets nearby, and also Bellini Close, lies only yards from the place where Seaforth House used to stand. It was also within two streets of the imposing barracks that housed the King's Liverpool Regiment. The two places were separated by a thoroughfare that would, in a few yards, become Derby Road.

In 1834, when he was already himself a Member of Parliament, the younger Gladstone would render a very valuable political service to his father. As the result of an Act of Parliament passed the year before, the slaves of the Caribbean, and of much of the rest of the British Empire, were now emancipated and those who owned them were handsomely compensated. In Sir John Gladstone's case, his payment, secured by his son, would total around £80 million in modern terms. It was the largest paid to a British slave-owner as a result of the new legislation. The Act had cleared the House of Commons and received the Royal Assent under the gaze of the Secretary of State for the Colonies, a post held at the time by the Honourable Edward Stanley, who would be the fourteenth Earl of Derby.

Just north of Rossini Street, on more or less the only incline offered by the flat, sandy marshland of those parts, there is Moor Lane Mill. Built in the same style as Marsh Mill but a couple of decades later, it too was used for the grinding of corn, and though its sails are long gone, its white tower and squat black cap are still there for anyone to see. The mill stands in Great Crosby, close to the point where that settlement meets its neighbour: another one named Thornton.

204824

4

The station behind him, Joseph walked south. The path rose under his feet and he will have turned his collar up against the gale. This would be one of the wettest months ever. He knew full well what he was going to do and, seeing the churchyard wall, he thought of the little lass who lay in a coffin of glass. He repeated that twice and was surprised at his nervousness.

Joseph was making for the old coaching inn at the edge of the square. It had served as a reading room and was where the news from Waterloo was first proclaimed. The inn was a courthouse for a good few years and he remembered that upstairs, standing in the one bay window, you could see the stocks and the post where they used to whip beggars. When did all that stop? The yard behind was where they held the cattle market and he fancied he could smell a bit of that on the wind.

Joseph heard them before he saw them, the great gaggle of men waiting to be ushered inside, all of them about to do something, surely, that would matter.

*

There is at least one place where traces of the life of Joseph Blackburn can still be found. That is in the dusty corner of the internet where the files are kept of men who served in the First World War. Those files have an antiquated look about them now, even when they are viewed electronically. They are full of forms that are plainly crumbling and that are printed in obscure fonts, and often filled out in a challenging, though elegant cursive script.

Joseph's file is a modest one, running to only a few images, and the information it contains is sparse and given tersely. Little seems to have happened to him that was considered remarkable. What the file does tell us, though, is that in December 1915, Joseph joined the British Army. He did so under the so-called 'Derby scheme'.

In August 1914, when the war began, the Army was a small one, numbering less than a quarter of a million men, with only seven divisions at home and four overseas. The Secretary of State for War, Earl Kitchener, was almost alone in the Cabinet in believing that the conflict would be a long one. He argued that fully seventy divisions, a force equivalent to that of Germany or France, would be required if it was to be brought to a successful conclusion.

There was, therefore, an urgent call for recruits, one reflected in that now-iconic poster. At least at first, the response to the call was dramatic. Kitchener had wanted a hundred thousand men, but by the end of September, almost half a million had enlisted in the Army – or 'Mob' – that would bear his name. In the months that followed, however, as the grim reality of the fighting became clear and public enthusiasm waned, the number of recruits fell sharply. By the end of the year, it was evident that Kitchener's ambitions could not be met by volunteers alone and the calls for compulsion were growing ever louder and harder to ignore.

In August 1915 there had been a national census, which sought to identify everyone aged between fifteen and sixty-five years who was not already in the armed forces. Carried out by each local authority, the census revealed that in England and Wales, there were approximately five million men of military age. Of those men, around a third were already in occupations essential to the war effort and could not, therefore, be spared, while of the remainder, as much as a quarter was assumed to be simply unsuited for service. It seemed, therefore, that the pool of potential soldiers contained fewer than three million men.

That autumn, the Army's recruitment problems increased and in the single month of September, due in no small part to the start of the colossal Loos offensive, fifty thousand British lives were lost. Those losses continued and by the end of the year, the expeditionary force of one hundred thousand men that had landed in France with such enthusiasm had been all but wiped out. On 8th October, Kitchener told the Cabinet that 130,000 men would be needed every month in order to cover "wastage" alone.

The Derby scheme was either a final attempt to avoid conscription or the beginning of preparations to introduce it. More properly known as the 'Group Scheme', it opened on 16th October 1915. Its author was Edward Stanley, the seventeenth Earl of Derby, who had been made Director General of Recruiting only five days before.

*

Edward George Villiers Stanley was born in London in 1865, the same year as Jessie Blackburn's mother and the year the railway came to Thornton. He was the eldest son of the sixteenth earl, whose own father had already been Prime Minister of the United Kingdom twice and would hold that office once more. (In his second period in office, the fourteenth earl had been both preceded and succeeded by Lord Palmerston, who was as good as a grandfather to Wilfred Ashley.)

The young Edward joined the Grenadier Guards as a lieutenant and served in that regiment for ten years. He took part in the second Boer War, where his roles included that of press censor, and he was aide-de-camp to the Governor-General of Canada, who happened to be his father. Edward Stanley entered Parliament at the general election of 1892, having successfully defended the constituency of Westhoughton. A Conservative, he served as a Treasury minister and as Postmaster General before succeeding to the earldom in 1908 and taking his seat in the House of Lords.

For much of his life, Edward Stanley was known as the 'King of Lancashire'. That, indeed, was the title of a biography of him written by Randolph Churchill, Sir Winston's son. Major Churchill was at one time a Member of Parliament for Preston and the successor there to at least six members of the Stanley family, and also to Sir Peter Hesketh-Fleetwood, who had occupied the seat exactly a century before.

In 1911 and 1912, the earl was also Lord Mayor of Liverpool, his most obvious connection with the city being through the family seat at nearby Knowsley Hall, and from July 1916, he would serve in the War Office. At first that was in a junior capacity, but from December of that year, in succession to Earl Kitchener, Lord Derby was the Secretary of State.

In August 1914, during the first, brief flush of enthusiasm for war, Lord Derby organised one of the most successful campaigns of recruitment into Kitchener's Army. In two days in Liverpool, some 1,500 men joined up and before long, four new battalions had been formed. The last of those, which would be the 20th Battalion of the King's Liverpool Regiment, was immediately placed under the command of Colonel Ashley. He was currently the Member of Parliament for Blackpool and, therefore, Joseph Blackburn's representative at Westminster.

The Derby scheme now focused upon men aged between eighteen and forty-one years who were not in an essential occupation, and it required each of them to make a solemn public declaration.

Canvassers visited those men, who had been identified from the August census, handed them a letter from Lord Derby, explaining the scheme, and asked whether they were willing to 'attest' to join the forces. Some willing men entered the Army straight away, while others were permitted to defer their service. Those men were allocated to one of forty-six groups, according to their age and whether they were married. They were promised that only entire groups would be called for active service, that each group would be given at least fourteen days' notice of its call and that single men's groups would be called before married men's. For their part, married men were promised that, unless conscription was introduced, their groups would not be called if too few single men attested.

The Derby scheme would not be an option for very long. On the very day it was introduced, the War Office announced that it would close at midnight on 11th December 1915.

*

The canvasser who visited Rose Cottage found its occupant willing to attest.

On Friday 10th December 1915, no more than forty-eight hours later, as the Derby scheme required, Joseph put his name down for military service. He did so in Poulton, a small, old town, once called 'the metropolis of the Fylde', which lies just below Thornton on the left bank of the Wyre.

At the Golden Ball, with the storm spattering the sash windows as it drove eastwards down Ball Street, Joseph answered questions put to him by a magistrate. The hubbub will have been even greater inside, under the low ceiling of the dimly-lit room, and he will have had to speak up to make himself heard. He said he was twenty-nine years and eleven months old and married, and that he lived on Raikes Road in Little Thornton. That is almost all we can know Joseph ever said about himself. When asked his trade or calling, he said he was a market gardener.

The details Joseph gave were entered on Army form B.2512, for *Short Service (For the Duration of the War, with the Colours and in the Army Reserve)*. He said he was willing to serve, *for the Duration of the War, at the end of which you will be discharged with all convenient speed.* He had been informed:

27

You will be required to serve for one day with the Colours and the remainder of the period in the Army Reserve, in accordance with the provisions of the Royal Warrant dated 20th Oct, 1915, until such times as you may be called up by order of the Army Council. If employed with Hospitals, Depots of Mounted Units, or as a Clerk, etc., you may be retained after the termination of hostilities until your service can be spared, but such retention shall in no case exceed six months.

Joseph indicated that he would serve under those conditions, *provided His Majesty should so long require [his] services.* He then made his last intervention in the surviving public record, signing *J. S. Blackburn* to confirm that what he had said was correct and that he was *willing to fulfil the engagements made.* The witness was one N. Musgrave, who we shall come across again.

Joseph then swore the following oath:

"I, Joseph Septimus Blackburn, swear by Almighty God, that I will be faithful and bear true Allegiance to His Majesty King George the Fifth, His Heirs and Successors, and that I will, as in duty bound, honestly and faithfully defend His Majesty, His Heirs and Successors, in Person and in Dignity against all enemies, and will observe and obey all orders of His Majesty, His Heirs and Successors, and His Generals and Officers set over me. So help me God."

The oath was administered to Joseph by the magistrate, who also signed the form, certifying:

The Recruit above named was cautioned by me that if he made any false answer to any of the above questions he would be liable to be punished as provided in the Army Act. The above questions were then read to the Recruit in my presence. I have taken care that he understands each question, and that his answer to each question has been duly entered as replied to, and the said Recruit has made and signed the declaration and taken the oath before me at Poulton-le-Fylde on this tenth day of December 1915.

The suffix 'le Fylde' is not Norman. It came in 1842 with the first national postal system and was added simply to distinguish this Poulton from one in Morecambe. The locals have, however, seen no reason to dispense with it in the two centuries since, even though the Penny Post is long gone.

5

In Joseph Blackburn's case, the effect of what he did was immediate. Under the group scheme, he was placed in Class A, which contained all attested men who had chosen to defer their military service. Then, because he had been born in 1886 and was married, he was allocated to Group 35.

Like other men in the same position, Joseph will have been paid a bonus of 2s 9d, the equivalent of a day's Army pay, and given a khaki armlet, bearing a crimson image of the royal crown. He could wear that wherever he went so that he wasn't taken for a coward and, perhaps, presented with a white feather. As the form he had signed provided, he will then have been sent home to await being called up.

On 11th December 1915, Joseph was formally assigned to the 4th Battalion of the Loyal North Lancashire Regiment. Based in Preston and nicknamed 'the Cauliflowers' after the shape of its badge, the regiment was the successor to one that had distinguished itself in the Boer War and the Crimea. Already during the present conflict it had gained honours not only at Mons and Ypres and on the Marne, but also for its efforts in Gaza and Baghdad and at Suvla Bay. Joseph was given number 204824 and then transferred to the Army reserve, but he would never see service with his first regiment.

*

Joseph was not the first member of his family to enlist in the military during the autumn of 1915. That distinction belongs to his nephew, Robert Blackburn. He was the son of Joseph's brother, also named Robert, who had left Thornton at least a decade before. And his was the branch of the family that had made its home in Seaforth, where Sir John Gladstone's modest mansion used to stand. On 21st September 1915, Robert Junior also joined the British Army. He did so in Liverpool, where Lord Derby had recruited to such stunning effect the previous year.

As his uncle would ten weeks later, Robert signed up for the duration of the war. He gave his age as nineteen years and thirty-seven days and his occupation as cabinetmaker, and he agreed that he would serve where required, either within the United Kingdom or outside it. Robert was immediately assigned to one of the so-called 'Irish' battalions of the King's Liverpool Regiment, although for him, military service would begin straight away.

The battalion Robert Blackburn joined was responsible for the training of new recruits and he was sent to the military camp at Weeton, which was then little more than a collection of tents in the flat, lush countryside to the south-east of Blackpool. While he was there, Robert will have been little more than five miles from his uncle's home in Thornton.

His service with the Liverpool Irish would not last long. On 11th October 1915, less than three weeks after he had joined it, Robert was discharged from the regiment. His own dusty file tells us that this was because he had *made a mis-statement as to age on enlistment and being under the age of 17 years.* On the day of his discharge, Robert Blackburn was still only sixteen years and eleven months old.

*

There has been a civilian settlement at Weeton for more than a thousand years, and the land in those parts had lain in the hands of the same family since 1400. That was the Stanley family, and by the 19th century, the Earls of Derby had taken to styling themselves 'Baron of Weeton'. For almost two hundred years, the village was home to another of the Fylde's windmills: one more white-and-black construction that occupied a slight incline just beyond the village. Still milling corn in 1915, its tower rose above the willow trees that are a feature of the area and its cap and sails will have been visible for miles around.

A public house has stood in the centre of the village since the 16th century and its name, the Eagle and Child, comes from the Stanleys' coat of arms. Two men taken from the pub in 1814 would be the last from the Fylde to be pressed into the Navy. They would also be among the last impressed men to die in battle.

In late Georgian times, Weeton was visited in the summer by a minstrel, who came from Lancaster and stayed for several weeks at the village's expense. The high-pitched, cheerful sound of his flageolet will have been heard into the early hours, carried on the warm breeze from the upstairs room of the Eagle and Child, where he played so that the people of the village could dance. So enthusiastically did they dance, in fact, that the ceiling of the room below began to sag. The minstrel's songs were seditious and, doubtless to the delight of his audience, he would loudly denounce the military and the way it came by its men. There must have been great surprise then when, after his sudden death in June 1815, he was revealed as the man who had told the press gang where likely recruits could be found.

*

On the very day that Joseph Blackburn became one of the Cauliflowers, Thomas Hume Dunlop, a musician who had lately been studying in London, also attested under the Derby scheme. He was the son of the Reverend Thomas Dunlop and his wife, Charlotte Maria Dunlop, and he too was sent to the Army reserve. A single man and younger than Joseph Blackburn,

Thomas would, on 22nd March 1916, be mobilised for military service and then posted to the 14th Battalion of the Cheshire Regiment. His father was the Congregationalist minister of Emmanuel Church in Bootle, near Liverpool, and he would die only a fortnight after his son's enlistment.

*

All these years later, we cannot know why, in December 1915, Joseph Blackburn chose to attest and then to enlist in the British Army and why he did not simply stay his hand and take his chances. Neither can we know why, when Joseph did enlist, he decided not to go to the Colours straight away.

Yet, it is striking that Joseph's fateful excursion to Poulton came only one day before the Derby scheme was due to close. The scheme would, in fact, be extended by a few days, reflecting the fact that, towards the end at least, it had proved popular. Between 10th and 13th December 1915, the number of men who attested was almost half the total number who did so throughout the entire life of the scheme.

In Joseph's case, it is possible that he always intended to fight in the war and simply hoped to be allowed to do so at a more convenient time. Alternatively, he might have wished to postpone not his service, but merely the point at which a final commitment would have to be made. It is, however, conceivable that Joseph wished to avoid military service altogether and that he thought that his best chance of doing so lay within the Derby scheme. Many men seem to have thought the same. If he did think that then Joseph, like those other men, was mistaken.

There is a further, perhaps more sinister possibility, and it is one that was mentioned during a debate in the House of Lords on 22nd May 1916. The speaker on that occasion was eager to explain why married men who attested, and therefore came forward voluntarily, should nevertheless have the right to ask a tribunal to exempt them from military service. The reason, he said:

"...Is this: that over and over again, throughout the country, the married man... was told, 'Unless you attest you will not be allowed to go before the Tribunals and will have no opportunity of pleading your case.' I hope that will not be denied, because I know it."

After a brief interruption, the speaker continued: "I have seen it over and over again... The man was told, 'If you attest you shall have the right of access to the Tribunals; if you do not attest you will be gobbled up without any powers of complaint'; and upon the faith of that assurance, made in the name of the Government right throughout the country, he did attest."

The speaker was Lord Salisbury, whom we shall encounter again before long. The brief interruption came in the form of a cry of "Hear, hear!" and its author was the Earl of Derby – he of the scheme.

*

We cannot know the truth of the matter from the documents that survive in the public realm. What we can say with some certainty, however, is that Joseph Blackburn did not wish to enter the armed forces in December 1915. He had not been swayed by the early, brief enthusiasm for war and on the day, more than a year later, when he attested, he knew that he would still not be required to serve for several months. In fact, and as we shall see, he would subsequently attempt to postpone his service for even longer.

Whatever his intention, it is likely that Joseph's domestic circumstances played a significant part in the course he chose to take. As 1915 came to an end, he was both a married man and the father of two young children. His daughter, Elizabeth, was little more than two years old, while his son, Joseph, had yet to reach his first birthday. Very recently, however, there had been a further, sad development in his life.

On 18th November 1915, only three weeks before he promised himself to the military, Joseph's mother, Elizabeth Blackburn, died. She was seventy-two years of age and had been carried off by Bright's disease, the name then given to several different disorders of the kidney. The disease had already claimed Emily Dickinson, Isambard Brunel, Madame Blavatsky and Bram Stoker, as well as Tsar Alexander III and, earlier that same year, Victor Trumper, the stylish Australian batsman. It is likely to have afflicted Elizabeth Blackburn for some time.

Elizabeth Blackburn died at Rose Cottage in Thornton, the home she had made with her husband, Thomas. He would remain there after her, at least for a little while, with their son, his wife and their children.

Another of Elizabeth's sons – named, like his father, Thomas Blackburn – was also, of course, living at Rose Cottage at this time. It seems, however, that Thomas Junior had a life, and a living, of his own. At least from the date of his mother's death, therefore, Joseph Blackburn was the only person to assist his father in his business; the business of the market garden. Soon, his circumstances would change once again.

*

Ultimately, the group scheme would come to be seen as a failure. Although it reopened on 10th January 1916, before closing finally on 1st March, Lord Derby's initiative secured for the military fewer than a million single men and only slightly more married men. Of those who might have attested, nearly two fifths of single men and more than a half of married men steadfastly refused to do so.

The first of the Derby scheme groups were called up on 20th January 1916 – earlier, perhaps, than their members had expected – and the next followed on 8th and 29th February. The last groups of single men were called on 18th March 1916 and the first ones of married men followed on 7th April.

Because of the group in which he had been placed, Joseph Blackburn will have known that he would be mobilised for military service alongside other married men born from 1880 to 1888. All other things being equal, therefore, Joseph would begin his military service on Monday 29th May 1916.

6

Joseph Blackburn's next public appearance is in the records of the Thornton Urban District Council. That was the local authority for the area in which Rose Cottage, and Raikes Road and Little Thornton, lay.

At the beginning of May 1916, Joseph made a claim under Lord Derby's scheme. In doing so, he will have hoped to be relieved from military service – the military service for which, six months earlier, he had put himself forward – and it was to the Thornton Local Tribunal that Joseph presented his claim.

The Thornton tribunal was one of more than two thousand that would operate throughout Britain until late 1918 and even beyond. They were created by urban district councils, and by rural district councils and borough councils, specifically to hear claims from men who were subject to the group scheme. At first, the tribunals had only a single, modest power. All they could do was remove an attested man from his appointed group and place him in a later one no more than ten groups hence. Even where the power was used, therefore, its effect would only ever be to postpone the man's call; never to cancel it.

The records of the Thornton local tribunal are kept with those of the council that created it, in Preston in a grey, Brutalist archive. That building contrasts sharply with its neighbour, the red-brick County Hall, which has gables and mullions, tall chimneys and pediments and is unmistakeably Victorian. The records comprise two ledgers – stiff, stout volumes, whose pages won't have been turned much in the last hundred years and are dried out and compressed. One ledger serves as a minute book, recording each session of the tribunal at which cases were heard or decisions made. The other contains a collection of letters, reflecting the tribunal's dealings with claimants and other parties, with institutions both legal and political and with the world at large.

Frustratingly, the Thornton records are incomplete. The minute book rarely gives either the names of claimants or the result of their claims, while the letter book contains copies of letters sent by the tribunal, but none of the ones it received. Those aren't, however, fatal problems, for when the information in the two books is combined, a much fuller picture emerges. That is certainly so for claims heard between January and November 1916, in the tribunal's first year of operation. In either the minutes or the letters we find the names of all but eighteen claimants and the likely result of all but two claims. For the most part, therefore, we can be confident about the tale the Thornton records tell.

*

The Thornton tribunal came into existence on 4th November 1915, when it also sat for the first time. Its birth and subsequent proceedings were diligently recorded by its clerk, Richard Bowman, who was an accountant in practice in nearby Blackpool.

Those assembled in the council chamber that Thursday evening heard Mr Bowman read a letter from the Local Government Board, *requesting appointment of a committee to act as a Local Tribunal for the hearing of claims arising from recruiting under Lord Derby's scheme.* The twelve councillors then resolved that five of their number – Messrs William Betney, Thomas Dewhurst, Thomas Robert Strickland, William John Titherington and Thomas Waring – should be appointed to the new tribunal. This news might have come as a surprise to Councillor Waring, because he wasn't present at that first meeting.

Neither the tribunal nor the council would be the limit of these men's civic obligations. Councillor Titherington, for example, was already a governor of the local secondary school and the manager of a hospital, and he was one of the town's Poor Law Guardians. He was also the treasurer of the Ratepayers' and Property Owners' Association. Councillor Strickland, meanwhile, also sat on the local sewerage committee and was an Overseer of the Poor. A local farmer, he shared the former duty with Councillor Waring, who was also a farmer, and the latter duty with Councillor Dewhurst. The latter councillor, meanwhile, was also a member of the local education board, where his colleagues included Councillor Betney.

These would remain the tribunal's members, and its only ones, until the last recorded session, almost three years later. Their appointment confirmed, the members then decided that Councillor Dewhurst should be their chairman. He was a local insurance agent and had sat on the council for a good few years. With that, the evening's proceedings will have come to an end. For the moment, the tribunal had no other business to transact and its next session could safely be left for nearly a month.

The members of the Thornton tribunal convened again on the evening of Monday 29th November 1915, *at the close of the War Relief Public Meeting*, when they were provided with several important documents. Almost immediately the session began, Mr Bowman handed out copies of the rules under which local tribunals would be required to operate and the first of a succession of lists, drawn up by the government, setting out the essential occupations that might entitle a man to exemption from military service. The minute book notes, however, that consideration of these documents *was left until a future meeting*. Members were also given a circular from the Local Government Board. That, too, would be the first of many. Before long, the Thornton tribunal would have not just the Local Government Board's letters and circulars to contend with, but also one of its inspectors.

The Local Government Board had been created in 1871, during the first of Mr Gladstone's four governments, and now, as then, its purpose was to supervise the law relating to public health, local government and the relief of the poor. The board was led by its President, a politician who was usually a member of the Cabinet, and its powers were extensive and near judicial in nature. It could, for example, impose binding legal obligations upon the councils and other public bodies that came within its reach.

The practical work of the board was done by its salaried officers, of which it had many different kinds, including secretaries, assistant secretaries, auditors, clerks and messengers. The board also had a myriad of inspectors, whose functions included visiting local authorities to ensure that they were performing both lawfully and satisfactorily.

In 1915, and also the following year, the President of the Local Government Board was Walter Hume Long. A Unionist politician, he had first held the post ten years before during the last of three governments headed by the third Marquess of Salisbury. Mr Long was now Member of Parliament for the Strand, which was the sixth seat he had held in a parliamentary career spanning four decades. For seven years, he had represented the West Derby constituency of Liverpool. His son, who was also named Walter, saw service in the First World War, ultimately with the 56th Infantry Brigade.

*

It was not until the session held on 10th January 1916, more than two months after the Thornton tribunal was created, that it dealt with its first claims. That was also the session at which members first encountered the military representative. He was the official with the job of attending hearings where men claimed exemption from military service, of contesting those claims and of arguing that the men who made them should be sent to the Colours instead. There is evidence that military representatives did their job enthusiastically and even, as we shall see, pugnaciously.

Military representatives were required to act only in accordance with official instructions issued by the Army Council, and they had little or no discretion of their own. Often, therefore, they found themselves challenging claims, or even whole categories of claim, regardless of the circumstances of the men concerned and irrespective of their own personal opinions. This stance would sometimes bring them into conflict with local tribunals and, as we shall see, with individual members of those tribunals.

The military representative who presented his credentials to the Thornton tribunal on 10th January 1916 was John Robinson, and when he did so, he also produced a letter from his superior, one Captain Booth, confirming his appointment. Thereafter, and until February 1917, when Captain Booth was promoted, either he or Mr Robinson would be present at almost every session in Four Lane Ends.

In time, another official, Mr Walsh, would begin attending those sessions. He was the agricultural representative and it would fall to him to argue the interests of the land and of food production. In an area such as Thornton, such as the whole of the Fylde in fact, that was no small task. Mr Walsh would often, therefore, find himself speaking in support of claims made by attested men and their employers and in opposition to the military representative.

7

The Thornton tribunal didn't actually hear from a claimant until its fourth session, which was held on 20th January 1916.

Proceedings that Thursday evening were opened by the clerk, Richard Bowman, and he told the members about four letters that had been received in the last few days. Three were from the Local Government Board and one of them enclosed a further, revised list of certified occupations. Then, at a little after seven o'clock, Fred Owen became the first man to present his case at Four Lane Ends. He had also been among the first Thornton men to make a claim for relief and he was promptly put back to Group 14. In other words, his mobilisation was postponed until 18th March.

It isn't clear what happened to Mr Owen subsequently and there is nothing to say whether he eventually went to war. In March 1916, as his postponement was about to end, he made a further claim. That and a subsequent appeal were dismissed, but his name doesn't appear on the list of Thornton dead. Fred Owen is significant, however, for it was in his case that the tribunal settled on a course it would often take in the weeks and months to come.

In January 1916, as it got used to its new role, the tribunal held three sessions. Thereafter, and save in March and May when there were two of them, there would be only one session a month for the rest of the year. Twelve cases had been considered at the first session, but only eight were heard at each of the two sessions that followed. On 31st January, the minutes note, *the date of the next meeting was left to the Clerk when any cases were ready for consideration.*

The next session in fact took place almost three weeks later, on the evening of 21st February, when a further six cases were heard. By then, it had become the tribunal's practice to list precisely that number of cases for hearing in a single session and to begin hearing them at 7.10pm.

Those first sessions at Four Lane Ends won't have been particularly taxing, at least for the members of the tribunal, for a mere ten minutes was allocated to each case and, all being well, proceedings will have concluded only just after eight o'clock. Before long, however, the pace would accelerate, as it became necessary for the Thornton tribunal, and all local tribunals, to consider claims not just from attested men, but also from those unattested men who had by now been caught by the Military Service Act 1916. Those men were, for the first time in the nation's history, conscripts.

*

Given the shortcomings of the Derby scheme and the sheer number of men who remained impervious to Lord Kitchener's blandishments – and, it seems, to the misrepresentations of recruiting officers up and down the land – it was obvious that voluntary enlistment had failed. On 14th December 1915, the Cabinet finally decided to put forward a bill introducing limited conscription and on 5th January 1916, five days before the Thornton tribunal considered its first case, that bill was introduced into the House of Commons. The Military Service Act 1916 came into effect three weeks later.

The chief impact of the new Act, and its main burden, was felt by unmarried men and by some widowers who did not have children. There were exceptions, for example for men in holy orders, those residing abroad and those who had been discharged on grounds of ill health. Otherwise, however, every such man was deemed to have enlisted in the armed forces, he was immediately transferred to the reserve and, crucially, he now came under military control.

As before, men who didn't want to serve, at least for the moment, might make a claim to their local tribunal. Those were the same tribunals that had been set up under the Derby scheme, but they now acquired greater, statutory powers. For the first time, they would be able to award an exemption from, and not merely a postponement of, military service, and they would sometimes be able to do so on grounds of a conscientious objection. Alternatively, a man could now claim that it was in the national interest for him to do other, non-military work and the Local Government Board was therefore asked to provide guidance on what that might mean. There would also be appeal tribunals for each county, which might correct errors made at the first stage, and the Central Tribunal, sitting in London, would give a final determination on points of law and principle.

The new Act therefore brought a subtle change to the work of the local tribunals, whose members might now find themselves having to decide not just when a man who had already enlisted should be called to the Colours, but whether a man who had not been a soldier should now be sent off to fight.

The Act would also apply to existing claims, made under the Derby scheme, and it would therefore cover the cases of attested men. They too would have access to the new appeal tribunals, as well as the Central Tribunal, and in their cases, too, it would now be possible for all tribunals, including local ones, to grant exemption from military service and to do so on an absolute, a conditional or a temporary basis. Joseph Blackburn was but one among a great many men for whom that change would be significant.

But even though the tribunals had now been established by Act of Parliament, there was one fact that could not be ignored. No matter how wise their members might have been and no matter how assiduous their deliberations, the tribunals' decisions, when they came, had no legal force. The government had, it is true, promised to respect those decisions and it would remain true to that promise throughout the war. The simple truth, however, is that although men were not sent to fight while they had exemptions in place, that was simply the result of an administrative arrangement, and one that might at any moment be brought to an end.

*

The records tell a fairly complete tale about the claim Joseph presented in May 1916. It was made on form R.53, which was for use by attested men who wished to seek exemption from military service, and it was the ninety-third in Thornton to have come from such a man. By the time it was lodged, however, the tribunal had also received fourteen claims under the new Act. They were the claims of the town's first conscripts.

8

At a special session held on 17th February 1916, the Thornton tribunal announced that from now on, it would be governed by the Military Service Act 1916 and would deal not just with attested men, but also with those who had suddenly found themselves required to fight. That was, however, the limit of the changes the tribunal decided it must make. Its members, chairman and clerk would remain precisely the same, despite the new statute, and they would all continue to come together in the council chamber at Four Lane Ends.

The first session at which the tribunal dealt with claims from conscripted men was the one held a fortnight later, on 2nd March. Eight of those claims were considered then, along with eleven from attested men. Thereafter, at least one such claim was heard at each session. Usually, in fact, the number was between three and eight and although, sometimes, it would be nine or ten, it was never more than that. In the three years of its life, the tribunal would deal with fewer than a hundred claims from conscripts, less than a third of the number that came from attested men. (That might, of course, suggest that in Thornton, the Derby scheme had attracted a large proportion of useable men; that it had been less unsuccessful there than elsewhere in the country.)

In order to accommodate the nineteen cases listed for hearing that Thursday evening, the beginning of the session was brought forward by an hour and, in another departure from established practice, the time allocated to each of them was reduced from ten minutes to five.

It is in the note of this session that the subject of appeals is first raised. At the beginning of the proceedings, Richard Bowman read out a letter, confirming both the creation of the Lancashire Appeal Tribunal and that it would be based in Preston. The letter came from County Hall and it was signed by Sir Harcourt Clare, who was the new tribunal's clerk.

*

Like Mr Bowman, Sir Harcourt would combine his tribunal duties with existing ones in local government. He was already Clerk of the Peace and Clerk to the Lancashire County Council – in effect, the chief legal and governmental administrator in the county.

By training and qualification, Harcourt Everard Clare was a solicitor, and by the spring of 1916, he had worked in local government for more than thirty-five years. At first, he had been the clerk – and latterly the chief clerk – of Liverpool City Council, for which he had overseen the building of a tramway and the installation of street lighting. During the 20th century, however, he had served the people of Lancashire and he would guide the work of many council committees, including the ones that arranged care for the mentally ill and the mentally handicapped. He would also serve on two national commissions, set up to consider local taxation and the acquisition of land for public purposes.

These were heady times for Sir Harcourt, for he had been made a baronet only a few days before. A portrait of him, painted later in the year to commemorate that great event, hangs to this day in the Crown Court building in Preston. Done in oils, in discreet shades of grey, brown and claret, the painting is the work of William Llewellyn, who would himself be knighted two years later. Like others by the same hand, it offers a three-quarter likeness of its subject, standing confidently in a frock coat, spectacles in his right hand and with his left hand resting on a fold of documents that might easily be a legal brief or a collection of title deeds.

Sir William Llewellyn would serve as president of the Royal Academy for a decade. Perhaps his most celebrated work is the state portrait, begun in 1911, that has as its subject Mary of Teck, Queen Consort of the new King George V.

For his home, Sir Harcourt held the tenancy of Bank Hall, a fine mansion in the village of Bretherton, which lies to the south of the River Ribble about nine miles from Preston. The hall dates back at least to Jacobean times. It was built of brick with elegant bays and Dutch gables and it had roofs of Cumbrian slate with lavish finials and tall, diamond-shaped chimney stacks. It also had a distinctive, sixty-foot clock tower and stood at the end of a long avenue that was flanked by lime trees.

An earlier owner of the hall, Anne Banestre, had married into the Fleetwood family and her husband, Sir Thomas, had once attempted to drain the surrounding marshes. That job proved something of a challenge, however, and it was only completed more than a century later by his descendant, Sir Peter Hesketh-Fleetwood.

The village lies on the southern boundary of the old Hesketh family estate and it is also home to an impressive windmill. Built in 1741, Bretherton Mill has a whitewashed tower supporting an octagonal cap that is painted black. It stands close to the point, in Rufford, from which the ancient wooden mill was transplanted to Warton, and it is almost equidistant from the windmills at Great Crosby (or Thornton) to the south-east and Thornton in the Fylde to the north.

Bank Hall, too, had been tricked out for the Diamond Jubilee, although the owner didn't paint it from top to toe in red, white and blue. She chose simply to plant a cedar tree in its already verdant grounds.

*

As a final piece of business that Thursday evening, the tribunal noted that two appeals had been received and then forwarded to Preston. They were the very first appeals against decisions made at Four Lane Ends and they had each come from the previous session.

By now, with the claims of conscripted men having been added to those of attested men, the workload of the Thornton tribunal had grown considerably. In March, the number of pending cases had become so great that the tribunal decided it would have to sit again that month, and a fortnight later, thirteen more claims were considered. At the same time, the tribunal noted that another nine appeals against its decisions had been received at County Hall.

In the single month of March 1916, therefore, the tribunal dealt with thirty-two claims for exemption. But that number would be dwarfed by the claims considered in the months that followed. Two sessions were held in May and fully fifty-three claims were dealt with in total, while in June, forty-three claims were determined during a single, no doubt hectic session.

Among the claims heard in May was that of Joseph Blackburn.

*

The chief provisions of the Military Service Act 1916 did not apply to married men. That was widely seen as inequitable, not least by the likes of Joseph Blackburn. They were men with wives and sometimes children, who, by attesting their willingness to serve, had answered Lord Kitchener's call. They had, however, answered that call without being compelled to do so and they could not, therefore, claim the benefit of statutory rights now made available elsewhere. It didn't help that those new rights could now be exercised even by unattested *single* men.

In an attempt to remedy this situation, the government

introduced a further statute, the Military Service (Session 2) Act 1916. This second Act came into effect on 25th May 1916 and it provided that in the case of married men, even those who had not attested could now be called to the Colours. Those men were also granted the familiar rights of appeal. They would be able to seek exemption from military service and they might do so by making a claim to the local tribunal.

It was, however, the changes made by the first Military Service Act, and not the second, that would have the greater effect upon Joseph Blackburn. Even though he had attested and was not, therefore, to be treated as a conscripted man, the local tribunal that heard his claim would no longer be constrained by the provisions of the old group scheme. If it were persuaded of the merits of his case, the tribunal would be able to award him some form of exemption. And the effect of that exemption might now be to defer, and not merely to postpone, his military service.

Joseph's claim was heard at Four Lane Ends on the very day the second Military Service Act came into effect. It is unlikely, however, that he made that claim in anticipation of the new Act. Although many married men who had previously been beyond the reach of the military could now be required to serve, Joseph was not among them. He was already an attested man and had been committed to serve since December 1915. After what he did, in the wind and rain in Poulton-le-Fylde, he had been placed in the appropriate group and was now awaiting developments. Joseph's claim to the Thornton tribunal is likely to have been made because he was due to be mobilised on 29th May 1916. That is a fact of which he would have been aware for more than six months.

*

As it was required to do, the tribunal sent a duplicate copy of Joseph's claim to the military representative, Captain Booth. In the tribunal's records, there is a copy of the letter with which that duplicate was enclosed. It is dated 9th May 1916.

The relevant ledger contains copies of a large number of letters sent by the Thornton tribunal. There are, in fact, well over four hundred of them and from the dates they bear it is clear that Mr Bowman was in the habit of dealing with new matters straight away. It is likely, therefore, that Joseph lodged his claim at Four Lane Ends on or very shortly before 9th May.

That would be consistent with the timetable Joseph was required to meet. Under the Derby scheme, an attested man who wished to seek exemption was subject to a straightforward requirement: his claim would have to be lodged not less than ten days before the group of which he was a member was due to be mobilised. In Joseph's case, therefore, he would have to act before 19th May 1916.

This is, however, another aspect of the case to be affected by the passing of the first Military Service Act. Now, all claims, even those by attested men, would have to be made within fourteen days from the day on which the man was called up. According to arrangements published under the Derby scheme, Joseph will have received his call-up papers on or about 27th April 1916. That would mean that if he wished to be exempted from service, any claim to that effect would have to be lodged by 11th May. It seems that, once again, Joseph was just in time.

*

Joseph might, perhaps, be forgiven if he was optimistic about his chances before the Thornton tribunal. The simple fact is that in some way, at least, his claim was likely to succeed. Across the country in mid-1916, local tribunals were granting exemptions from military service to large numbers of men; to rather more of them, in fact, than the government had hoped.

In the first three months of the year, while almost two hundred thousand attested men had gone to the Colours, five times that number had managed to have their call-ups postponed. This was a position the first Military Service Act did little to change. Of the 1.2 million men suddenly deemed enlisted in the military, 750,000 applied for exemption, while in the first month of the new county appeal tribunals, almost sixty thousand men were exempted, more than a third absolutely, and fewer than twenty-six thousand men were secured for the war.

The government was therefore faced with another worrying shortfall in recruits. Its response would, however, create as many problems as it solved. The terms of the old Derby scheme were adjusted and the call-up of attested men gathered pace, but an increase in the number of men called brought a corresponding increase in the number who would seek to be made exempt.

And there is a second reason why Joseph Blackburn might be forgiven for being optimistic about his claim. That reason has to do less with national circumstances than with his own domestic position.

Joseph's mother, Elizabeth Blackburn, had died at the end of 1915, shortly before he attested his willingness to serve. Now, however, his circumstances had changed once again, and again, they had done so for the worse.

On Sunday 16th January 1916, a matter of days after the Thornton tribunal considered its first claims, Joseph's father, Thomas Blackburn, died. The cause of his death was certified as chronic rheumatoid arthritis, and the place, Rose Cottage. His occupation was given as market gardener.

The mechanism by which rheumatoid arthritis causes death remains unknown and would certainly have been so in 1916. Whilst it is possible, and even likely, that the disease weakens the heart and prompts cardiac arrest, that process was neither described nor even hinted at on Thomas Blackburn's death certificate.

This sad event might, however, help to explain Joseph

Blackburn's decision to attest for military service under the Derby scheme. Like the Bright's disease from which his mother died, the rheumatoid arthritis that claimed his father is a chronic illness. The effects of that illness upon Thomas will have become progressively more evident both to him and to his son, and each man will surely have known that before long, Joseph would have to run the market garden alone.

The event also resembles one in the life of Thomas Hume Dunlop. He was the musician from Liverpool who had enlisted at the same time as Joseph and whose father died a fortnight later. That is not the only way in which the two men are linked.

Thomas Blackburn left an estate worth nearly £300 and in the records noting that fact, his son, too, is described as a *market gardener*. That is how Joseph had described himself, of course, at least since December of the previous year, when he enlisted in the British Army. The death of his father and the fact that it had occurred so close to that of his mother was something that surely would not be lost on the members of the Thornton tribunal.

9

On 25th May 1916, three days after Lord Salisbury spoke in the House of Lords, the Thornton local tribunal decided that Joseph Blackburn should be given a temporary exemption from military service. The surviving records don't tell us why it did so or whether the recent deaths of his parents were taken account. The effect of the decision is, however, clear: Joseph would not be required to join the Colours, or to take his place in the Great War, until at least 30th September 1916. That is fully four months after the date upon which, under the Derby scheme, his group was due to be mobilised.

Given the significance of his claim, at least to him, and given also that the council chamber in Four Lane Ends was barely a mile from his home, it is likely that Joseph appeared in person before the tribunal. It is also likely that, making the most of the five minutes allotted to him, he presented his case himself. He would certainly both attend and speak at another such session almost eight months later.

We cannot be sure of that, however, because, somewhat unusually for one at which claimants were heard, the session on 25th May took place in the afternoon. That might have been inconvenient for a working man, even one working on his own account. Given the time of year, there was probably a great deal to be done at Rose Cottage.

Joseph's claim was heard on the very day the second Military Service Act came into effect and his exemption was one of twenty-six the tribunal granted then, all but one of them to attested men. Of those exemptions, nine were limited in time with the one given to Joseph being by some way the longest. Five claimants, all of them attested men, had their appeals rejected.

Joseph wasn't, however, the only man in his trade to have a claim considered that Thursday afternoon. He wasn't even the only one to be granted an exemption. The same result was achieved by William Crook Sefton, who was also an attested man. In fact, Mr Sefton was more fortunate than Joseph, for his exemption was not temporary, but conditional. He would remain out of the military not for a week or two, or even a month or two, but *so long as he remains a market gardener*. The records don't say why that indulgence couldn't also have been afforded to Joseph Blackburn.

There is a further question on which the Thornton records are silent. Nowhere in the minutes or copy letters is there any reference to a tribunal claim made by one of Joseph's brothers, cousins or uncles; those among his male relatives likely to have been of an age for military service. Some caution is required here, however, because of the limitations of the records. Those limitations might be modest, but at times they have a very real effect. There are, for example, a number of cases in which the claimant's name has been lost but it is plain from what remains that he worked on the land. That is particularly true of cases heard in May 1916, and it is therefore possible that another Blackburn man, or a Bennett man, made a similar claim at the same time.

After the sessions held in May 1916, and also in June, the pace eased a little at Four Lane Ends. Even in the autumn of that year, however, the number of claims dealt with in each of the monthly sessions was always in the low twenties.

When they convened on Tuesday 12th September 1916, the members of the tribunal were told by their clerk of a letter that had been received from a Mr W. P. Elias. He was one of the Local Government Board's inspectors. For some time, in fact, he had been the board's General Inspector for the North-Western Poor

Law District, but while this might be the first time his name appears in the Thornton records, it certainly won't be the last. Mr Elias' letter contained a disarmingly modest request. He asked to be sent *reports at intervals on work of tribunal.*

*

The holder of his present post for a little over two years, William Pritchard Elias was by now an experienced scrutineer of local government. He had been born in 1870, on Anglesey, and had studied classics and modern languages at Oriel College, Oxford. Like Sir Harcourt Clare, he had trained and qualified as a solicitor, and he had also practised as one, in a small town on the North Wales coast.

Mr Elias came from agricultural and merchant stock. His grandfather had farmed in Caernarvonshire and acted as land agent to the local gentry, while his father, Thomas, had found success as a brewer and wine-seller. Thomas Elias was also a well-known genealogist and antiquary, and he was staunch in his support of both the Established Church and the Conservative party.

For William Elias, his job involved what must sometimes have seemed an endless round of meetings with Poor Law guardians across the north-west of England. His brief was a wide one, however, and it wasn't confined to the relief of the adult poor. The surviving records find him visiting Culcheth near Wigan, for example, and pronouncing himself *exceedingly disappointed* with the quality of accommodation provided for deprived children. They also find him in Burnley, and later in Chester, calling for the indigent to be ejected from the workhouse so that room might be made for disabled soldiers. And neither was that the geographical limit of his work.

In June 1914, when he had been in his new role for less than a month, Mr Elias presided over a three-day inquiry into the conduct of an officer of the Salford guardians whom they had recently chosen to dismiss. It was said that the man had sold furniture belonging to an inmate of the workhouse. His alleged offence wasn't, however, to have sold the furniture, but to have done so at less than its true value. Later that month, William Elias found himself drawn into a heated argument among the South Manchester guardians about the provision of accommodation for sick children and whether tents might suffice. Prefiguring later events, the guardians' clerk would explain that, *in the course of a long conversation with Mr Elias... the whole matter was thoroughly thrashed out.*

Mr Elias was also fond of giving culinary advice. In January 1916, for example – the month in which Joseph Blackburn's father died and the Thornton tribunal considered its first claims – he can be found telling the Clitheroe guardians that they should reduce the amount of meat served to workhouse inmates. A fortnight later, he sent the guardians in Penrith a recipe for bread made with potato instead of flour, explaining that it would be lighter than conventional bread, but also wholesome and economical. This suggestion prompted a lively discussion in Cumberland, with one of the guardians demanding that there be no such experiment and another saying he had heard that potato bread gave people boils. Those were not the views of the majority, however, and a decision was taken to add Mr Elias' new concoction to the menu.

The wise counsel of the Local Government Board was not always welcomed, however, whether it concerned the baking of bread or other, less gustatory matters. In May 1914, for example, Mr Elias had been caught up in a dispute with the Rochdale guardians over a practice that had been adopted in the town's workhouse. In short, destitute people were being turned away if they refused to be bathed. The inspector told a meeting of the guardians that the practice was unlawful, even though it was permitted by a regulation they had themselves drawn up, and he advised that the regulation be omitted. The mood was not, however, receptive. The minutes note, tersely:

> *It was decided to respectfully inform the Local Government Board that the Guardians find themselves unable to comply with their request for the regulation to be omitted, being of opinion that it is a proper one.*

And there was a similar reception for advice Mr Elias gave the following year, thirty miles away. In November 1915, he attended a meeting on Merseyside at which thoughts soon turned to a current controversy. As a newspaper report of the time notes, under the heading *CHILDREN IN CELLS*:

> *At the fortnightly meeting of the Prescot Board of Guardians, Mr W. P. Elias, the Local Government Board inspector, said, in regard to a complaint which had been made against an official of the workhouse concerning the treatment of two boys of tender years, who had been placed in cells and given oakum to pick, that there was no breach of the regulations. He personally thought that that was not the kind of work he would have put boys to, but he knew it was inconvenient to find suitable accommodation at once for children accompanying people who came in late. These two boys were not very much prejudiced, he added, as he understood they were runaways.*
> *Mr Crowther – What I want to know is: was the master exceeding his duty in doing what he did?*
> *Mr Elias – Not according to your own regulations. It was not a task I should have given, but I don't think they suffered much. I have spoken to the master and given him my opinions, and I don't think it is necessary to go further.*

Mr Crowther – Under the Children Act it is unlawful to put young children into a cell.

The Inspector – The word 'cell' in a police sense and workhouse sense is quite different. It has no bearing on this at all.

Mr Crowther – As a guardian of the poor, I am not satisfied with what the inspector says.

The Chairman – You are pressing this too far.

Mr Crowther – If you rule me out of order I'll sit down.

The Chairman – Well, all right; you are out of order. Now sit down (laughter).

Mr Crowther – Well, you haven't allowed me to reply to the inspector.

The incident then terminated.

Animated discussions such as this, and protracted debates about the precise import of rules and regulations, would become very familiar to William Elias.

*

From the surviving records we know that Joseph Blackburn made one more claim for exemption. That claim, which was again set out on form R.53, was presented to the Thornton tribunal in mid-September 1916, shortly before the exemption granted to him in May was due to expire. The claim was allocated the reference number 164, it was copied and, on 18th September, the copy was again sent to Captain Booth.

In making this claim, Joseph will have wished to extend his existing exemption and, if not to avoid military service, at least to postpone it for a few more months. It is plain that, for the moment at least, he did not wish to go to the Colours.

The next session to be held after the claim was received was that of 10th October, when the minutes note that the claim was *adjourned until further instructions received*, and that the man himself was directed *to go before Medical Board.*

At that session, the Thornton tribunal received a large number of letters, including one from the Local Government Board enclosing *further instructions.* The members were also read a telegram from the recruiting officer in Lancaster, which was dated 4th October and advised that the cases of men working in agriculture, in dairy farming or on smallholdings should be postponed. The same advice was given about the cases of men working in market gardens, and it reflected a significant change of emphasis.

In the autumn of 1916, there was considerable official concern about the state of agriculture in Britain and the limited yield coming from the land. In September, the Board of Agriculture and the War Office agreed that no more farm workers should be taken into the military until a comprehensive survey of the remaining workforce could be made. On 5th October, it was announced that no man still engaged on the land should be called up before the New Year and the following day, the Local Government Board issued formal instructions to that effect.

It is easy to see what the War Office might have hoped to achieve from its negotiations with the Board of Agriculture. By the end of June 1916, almost three quarters of a million men had made claims to the local tribunals, seeking exemption from military service. That was only slightly fewer than the number of men who had joined the Army, and the problem didn't end there.

When their cases came before the local tribunals, most men were awarded at least some form of exemption. That was true as much of the Thornton tribunal as of local tribunals across the country, and we have seen that it was especially true in the case of Joseph Blackburn. Usually, the exemptions men received were temporary, for a few weeks or a few months.

Often, however, the exemptions were conditional, on the men's domestic or employment situation remaining serious enough to warrant their being kept at home.

By October 1916, well over a million men had been exempted from service or were waiting for the tribunals to deal with their claims. In November, the Army Council concluded that almost a million new recruits would be required in the following year, and it noted that at current rates, recruitment would fall short of that figure by nearly a quarter.

*

Although they might seem to have anticipated the Local Government Board's instructions, the recruiting officer's telegram and the Thornton tribunal's decision to adjourn Joseph's case are consistent with the change in official policy. It was one that had been predicted for some time. And it was not only in that case that the tribunal decided to act, or to refrain from doing so. On 23rd October, the clerk sent a letter to Mr Walsh, the agricultural representative, stating:

> *We are waiting for official instructions respecting the cases of Agricultural men. Decision seems to be that they will not be pulled up before the 1st of January 1917 but the intention is to deal with the cases before that date.*

At its next session, on 15th November 1916, the Thornton tribunal adjourned Joseph's case again, this time until New Year's Day. That, of course, was the day mentioned in the interdepartmental agreement reached the month before. In fact, Joseph's second claim would be considered, and the next tribunal session would take place, a little after that.

164

10

With no breeze to impede it, and with the warmth of the night doing nothing to discourage the listeners, the cheerful notes of the piccolo will have been audible even at the end of the drive. There will have been laughter, lots of that, and the sound of a sentimental ballad, and then there will have been a broad and familiar Lancashire accent.

The old hall had been lit up all night, at least from within, and suddenly, some low lights seemed to approach. The droning of engines grew louder and then, indistinctly against the dark sky, the great iron gates began to open.

*

As 1916 came to an end, Joseph Blackburn might have been as optimistic about his second tribunal claim as he was entitled to be about his first. His personal circumstances had improved little in the last few months, following the deaths of his mother and father, and the demands upon him, in the unyielding months of winter, will have been no less onerous.

There was, however, a further reason for optimism in Joseph's case; one that had become firmer since May and that had less to do with his own life than with what was happening at Four Lane Ends. It was clear that the Thornton tribunal would be broadly sympathetic to the claims it received and that was especially so of claims from men who, as many in the area did, worked on the land.

The session held at the beginning of the year, on 10th January, had been the first at which the tribunal dealt with claims. At that point, of course, those claims had all come from attested men and not one of them was dismissed. Several cases were, however, held over to the next session, with the direction that the man concerned should present himself so that he might be heard. The tribunal convened again on 20th January, four days after the death of Thomas Blackburn. At the session held that evening, eight men whose cases had first come up ten days before had their call-ups postponed. While those postponements were usually to 29th February – this being a Leap Year – or even 18th March, one man, Frank Butcher, fared less well. He would have to go to the Colours in a mere nineteen days.

At the same session, in the case of Albert Hodgkinson, the tribunal decided to 'star' the man – in other words, to acknowledge that his occupation was an essential one and that he should not, therefore, be required to fight. Mr Hodgkinson's starring does not appear to have served him particularly well, however, for five months later he would find himself before the tribunal again. On that occasion, although he was granted the further exemption he plainly felt he required, it was merely conditional.

The final session of the tribunal in January 1916 was held on the 31st of the month. That day, three men – including William Lawrenson and John Cowell – were starred, another man was recognised as enjoying that status already and a further three men had their call-ups postponed until 18th March.

Here, once again, starring seems to have proved of limited value, at least in the cases of two of the men. On 25th May 1916, when Joseph Blackburn's second claim was considered, Mr Lawrenson felt it necessary to come back before the tribunal and he was given a conditional exemption for his trouble. He would not need to fight while he remained a cowman. On 12th September, Mr Cowell, too, would be given a conditional exemption. Despite that, and even though, at one time at least, Mr Cowell had been deemed to be performing essential work, it is plain that he eventually found himself in combat. His name appears on the roll of Thornton's war dead.

In the minutes of the tribunal, one claim heard on 31st January 1916 is the first to be recorded as *not assented to*. Made under the Derby scheme, it was at least the twentieth the tribunal had considered. The man who made the claim was John Morton and it seems that, having failed to gain the exemption he sought, Mr Morton was received into the 1st Battalion of the King's Own Royal Lancaster Regiment. Thereafter, events unfolded with what must have seemed bewildering speed. On 17th October 1917, Private John Waddington Morton was killed in action. He was twenty-four years of age.

At the next Thornton session, on 21st February 1916, a further three claims were not assented to by the tribunal. On that occasion, however, there were two other claims – the first, in fact – in which the man concerned was given not merely a conditional or a temporary exemption from military service, but an absolute one. One of those men was John Butler. He does not appear to have profited from his absolute exemption, however, for on 27th April 1917, he found it necessary to present himself before the Thornton tribunal again. He was directed to attend for a medical and then, on 5th October, he was given exemption until 31st December. Mr Butler's final appearance in the Thornton minutes comes in those for the session held on 31st January 1918, when he was given a further exemption. That one, however, was merely conditional.

It was the session held on 21st February that produced the first appeals to the new Preston tribunal, and one of them was about a claim the Thornton tribunal had already dismissed. The case concerned Thomas Cartmell and the appeal was made by his employer, a local dairy farmer named William Cartmell. Farmer William was Thomas' father, as well as his employer, and he was also an elected member of the Thornton Urban District Council.

Mr Cartmell's membership of the Thornton council seems not to have impaired his relationship with the town's tribunal. On 4th March 1916, the tribunal's clerk, Richard Bowman, replied to a letter that he had sent. Mr Bowman was also the clerk to the council, of course, and he wrote:

I submitted your letter to the Military Representative and the Tribunal, but they were unable to find anything in the instructions which would enable them to amend the decision arrived at previously.

A fortnight later, in a further letter to Councillor Cartmell, Mr Bowman wrote:

I have arranged with Captain Booth that your son need not report himself until his appeal has been settled. Will you kindly let me have the enclosed Appeal Form, duly filled up, at my house by tomorrow (Sunday).

The solicitous approach Mr Bowman adopted towards Councillor Cartmell is unique in Thornton. The surviving records contain no other example of an appeal, or even a claim to the local tribunal, being lodged at the home of the tribunal's clerk. It is not clear whether any other man's appeal was received at the weekend.

As Richard Bowman's second letter anticipated, Thomas Cartmell had not been called up by the time his appeal was considered. That will have been in the first half of August 1916, for at its session on the 17th of that month, the Thornton tribunal heard that its original decision had been set aside in Preston and Thomas had been exempted from military service until the end of November. It is not clear whether Councillor Cartmell had any influence at County Hall or whether, for example, his son's appeal form was received at Bank Hall, on a Sunday.

The Thornton records contain one further mention of Thomas Cartmell. It seems that in November 1916, as his first exemption was due to expire, he asked the Preston tribunal to grant him a second one. The form upon which Thomas made his request was forwarded to County Hall on the 27th of the month, which was a Monday, and, given the speed with which Richard Bowman worked, it is likely that Thomas Cartmell's appeal had again been received over the weekend.

This was not the only indulgence the Thornton tribunal saw fit to grant to the Cartmell family. The man who, on 31st January, the tribunal had deemed already starred was James Cartmell – Thomas' brother and another of Councillor Cartmell's sons.

The Thornton local tribunal would remain receptive to the claims it received, even after the introduction of the Military Service Act 1916. In fact, the new statute seems only to have increased the range of options. The Act came into effect on Thursday 2nd March 1916, on which day, and perhaps by coincidence, the tribunal held another of its sessions. As was customary, proceedings began with the reading out of correspondence received. This included the letter from Councillor Cartmell in which he complained about the treatment of his son. According to the minutes, the correspondence also included a directive from the Local Government Board about the new Act and, finally, *two anonymous letters re: proceedings of Tribunal.*

Once the members got down to business, it became clear that their approach was not to change. Of eleven attested men whose cases were dealt with that evening, one was given an absolute exemption and nine received exemptions either for fixed periods, ranging from one month to three, or on condition they remained a *ploughman and horseman*, a *cowman and shepherd* or a *slaughterman*. At that session, and for the first time, the Thornton tribunal also considered claims from conscripted men. There were eight of them and in one the man was given an absolute exemption, while in another the man was exempted on condition that he remain, again, a slaughterman. One man, meanwhile, was made exempt from service for two months and five claims were dismissed.

It is striking that at this, the first session at which the two types of claim were considered, conscripted men were markedly less successful than attested men. That happened in other local tribunals too, and it has been attributed to a feeling among members that men who were now subject to the Military Service Act should have enlisted voluntarily before they could be compelled to do so. If there was such a feeling, and if it did affect the decisions the tribunals made, that would support the representations said to have been made by those who sought recruits under the Derby scheme – men who had attested *did* receive more sympathy than some of those who had failed to do so, even if the latter were certainly not denied the right to appeal at all. Those representations would, of course, be condemned as misrepresentations, not least by Lord Salisbury and Lord Derby.

The next Thornton session was held a fortnight later, on 16th March 1916, when, of nine claims concerning attested men, only two were dismissed and seven were rewarded with exemptions of up to eight weeks. At that session, a further four conscripted men had their claims considered – two of those claims were postponed, one was referred to the neighbouring tribunal in Blackpool and in one claim, the man concerned was awarded a two-month temporary exemption.

11

Many Thornton men who sought exemption from military service worked in agriculture, and that is also true, more generally, of men who lived in the town and on either side of the River Wyre. From the descriptions left in the records of the tribunal, we know that those men were slaughtermen; farmers, tenant farmers or farm bailiffs; stockmen, cowmen or milkers; or shepherds, horsemen or ploughmen. Often, in fact, the men worked in some combination of those trades.

Not surprisingly, therefore, and as the exemptions granted in March 1916 demonstrate, these were the occupations in which the men were required to remain if they wished to be exempted from military service. Sometimes, though, a further condition was imposed: the men would have to take part in the activities of the Volunteer Training Corps.

*

With war, and especially with the introduction of conscription, there had come a call for all men to be found a way to serve, including those above military age or in essential occupations. The response to that call was the creation of a large number of volunteer defence organisations. Though doubtless well-motivated, those organisations were informal and probably illegal and by September 1914, a central committee had been established to supervise, and perhaps restrain, their efforts. It was that committee which would give the organisations their collective name.

At first, the various Volunteer Training Corps were highly

selective and membership was open only to men who could demonstrate that they had good reason for not enlisting in the regular armed forces. That soon changed, however, and in March 1916, with the coming of the first Military Service Act, local tribunals acquired the power to order a man to join a VTC. By February 1918, the corps would have over a quarter of a million members, fully a third of whom had not joined willingly.

Each VTC was self-supporting and its members had to provide their own uniforms, which could not be khaki in colour. Members were also required to wear a red armband, bearing the letters *GR*. That stood for *Georgius Rex* and certainly not, as some wags unkindly claimed, for 'George's Wrecks', much less 'Government Rejects'. Members of the VTC trained – incessantly it was sometimes said – in drill and also in the use of firearms, and on occasions they were asked to perform duties to do with home defence. At first, the only weapons they had were dummy rifles from the local Territorials. During 1917, however, real guns and then machine guns would be issued to volunteers.

*

The need for men to be adept at drill was sometimes balanced, in Thornton at least, by other, perhaps more pressing considerations. Not surprisingly, they were usually considerations of the land. One notable case concerned a man named Herbert Mottershead. He was the gardener to a prominent businessman, Thomas Silcock, whose family had run the undoubtedly haunted bone mill out on Skippool quay and manufactured fertiliser from the guano the tiny port for a while received from Africa.

On 15th November 1916, when the Thornton tribunal gave Mr Mottershead an exemption from military service, it also said that he should join the VTC. That condition appears to have been considered too onerous, however, for in May the following year, the tribunal's clerk, Richard Bowman, wrote to Mr Silcock, referring to the most recent meeting and stating, *it was resolved that your gardener Mottershead be allowed to engage in work on the land instead of joining the VTC*. It would be some time before this information reached the local corps, for it was not until 31st July 1917 that Mr Bowman informed Captain Musgrave at the Drill Hall in Blackpool that the tribunal had *allowed Mr Mottershead to put in all his spare time on the land, instead of joining the VTC*. Herbert Mottershead survived the Great War and he would continue to live in Thornton, and to serve the Silcocks, for many years to come.

As 1916 wore on, the Thornton tribunal continued to grant men exemptions from military service. At its session on 4th April, for example, it concluded seven claims, all of which came from men who had attested under the Derby scheme. The tribunal awarded temporary exemptions in four cases and conditional exemptions in two more, and it dismissed only one claim. At the first of its two sessions in May, meanwhile, the tribunal granted exemptions in twice the number of claims it dismissed, while in the second session it dismissed five claims but granted exemptions in fully twenty-six.

A high point of sorts was reached at the extremely hectic session of 27th June, when the tribunal granted exemptions in thirty-nine claims and dismissed only two. Although the number of claims diminished, this trend continued in the months that followed. One claim was dismissed in each of the July and August sessions, but exemptions were granted in a further seven and four claims respectively, while in September and November, the ratio was twelve to two. In the last two thirds of 1916, the tribunal dismissed only a fifth as many cases as it granted exemptions.

A number of Thornton men received their exemptions because they had found work in the chemical industry.

*

The United Alkali Company had been formed in 1890 from almost fifty firms in Lancashire and the north-east of England, and in Scotland and Ireland. Those firms all used the famous Leblanc process to make sodium carbonate, a substance crucial at the time to the production of soap, textiles, paper and glass. Before long, the company would be the largest manufacturing concern in the country and for a while at least, it was the largest one in the world. Among the old firms of which it was comprised was James Muspratt and Sons, which had been based at Widnes in Cheshire and was the first to use the Leblanc process on anything like an industrial scale.

Since the mid-19th century, there had been a rival for the Leblanc process in the Solvay one, which used simple brine and was considered a good deal more efficient. That process was being used to increasingly impressive effect by Ludwig Mond and John Brunner, whose factory was also in Cheshire. Their organisation – Brunner, Mond and Company Limited – was not part of the new concern.

One of the first businesses to be purchased by the United Alkali Company was the Fleetwood Salt Company. For centuries, significant brine deposits had been known to exist on the east bank of the River Wyre, close to the village of Preesall, and from at least the 16th century they were being used to produce salt. In 1889, the Fleetwood Salt Company gained a monopoly over the deposits and it was soon pumping brine across the river to the processing works it had built in Thornton. In time, those works also came to adopt the Solvay process and in taking control of them, the United Alkali Company could expect to enter into direct competition with Brunner Mond.

After the First World War, the United Alkali Company, together with other British chemical concerns, would find itself losing ground to leaner and more dynamic competitors, especially in Germany and the United States of America. The trade depression that followed, combined with technological advances with which the company failed to keep abreast, led to a sharp decline in its market share. In 1926, the United Alkali Company would combine with several others to form Imperial Chemical Industries Limited. One of those other companies was Brunner Mond.

*

In the year of 1916, then, the Thornton tribunal considered the claims of local men at sessions held between 10th January and 15th November, and in dealing with those claims, it often did so sympathetically. The surviving records demonstrate that in at least 150 cases, the man's call-up was postponed or he was given some form of exemption from military service. In only thirty-four cases was a claim refused in such a way that the man would be required to go to war.

Although, in some cases, it did have that effect, in most cases the granting of exemption did not keep a man out of the armed forces forever. It was an intermediate step, usually taken, in Thornton at least, in order to balance the competing interests of the war and the land. If, of the two more decisive alternatives, dismissal was rare, the other was even rarer.

In its first year of operation, the Thornton tribunal awarded only three absolute exemptions, two at the fourth session at which cases were considered and the other at the fifth. The second absolute exemption was awarded to William Cartmell. He was a brother of Thomas Cartmell and James Cartmell, and another son of Councillor Cartmell, the man of whom the Thornton tribunal appears to have been so solicitous. William was given his absolute exemption at the session held on 21st February 1916. That was the same session as the one at which his brother Thomas' claim was dismissed.

There is a further striking feature of the approach the Thornton tribunal took during its first year of operation, and that it took, in particular, at sessions held towards the end of that year. The tribunal became very willing to adjourn the hearing of cases, not least, and as we have seen, because of uncertainty about the position of men who worked on the land. So great had that uncertainty become that on 10th October 1916, ten claims, including the second one brought by Joseph Blackburn, were put aside for another day.

Those claims were more than half the ones listed for hearing on that occasion and they made up the largest number adjourned at any of the Thornton sessions. The tribunal's first adjournment had not come until 16th March 1916 and those that followed did so at a rate of no more than three a session, even during the hectic months of late spring and early summer. Now, cases were put aside without any explanation or so that claimants, such as Joseph, could go before the medical board. One case was mysteriously adjourned for the man concerned to *see Captain Booth*. It is not clear what happened when the meeting took place, but the next note of the man's case states, with troubling finality, *appeal withdrawn*. The result, as the New Year came in, was that a backlog of cases was building up at Four Lane Ends.

12

When, on 9th January 1917, the members of the Thornton tribunal came together at the council offices at Four Lane Ends, it was for the first time in the New Year. The session that day began at 6pm, in accordance with the practice the tribunal had followed since March 1916, when it began receiving the claims not just of attested men but of conscripted men as well.

All members of the tribunal were present that Tuesday evening, together with the military representative, Captain Booth, and his assistant, Mr Robinson; and once again, Councillor Dewhurst was in the chair. Mr Walsh, the agricultural representative, was not, however, present. The chairman announced that he was suffering from *a severe illness*, but also that he was *progressing satisfactorily*. Councillor Dewhurst then wished everyone present a happy and prosperous New Year and expressed the hope that the terrible war would be over before the year was out.

The first order of business was the wealth of correspondence the tribunal had received over the festive season. That included a letter from the Army's Western Command in Chester, concerning *the substitution of labour*, and one from the local Superintendent of Police about *exempted men who are Special Constables*. With regard to the second matter, the minutes state that it was *Resolved: that the previous decision be adhered to*. In addition, and as was by now usual, the Thornton tribunal had received a number of missives from the Local Government Board. These included two letters about 'drawers-in' in the cotton trade, a publication entitled

Women's War Work and instructions on the subjects of men under twenty-six years of age and the distribution of manpower.

The tribunal had also received from the Local Government Board a copy of the current list of certified occupations. Helpfully, the board had included its own guidance, drawn up days before, on the new additions to that list. The tribunal would be able to put both documents to good use later in the evening.

Councillor Titherington then raised a matter that had clearly exercised him greatly. It seems that some of the cases adjourned at the last two sessions of the Thornton tribunal and set down for hearing at this one had, in the interim, been the subject of appeals to the county tribunal in Preston. Those appeals had been made by the military representative and, as a local newspaper would report, that man was now invited to account for his actions.

*

THE RIGHT TO APPEAL
THORNTON TRIBUNAL ANNOYED
Members Complain of Discourtesy
MILITARY REPRESENTATIVES' ACTION CRITICISED

Councillor Titherington said he wanted the matter dealt with now. He did not think it was any use the members of that tribunal sitting there, if their decisions were going to be opposed in the way they had been.

He thought it was totally wrong, after gentlemen had given their services to try to do the best they could for their king and country, that their decisions should be overruled. They might just as well stay at home. He wanted to know why these applications took place. If that kind of thing was going to occur, he was not venturing out these cold evenings and wasting his time and services.

The chairman said no one was more surprised than he had been to find seven of their cases appealed by Captain Booth. Although he was perfectly within his rights in making the appeal, it made their work as a tribunal useless.

Councillor Titherington – If we do something wrong, the Tribunal ought to be notified, so that we can have a chance to rectify ourselves, but to do such things as have been done by the military representative passes my comprehension.

Captain Booth – You are quite wrong in thinking I am trying to do something beyond the Tribunal's backs.

Councillor Titherington – I have not mentioned any names at present.

Captain Booth – I wish you would.

Continuing, he said that where a tribunal gave an adjournment, it was equal to a temporary exemption. He had the right to appeal against any other decisions, just as an applicant had a right to appeal against the decision of the tribunal.

"When I objected to these men getting exemption," he added, "you said, 'You know what to do.'"

Councillor Betney said he thought it was himself who said that Captain Booth had a right to appeal. Captain Booth was not present at the tribunal, and Mr Robinson stated that he did not know what Captain Booth would have said on the tribunal's decision had he been present. They thought it discourteous that Captain Booth did not tell them he was going to appeal against their decision.

Captain Booth retorted that that was the last thing he would think of doing. He was absolutely within his rights in challenging any decision, and there was no discourtesy on his part.

Councillor Betney – It appears that when these cases were taken to the Appeal Court, the military representative was told he was wrong in bringing them there. Is that not so?
Captain Booth – Not that I know of.
The Chairman – We only adjourned these cases on the latest instructions we had received. If Captain Booth appeals against our decisions, they don't come back to us.

Councillor Titherington said he asked the clerk if they were working from the last instructions received, and he assured them that they were. If these were further instructions, why were the tribunal not made acquainted with them?

Captain Booth – I do not supply you with instructions. You get them from the Local Government Board.

Councillor Strickland said that their last instructions were that agricultural cases as well as market gardeners should be adjourned. He had nothing to say against what Captain Booth had done, but there was one tremendous drawback, to his mind. They had four representatives sitting there who were familiar with the circumstances of the various applicants and after they had listened and decided a case on its merits, it was taken out of their hands. So far as Captain Booth's action was concerned, he did not think they had a right to speak.

Councillor Titherington – Then why waste our time here?
The Chairman – I think we have a right to speak or act, apparently. All market gardeners and farmers were to be exempted until the 1st January, and milkers until some other time.

The clerk said the telegram he had read dealing with the subject came from the military headquarters in Lancaster. It was to the effect that these cases should be postponed until further instructions had been received.

Councillor Betney said that if the military representative had told him he was dissatisfied with their decision, he would have been the first to help him. A farmer came up to him and asked him how it was that they had been brought before the Preston tribunal when the cases had been adjourned by the local tribunal.

Councillor Titherington said the tribunal could stand it, but it was not fair to their clerk. He was given the latest instructions, and they tried to work upon them. They did not want to keep anyone back who was eligible to go.

Captain Booth – It means that in order that I may please this Tribunal, I have apparently to neglect my duty, but I cannot do it. I respect this Tribunal, but at the same time I have to do my duty, however unpleasant it may be.

Councillor Titherington again pointed out that the tribunal had worked on the latest instruction received. They were told to exempt farmers and market gardeners until the 1st January, and they had done that. If there were some later instructions given, they had not received them.

Councillor Betney – You have always told Tribunals when you were going to appeal against their decisions?
Captain Booth – No, certainly not. In some cases, where I have been asked whether I was going to appeal against the decision, I have said that I was.

Councillor Betney said he had seen it in the papers where a military representative had said that he would have to appeal against a decision of the tribunal.

Captain Booth – And probably he has not done so.

Councillor Betney said he felt hurt at the way this thing had been managed. It appeared to be rather a sneaky way of going about things. They did not know anything until they were told by the men who had been brought before the Appeals Tribunal.

Captain Booth – Your clerk knew.
Councillor Betney – But we did not know.
Captain Booth – It is the same with an applicant. If he is dissatisfied with the finding of the Tribunal, he can appeal, and if I am dissatisfied with your decision I can also appeal. An applicant can put in an appeal and not inform you. It is a matter of procedure, and not discourtesy.

Councillor Strickland maintained that a man who was placed on a farm under the substitution scheme was as fit to fight as the man they took off. He knew what farming work was, and how hard it was.

Councillor Betney said that although these decisions had been appealed against, they knew of men who should have gone about the end of September but who were knocking about the district yet, or had been up to the last few days.

Captain Booth – I am here to do my work, and have nothing to do with the work of the recruiting officer. If these men have not been taken off, it is nothing to do with me. With regard to what Councillor Strickland had said, he remarked that a substitute could not do the same amount of work on a farm as the person whose place he took, but he could help to carry on the farm until the war was over.

*

Councillor Betney was wrong to say that Captain Booth had not attended the previous session of the Thornton tribunal. Both the captain and his assistant – and also, indeed, the agricultural representative and the councillor himself – were present in Four Lane Ends on 15th November 1916. Captain Booth had, in fact, attended every sitting there since April.

But the councillor was more accurate in his description of the attitude at County Hall to the appeals Captain Booth had made. This little spat, furthermore, was emblematic of the relationship between the Thornton tribunal and the military representative and it would become more so as the year went on.

The debate having subsided, tribunal members were told by their clerk, Richard Bowman, of eleven appeals from their decisions that had now been dealt with by the appeal tribunal. Those included the appeals members had just discussed with the military representative, which had now been returned to Four Lane Ends from County Hall. The outcome of ten of those appeals is readily apparent from the Thornton records. Most, if not all, had been made by Captain Booth and in nine of them, the Preston tribunal had found for the man and against the armed forces.

The tribunal then began to consider its cases. There were fifteen of them, twelve concerning attested men and three concerning conscripts.

13

The cases considered on 9th January 1917 are very similar to the ones the Thornton tribunal had dealt with in March the previous year, and each of them will again have been allocated a mere five minutes of hearing time. These were mostly the cases adjourned by the tribunal in the autumn, so that it might receive further official instructions or the results of medical examinations. One of them was Joseph Blackburn's second claim, which he had made more than three months before. That case was not among the ones the military representative had taken to Preston in the interim.

Of the other fourteen cases that evening, one was withdrawn, one was dismissed and twelve were decided in favour of the claimant. In thirteen cases, including the one withdrawn, the effect of the tribunal's decision was to exempt the man concerned from military service. In the case that was withdrawn, the man had already been given a conditional exemption and the tribunal simply confirmed that it would continue to apply. Four of the exemptions were made conditional upon the man finding or remaining in work of national importance, while one of them was granted to someone who had recently started work at the United Alkali Company. In the remaining eight cases, the man's exemption was made conditional upon his joining, or remaining in, the Volunteer Training Corps.

There is one other feature of those cases that is striking: in none where it was conditional on the man doing work of national importance, and in only two cases where he was required to join the VTC, was the exemption awarded also limited in time. In fully eleven cases, the exemption, though conditional, was also indefinite and it would therefore remain in place while the man's circumstances stayed the same.

*

Having given Joseph his five minutes, the members of the Thornton tribunal made a clear decision:

> *Exempted to 31st March conditionally on remaining in present employment. To join the VTC.*

The employment in which Joseph would have to remain was that of market gardener. That calling had been his for a number of years and, at least since the death of his father a year before, it is one he will have been following on his own account.

On that Tuesday evening, then, deep in the heart of winter, Joseph Blackburn received precisely what all but one of the men whose claims were heard alongside his received: an exemption from military service. He would not have to go to theArmy that month, or in the month that followed or the month that followed that.

The condition attached to Joseph's exemption was equally common; as they would be nationally, a great many men in Thornton were directed towards the VTC. It was, however, much less common for a Thornton man to have a time limit imposed upon his exemption from service. And it was uncommon for a man to be given an exemption that was both temporary and conditional. A good few men received conditional exemptions in succession to temporary ones and vice versa, but concurrent limitations were rare. In the fifteen sessions held before the tribunal considered Joseph's second claim, only five men were given an exemption that was limited in those two ways at the same time. Those men's cases had been considered at consecutive sessions the year before – four on 4th

May and one three weeks later, when Joseph's first, temporary but unconditional exemption was granted. But whatever its limitations and however uncommon it might have been, the exemption granted to Joseph on 9th January 1917 would be his last one.

*

We cannot, again, be sure whether Joseph appeared in person at Four Lane Ends. The minutes name only the members who were present that evening, together with the clerk and the military representative and his deputy. It seems reasonable, however, to assume that Joseph did attend the hearing of his case. Councillor Dewhurst and his colleagues plainly had significant information about him and, as we shall see, some of that information was very specific in nature. Save for the form we know Joseph completed at the beginning of his claim, it is difficult to think of any other source from which that information might have come.

There is certainly nothing in the minutes to suggest that Joseph made a written submission to the tribunal, and nothing in the copy letters to suggest that such a document was ever received. In addition, the timing of the 9th January session is unlikely to have been inconvenient for Joseph. Unlike the one held the previous May, at which his first claim was considered, it began only after the day's work will have been done.

There is one thing, however, of which we can be sure: when it considered his case a second time, the Thornton tribunal paid very close attention to the facts and, indeed, the current circumstances of Joseph's life. That might not be obvious from the records, but it is abundantly clear from the emphatic, public statements members of the tribunal would subsequently feel impelled to make.

Before long, the evidence heard in the council chamber at Thornton would be brought into question and the decision itself would come to be impugned. What members of the tribunal said as part of that process, however, allows us to be confident that on the final occasion they made a decision about Joseph's case, they were satisfied that he was a market gardener and that such was his principal occupation. In fact, the tribunal also concluded that Joseph worked hard on the land and produced two crops a year, and that he had spent more than £30 on seeds in the last twelve months. Given what was to come, those were significant findings.

Joseph might, in fact, have told the Thornton tribunal rather more than its members subsequently chose to recall. In reporting the session of 9th January 1917, one local newspaper noted the hearing of the following case:

> A market gardener and fruit grower (30), who had passed for general service, again appealed for conditional exemption. In reply to Captain Booth, he said he had 3 roods 20 perches of ground, and 500 feet of glass. He had had the place for 14 years. He worked four days on the land, and spent two days hawking his produce and fruit he purchased. Temporary to March 31st.

Although this report does not name the man in question, the age and occupation given for him, and the fact that he had been passed (fit) for service and was given an exemption, are all details that match those of Joseph's case. And those details do not match any other case considered in Four Lane Ends that evening.

If the report is indeed about Joseph's case, we can be sure, from the exchange with Captain Booth, that he was present when it was heard. The nature of that exchange suggests, in fact, that the case took up rather more than five minutes of the tribunal's time. We also discover that the size of Joseph's holding was equivalent to approximately seven eighths of an acre, which is a little larger than half a modern-day football pitch. And it is significant that while Joseph conceded that he hawked his produce, he also said he did so for only two days a week.

In performing its proper, judicial function, the local tribunal was required not only to find facts, but also to apply to those facts the relevant law. In this case, the law was contained in regulations whose precise wording allows us to conclude that Councillor Dewhurst and his colleagues were also satisfied that Joseph's personal labour or superintendence was indispensable for the proper cultivation of his holding and that such cultivation was expedient in the national interest. But those specifically legal conclusions would be of minimal significance.

*

The decision made by the Thornton tribunal was put into effect almost straight away. Six days after the hearing, Richard Bowman, the clerk, sent out a letter confirming Joseph's fate. The letter, like the one about Albert Mottershead, was addressed to Captain Musgrave of the VTC in Blackpool. The good captain had been the recipient of other letters from Mr Bowman and it is likely that he was also the N. Musgrave who, in Poulton in December 1915, witnessed Joseph's signature having watched him attest his willingness to serve. He was probably also a recruiting officer, and Mr Bowman now informed him:

> *JS Blackburn was among the men given a temporary exemption and required to join the Voluntary [sic] Training Corps.*

It isn't clear why Mr Bowman's letter omits to mention the conditional exemption that Joseph had also been given. Neither do the records tell us whether Joseph ever took part in the activities of the VTC. If he did so, however, it can't have been for very long.

*

The surviving records do not include any of the forms Thornton men had to complete when they made their claims for exemption. We know little, therefore, of the circumstances of those men or of the grounds upon which their claims were based.

That is equally so in Joseph Blackburn's case, and it is possible that what he hoped to be granted was an absolute exemption, maybe on the grounds of a conscientious objection to military service. Although possible, that it is highly unlikely. The Thornton records suggest that, like the majority of men who came before the local tribunals, Joseph sought more modest relief, based upon his domestic or professional circumstances. Because of the decision the Thornton tribunal made, he could now be sure that he would not be required to join the Colours, at least until the spring.

Whether that outcome pleased Joseph or dismayed him, it can't have come as a surprise – he had been granted a temporary exemption before, for three months, and that exemption had served him very well. Joseph was still at Rose Cottage, and in his garden, almost eight months after other members of his Derby scheme group had been mobilised for active service. But in early 1917, in Thornton at least, that was by no means uncommon.

One man whose case came before the Thornton tribunal at the same time as Joseph's was a conscript named Alfred Taylor. The tribunal had already granted him one extension, the effect of which was to prolong a two-month exemption granted in March 1916 to at least the end of November. The fortunate Mr Taylor would now gain further relief, until 28th

February the following year, which meant that his exemption from military service lasted for at least six times its original length.

A third man whose case was considered on 9th January 1917 fared even better. In total, George Bond would manage to obtain at least six extensions of an original one-month exemption from military service. As a result, that exemption was still in effect more than a year after it had been granted. Following a successful appeal by the military representative, Mr Bond went back to Four Lane Ends and obtained a further exemption, so that he remained at large fifteen months after the tribunal had first considered his case.

Like Joseph Blackburn, Bernard Ingle was a market gardener and had attested his willingness to enlist. In his case, a two-month exemption, granted on 2nd March 1916, was extended at least twice, so that he too was still at large fifteen months later. After Mr Ingle had obtained his second extension, an appeal in his case was heard in Preston. That appeal, which was probably made by the military representative, was granted, but only if the authorities could find a substitute for the man. That was clearly a difficult task, for Bernard Ingle was still in his garden in June 1917.

Mr Ingle's case seems to have caused some consternation in official circles and the Thornton tribunal eventually felt obliged to explain its position. On 12th March 1918, the tribunal's clerk sent a letter to the Lancashire War Agriculture Committee. The secretary to that committee was the ubiquitous Sir Harcourt Clare, and Richard Bowman told him:

My tribunal have always been of opinion that this man was whole-time engaged on work of national importance in connection with the cultivation of land for production of foodstuffs.

Those words, of course, carry distinct echoes of earlier events not just in the case of Bernard Ingle, but also in the case of Joseph Blackburn. When they were written, their significance will have been hauntingly apparent to all concerned.

*

The first session of the New Year was followed by another nine days later. When, on the afternoon of 18th January 1917, proceedings opened again, the members of the Thornton tribunal were given some significant news. Having heard of a further circular, received from the Local Government Board, they were told by Richard Bowman that the decision they had made about Joseph Blackburn was now the subject of an appeal by the military representative. On the same day, Mr Bowman sent the relevant papers to County Hall in Preston.

On Sunday 28th January 1917, Walter Long was killed in action at Hébuterne on the Western Front. A one-time middleweight boxing champion of the British Army, Brigadier-General Long of the 56th Infantry Brigade was the son of Walter Long, who was by now Secretary of State for the Colonies, but had previously been President of the Local Government Board. He was thirty-seven years of age.

14

Sir Robert and Sir George

When they joined the Central Tribunal in Westminster, George Talbot was a prominent barrister and Robert Carlyle was retired.

Robert Warrand Carlyle was born in 1859, in Brechin in Scotland. He was the elder son of the Reverend James Carlyle, a Presbyterian clergyman, who had served as chaplain in Bombay. Robert's mother, who happened to be called Jessie, came from Aberdeenshire.

The young Robert was educated at Glasgow University and at Balliol College, Oxford, and he entered the Indian Civil Service in 1878. Like his father, he would serve in the subcontinent for a good few years. At first, he was a tax collector and sometime magistrate in states in the east of India, but in 1902, he was appointed to lead the Bengal Police. Three years later, he became Chief Secretary of the region and by 1907 he was, in effect, the Indian Minister of Agriculture.

Although he favoured low taxation, Robert Carlyle presided over increased investment in the land and an expansion in co-operative credit, which aimed to make funds available to rural areas not well served by the larger, commercial banks. As his government portfolio also included public works, he was responsible from 1911 for the planning and building of the imperial capital at Delhi. The foundation stones of the new city were laid that same year by King George V, who had only recently ascended the throne and also become Emperor of India. The city would be primarily the work of Edwin – later

Sir Edwin – Lutyens. It was also in 1911 that Robert Carlyle was knighted and that Queen Mary first sat for William Llewellyn.

Four years later, as Joseph Blackburn's son was born, Sir Robert Carlyle retired to Essex. Already an expert in the philosophy of the Middle Ages, he collaborated on later volumes of his brother Alexander James Carlyle's mammoth history of medieval political theory. Sir Robert would die in Florence in May 1934.

Thomas Hume Dunlop, the musician who enlisted for military service the day after Joseph Blackburn did the same, was Sir Robert Carlyle's nephew. He arrived in France in July 1916 and was posted to the 10th Battalion of the Cheshire Regiment. On 10th October, Private Dunlop received the gunshot wounds from which he soon died. That was the same day that Joseph Blackburn's second claim was heard at Four Lane Ends.

Thomas Dunlop was thirty-six years old when he died. He is buried in the vast military cemetery at Étaples, which is the largest of its kind in France and the final resting place of more than eleven thousand men killed in the First World War. Like much of the city of New Delhi, the Étaples cemetery was the work of Edwin Lutyens and it would be the largest of the 136 he designed. In time, Sir Edwin would become President of the Royal Academy, the immediate successor to Sir William Llewellyn, who could count not just Queen Mary, but also Sir Everard Clare among his subjects. It is likely that Thomas Dunlop died in one of the many hospitals located on the edge of Étaples, close to the sand dunes and within sight of the sea.

*

George John Talbot was also an Oxford man, though of a slightly later vintage. His father, John Gilbert Talbot, was the son of the Earl Talbot, and his mother, Meriel Sarah Lyttelton, was the daughter of the fourth Lord Lyttelton.

Born in 1861, the year before Joseph Blackburn's father-in-law, George Talbot was one of ten children. Through his mother, he was an ancestor of Diana, the Princess of Wales, while through his father, he was a descendant of John Stuart, the third Earl of Bute, who in 1762 became Prime Minister of Great Britain. That was the year which saw Joseph's great-great-grandfather serving ale at an inn close to Blackpool.

George Talbot's uncle, the Right Reverend Edward Talbot, was, at one time or another, Bishop of Rochester, of Southwark and of Winchester. Bishop Edward's son, Gilbert Walter Lyttelton Talbot, a lieutenant in the 7th Battalion of the Rifle Brigade, was killed in action on 30th July 1915, at Hooge, a small village on the Menin Road around two miles east of Ypres. He was twenty-three years of age. Lieutenant Talbot was George Talbot's cousin and he is buried in the Sanctuary Wood Cemetery at Ypres, which is another of those designed by Edwin Lutyens.

John Gilbert Talbot, George Talbot's father, was a Conservative and a Member of Parliament, having been elected to serve the constituency of West Kent at the general election of 1868. He held that seat for ten years, before resigning it in order to fight a by-election in the Oxford University constituency, and the seat he won then he held until January 1910, when, at the general election, he stood down. Between 1878 and 1880, at the end of Benjamin Disraeli's second and final government, John Talbot served as Parliamentary Secretary to the Board of Trade.

Educated at Winchester College and at Christ Church, Oxford, George Talbot obtained a first-class degree in Classics in 1882 and was appointed to a fellowship at All Souls College four years later. Having been called to the bar, he specialised in presenting cases for parliamentary commissions. He would be a member of the Royal Commission on London Government in the early 1920s and also Chancellor of the Dioceses of Lincoln, Ely, Lichfield and Southwark. Like Sir Robert Carlyle, Mr Talbot would leave behind a number of written works, including *Law and Practice of Licensing and Modern Decisions on Ritual.*

George Talbot took silk in 1906 and would be made a High Court judge in 1923. He would receive a knighthood the following year, become a Fellow of Christ Church, Oxford, and in 1937, when he retired, be appointed to the Privy Council as his father had been. Sir George died in 1938, at the age of seventy-four years.

15

From early 1916, there were more than eighty appeal tribunals across Britain, each of which was set up by the local authority for the county it served. Although these new county tribunals owed their existence to the Military Service Act 1916, they would deal with appeals not just from conscripts, but also from men, such as Joseph Blackburn, who had promised to enlist and hoped merely to gain some limited relief.

In either case the appeal tribunals would have similar powers – they could grant a man exemption from military service and they could do so absolutely, temporarily or subject to conditions. They would, however, be required to consider each case afresh and they would neither be constrained by the decision of the local tribunal, nor bound to accept facts that had been found proved at the earlier stage.

The Lancashire Appeal Tribunal came into existence on 9th March 1916, some months, in other words, after the Thornton tribunal and the other local tribunals had begun hearing claims. Although it existed for almost three years and will have worked diligently throughout its life, and although its proceedings will have been properly recorded at the time, no trace remains of the hearings conducted by the Lancashire tribunal. Much the same is true of appeal tribunals across the land. All we have, at least in the case of appeals by Thornton men, is whatever remains of the notes the local tribunal chose to take.

The Lancashire appeal tribunal served four discrete areas, coinciding with the Quarter Sessions divisions; the areas into which the county had, for centuries, been divided for the purpose of administering criminal, and sometimes civil, justice. Those areas were Lonsdale in the north, Preston in the middle, Salford in the south-east and West Derby in the south-west. (The ancient hundred of West Derby began at the Ribble Estuary where that of Amunderness, and within it the Fylde, came to an end.) Discrete appeal tribunals would, in fact, sit in each of those areas and would be based in Lancaster, Preston, Manchester and Liverpool respectively.

The chairman of the Lancashire tribunal was the Right Honourable Lord Richard Frederick Cavendish, and he would also serve as chairman of the discrete tribunal for the Lonsdale area of the county. In time, in fact, he would go on to perform judicial work on a national scale.

*

Born in 1871, Lord Cavendish was a British aristocrat and politician, who lived at Holker Hall near Grange-over-Sands, where his descendants reside to this day. His father was the third son of the seventh Duke of Devonshire and the young Richard was educated at Eton College and at Trinity College, Cambridge.

Richard Cavendish entered the House of Commons in 1895, when he was elected Member of Parliament for North Lonsdale. At first, he was a member of the Liberal Unionist party, which had been formed nine years before by Liberals who opposed their leader W. E. Gladstone's conversion to the cause of Irish Home Rule. In Parliament, the party was allied to the Conservatives, with whom it formed a decade-long coalition government. That government was headed by Robert Gascoyne-Cecil, the third Marquess of Salisbury, who would be the last British Prime Minister to lead his administration from the House of Lords. Its leader in the House of Commons was Arthur Balfour, Lord Robert Cecil's nephew, who would eventually succeed his uncle both as leader of the Conservative party and as Prime Minister. For a while, the leader of the

Liberal Unionists in the House of Lords had been the fifteenth Earl of Derby, whose wife had previously been married to the second Marquess of Salisbury.

Beginning in 1903, a fissure had opened up within Liberal Unionist ranks, not least on the issue of Tariff Reform, a cause now favoured by the party's leader, Joseph Chamberlain. In the next few years, a large number of party members left to join the Liberals and in 1904, Richard Cavendish became one of them. By far the longest of his six recorded Parliamentary speeches were the two delivered, in February 1904 and March 1905, in support of Free Trade and against Protectionism. At the general election of 1906, however, Mr Cavendish was one of the very few members of his new party to lose their seat. He did so to the Conservative candidate by a mere 179 votes, and he would not return to the House of Commons.

Lord Cavendish chaired the Royal Commission on Systems of Election, which reported in 1910 and recommended, amongst other things, immediate abolition of two-member parliamentary constituencies and the introduction of a form of proportional representation. Having been proposed as a peer in the event that what became the Parliament Act 1911 was rejected by the House of Lords, he was made a Privy Councillor in 1912.

As might, perhaps, be expected, Lord Richard Cavendish is the subject of a large number of portraits. One of them, a photograph, would be made by Walter Stoneman in 1938 and now forms part of the National Photographic Record. That portrait is kept at the National Portrait Gallery, with two others of Lord Richard made forty years before.

*

The Lancashire Appeal Tribunal had as its clerk the new baronet, Sir Harcourt Everard Clare, and its thirty-eight members included not only a peer of the realm, but four knights or baronets, a Member of Parliament and seventeen Justices of the Peace.

The chairmen of the discrete Salford and West Derby tribunals were Joseph Maghull Yates and Arthur Stanley Mather respectively. Mr Yates was a barrister and King's Counsel and the stipendiary magistrate for Manchester; while Mr Mather was a solicitor and, when the Lancashire tribunal was formed, the incumbent Lord Mayor of Liverpool. The four appeal tribunals also included other men with legal knowledge. In Salford, for example, His Honour Judge Francis Hamilton Mellor was a county court judge and Sir William Cobbett was a solicitor, while in Lonsdale, James Clarkson was a chairman of borough justices.

Mr Clarkson was also a retired official of the Co-operative Society and right across the county, representatives of commerce and industry were present in appreciable numbers. In the tribunal that sat in Salford, for example, Sir William Stephens was a yarn merchant, Charles Ainsworth was engaged in cotton spinning and William Carnforth Robinson came from a textile federation; Sir James Edward Jones was a general merchant; and Henry Whitehead was said to be engaged in banking and general commerce. Also in that tribunal, Charles Ward was qualified for service on several grounds, being an alderman, a retired tinplate worker and a director of companies.

In West Derby, meanwhile, John Francis Gillott was general manager of the Wigan Coal and Iron Company Limited, and there was also Maxwell Hyslop Maxwell. An alderman of the city of Liverpool, Mr Maxwell was a member of the Liverpool merchant family of that name, which had interests in the Caribbean and in the trade in rum, coffee and spices. The family's endeavour had ensured that the port of Liverpool supplanted that of Skippool and the resources it provided had helped Simón Bolívar to great success in much of South America. Maxwell Maxwell was a director not only of the family firm, but also of the Cunard Company, the Royal Insurance Company and the Liverpool Overhead Railway Company. The tribunal could also claim as a member Max Muspratt.

*

Max Muspratt was made Lord Mayor of Liverpool in 1916, the immediate successor in that office to Arthur Mather, who was now his chairman on the West Derby appeal tribunal. A recent predecessor of both men was the seventeenth Earl of Derby, who had occupied the office from 1911 to 1912, the last of thirteen Stanleys to do so since the time of Queen Elizabeth I.

Mr Muspratt was born in Seaforth, near Liverpool, where Joseph Blackburn's brothers, Robert and William, were now living and from where his nephew, Thomas, had gone to the Army. For the first years of his life, Max Muspratt lived at Seaforth Hall, the modest, neo-Grecian mansion that his grandfather, James, had, like the Fleetwood family before him, built on shifting sands within sight of the Irish Sea. James Muspratt was the first person in the country to make alkali by the Leblanc process on anything like an industrial scale, and Charles Dickens and Richard Brinsley Sheridan were only two of the many notable people to whom he had played host.

The place where Seaforth Hall once stood is now occupied by the Gladstone Dock, for whose building the hall was razed to the ground. From that place to Rossini Street, and the house in which Robert and William Blackburn lived, is but a short walk. The same was true during the Great War of the journey from Seaforth Hall to the town's imposing barracks.

In 1910, between the first general election and the second, Max Muspratt was the Member of Parliament for the Liverpool Exchange constituency. At first a Liberal, he would later join the Conservatives.

As the Great War began, Max Muspratt was chairman of

the United Alkali Company, whose interests had for some time included the chemical works on the marshes between Thornton and the River Wyre. Amongst other things, the company produced the chlorine gas that would be used to such devastating effect across the Western Front, and it was at the Burn Naze works that the company made its chlorine. During the war, Max Muspratt was an adviser to the Ministry of Munitions and it was in recognition of that service that he would later be created the first Baronet Muspratt of Merseyside.

A matter of yards from Rossini Street in Seaforth, running sometimes parallel with it and sometimes at a right angle to it, is Muspratt Street. At no point do the two streets converge.

16

Among the members of Lancashire's four appeal tribunals there were several representatives of landed interests. In Salford, for example, Charles Hardy was an agent of Lord Ellesmere, while in West Derby, Robert Anderson was said to be an estate manager. Mr Anderson was, in fact, a qualified surveyor and the estate he managed belonged to the ubiquitous Lord Derby.

Knowsley Hall is a stately pile a few miles east of Liverpool. Designed in part by Robert Adam, it stands in nearly three thousand acres of parkland that was landscaped by Lancelot 'Capability' Brown. The hall is the seat of the Stanley family, which was a favourite of various Tudor kings, fought on the side of King Charles and has produced Earls of Derby since the fifteenth century. The family's military exploits are commemorated in a number of ancient ballads, including *The Ballad of Bosworth Field* and *The Famous History of Flodden Field*, and its support for the Royalist cause brought it into one of the notable skirmishes of the Civil War. In April 1643, at Whalley near Blackburn, troops led by James, the seventh earl, were ambushed by a smaller Parliamentary force and driven out of the village. The earl's retreat did not, however, end there. This had been merely the latest in a dispiriting series of defeats and he soon withdrew to the Isle of Man. (He would do so again the following year, when the Royalist cause was defeated in the north.) Of the Stanley family's many politicians, none was more eminent than the fourteenth earl, who was Prime Minister of the United Kingdom on three occasions. His son – and also his grandson, the seventeenth earl – served as Secretary of State for War, with the latter holding that office twice, either side of a spell as the country's ambassador to France. The Stanleys were great supporters of horse racing and ice hockey, and great patrons of writers such as William Shakespeare and Edward Lear.

And there were other men within the Lancashire tribunal who had expertise relevant to their new, judicial task. In Lonsdale, for example, George Tyson was a tenant farmer and it was noted of Gerald Garnett that he *has a thorough knowledge of requirements of hill farmers*. As the law required, there were also several representatives of labour. William Evans, for example, who sat in Lonsdale, was the local secretary of the National Federation of Blast-Furnace Men, and in Salford, Charles Kean was president of a trades and labour council. In West Derby, meanwhile, the members of the tribunal included Stephen Walsh.

In one of the few remaining documents of the Lancashire Appeal Tribunal, Stephen Walsh is described as a *Miner's representative* but he is also said to have *no business*. That is neither accurate nor fair. By 1916, when the appeal tribunal came into being, Stephen Walsh had been a Member of Parliament for ten years. He represented South West Lancashire in the Labour interest and would continue to do so until 1929. His constituency comprised much of the old hundred of West Derby and it had previously been part of the one for which W. E. Gladstone was the member immediately before he became Prime Minister.

Mr Walsh had, it is true, been a miners' union officer and indeed a miner. He claimed first to have gone down a pit at the age of thirteen and to have been paid 10d for a ten-hour shift. He would serve as the miners' agent for the Wigan district and as vice president of the Lancashire and Cheshire Miners and, from 1922, of the Miners' Federation of Great Britain.

In 1917, Stephen Walsh joined the coalition government of David Lloyd George. He was a junior minister first in the Ministry of National Service and then, from June of that year, at the Local Government Board. That was the office Mr Walsh held while he was a member of the Lancashire tribunal, which was a judicial body for which his own department was politically responsible. (The concept of conflict of interest was perhaps less developed than it is now.)

So strong was Mr Walsh's loyalty to the government that he refused to disavow it, even after his party withdrew its support for Lloyd George. As a result, he would find himself facing an official Labour candidate at the general election of 1918 and being constrained to stand on a 'Coalition Labour' ticket. He would do so successfully and his political career would continue to flourish thereafter. For much of 1924, Stephen Walsh would be Secretary of State for War under the first Labour Prime Minister, Ramsay MacDonald. He was in that post the immediate successor to the seventeenth Earl of Derby.

For a while, Mr Walsh also served as vice president of the British Workers' League. That was a 'patriotic labour' organisation whose supporters included Robert Blatchford and also H. G. Wells among other luminaries. The league promoted Britain's involvement in the First World War, while some of its supporters broke up pacifist meetings, and in time it took an emphatic rightwards turn.

The Lancashire Appeal Tribunal also included a number of politicians who operated on a local, rather than a national scale. In Lonsdale, for example, Mr Alfred Brown was a town councillor and Mr William Briggs was the Mayor of Lancaster. Although, again, the latter was recorded as having *no occupation*, he had in fact been a pharmacist in the city. Alderman Briggs would remain in office until 1919 and a portrait of him hangs in the mayor's parlour at Lancaster town hall.

In West Derby, meanwhile, another member of the appeal tribunal was Peter Peacock, who was the current Mayor of Warrington. Mr Peacock had taken that office in 1913 and he would continue to hold it throughout the war. He is now most celebrated, outside Warrington at least, for having two families, each of which was unknown to the other, and for being the – then barely acknowledged – father of the critic and writer Kenneth Tynan. A portrait of Sir Peter, painted by John A. A. Berrie, hangs in Warrington Art Gallery.

John Archibald Alexander Berrie studied at the Royal College of Art and was a noted portrait painter in the first half of the 20th century. His subjects included not just Mr Peacock, but at least four other mayors of Warrington, together with at least eleven mayors of Wallasey and sundry other municipal worthies. Mr Berrie also painted Edward, the Prince of Wales; the American golfer Bobby Jones; and the aviatrix Amy Johnson. On at least three occasions, he painted Margaret Beavan, who would be the first woman Lord Mayor of Liverpool, and in 1935, his portrait of Queen Mary would be presented to her husband. John Berrie's portrait of King George himself, done in 1931, is one of the few for which its subject ever agreed to sit. It was commissioned by the 2nd Battalion of the King's (Liverpool) Regiment; the one in which Joseph Blackburn's cousin, Robert, would very briefly serve.

*

The town of Thornton was served by the discrete appeal tribunal that sat in Preston. That tribunal also heard appeals from the other urban districts of Lancashire; from the county boroughs of Blackburn, Blackpool, Burnley and Preston; from the non-county boroughs, such as Accrington, Chorley and Clitheroe; and from the rural districts of the county. For its chairman, the Preston tribunal had Mr James Openshaw, who, a surviving document states, *takes Second Court at Quarter Sessions.* In fact, he was the deputy chairman of those sessions and would shortly become their chairman.

Like Lord Richard Cavendish, James Openshaw was born

in 1871 and educated at Trinity College, Cambridge. The young James was a Harrow boy, however, and also a prize-winning fencer. He qualified as a barrister and practised at the criminal bar, but even though he was now a judge, he gave farming as his occupation. Mr Openshaw lived at Hothersall Hall in Ribchester, a Victorian Gothic house inherited from his father that was surrounded by farms covering almost two thousand acres. He would receive a knighthood in the New Year's honours of 1928. A portrait of Sir James, with the customary gown, wig, collar and bands and in the customary shades of grey and brown, still hangs in the Crown Court in Preston. It was painted in 1935, again by John A. A. Berrie. The portrait makes a suitable companion for the one of Sir Harcourt Clare that also hangs there.

*

When, in January 1917, Joseph Blackburn heard about Captain Booth's appeal, the news will have come from the Thornton tribunal, which will itself have received it from the military representative and from County Hall. And when he heard the news, Joseph might once again have been optimistic about his prospects.

It is difficult to know what happened to cases that went to Preston – how many appeals succeeded, for example, and why – and the lack of any records means that we have to rely upon any notes the relevant local tribunal happened to make. In Thornton, thankfully, the records are of some assistance. They show that of twenty-nine appeals against decisions of the tribunal during its first year of operation, nineteen were dismissed. As for the decisions made at Four Lane Ends on 9th January 1917, three of them were the subject of appeals: one by the man concerned and two by the military representative. We know that the man failed and that the other appeals concerned Alfred Taylor and George Kings.

Mr Taylor was the man who managed to remain exempt from military service for a year. The extension granted to him on 9th January, and that would be good until the end of the following month, was conditional upon his joining the VTC. At its session on 27th February 1917, however, the Thornton tribunal noted that in Mr Taylor's case, the appeal by the military representative had succeeded. The same is true in the case of Mr Kings.

The names Alfred Taylor and George Kings do not appear subsequently in the records of the Thornton tribunal. The name George H. Kings can, however, be found among those of the town's dead. Driver George Henry Kings, of the Royal Army Service Corps, died on 24th April 1917, less than two months, it seems, after his lengthy exemption from military service finally came to an end. He was thirty-four years of age and now lies at rest in the churchyard of Christ Church in Thornton.

17

Sir Francis and Sir Algernon

When they went to Westminster, Sir Francis was a lawyer and administrator and Sir Algernon was a prominent businessman.

A barrister by profession, Francis Charles Gore became the Recorder of Canterbury in 1893, and from the following year until 1911, when he retired and was knighted, he served as Solicitor to the Board of Inland Revenue. He would die in 1940, at the age of ninety-three years.

Francis Gore was born in 1846 and he was therefore the rough contemporary of Joseph Blackburn's parents. He was the oldest son of Charles Alexander Gore, whose brother was the fourth Earl of Arran. He was also, therefore, a cousin of the fifth earl and also of the earl's daughter, Lady Cicely Gore, and that connection would soon become significant. Sir Francis had four siblings: two brothers and two sisters. The younger of his brothers was Charles Gore, a distinguished theologian, who was Bishop of Birmingham for six years until 1911 and Bishop of Oxford for eight years afterwards.

The elder of Sir Francis' brothers was Spencer William Gore, who in 1877 won the men's singles title at the first All England Lawn Tennis Championships. Spencer W. Gore in fact held a low opinion of lawn tennis, and he entered the Wimbledon tournament only because it was to be held close to his home and he hoped to win enough money to buy a horse-drawn roller. He also played cricket for Surrey and the banjo for amusement. Among his sons, and the nephews of Francis Gore, was Spencer 'Freddie' Gore, the noted artist and leading light of the Camden Town Group, who died of pneumonia in March 1914.

One of Sir Francis Gore's two sisters was Caroline Maria Gore. She married Henry Arthur Lascelles, a distinguished soldier, who fought in the Indian Mutiny and the Ashanti campaign and died in 1913. The couple had three sons who were involved in the First World War. Francis William Lascelles, a captain in the Sussex Yeomanry, was wounded in the conflict and awarded the Military Cross, while Henry Francis Lascelles fought with the Welsh Guards and received the Croix de Guerre. The couple's remaining son, John Frederick Lascelles, was a second lieutenant in the Rifle Brigade and a member of the Royal Flying Corps. Lieutenant Lascelles was killed in action on 31st July 1915 at the age of nineteen years. He died the day after Gilbert Lyttelton, the cousin of George John Talbot, who would soon become his uncle's colleague.

Sir Francis had three sons of his own, the eldest of whom, Arthur Charles Gore, rose to the rank of lieutenant in the Connaught Rangers and fought in the Boer War. Charles Henry Gore was Sir Francis' second son. Educated at Trinity College, Oxford, he was a major in the Royal Army Service Corps, served in the Middle East during the First World War and became Director of Supplies and Transport of the Egyptian Army. Sir Francis Gore's third son was John Francis Gore, who was also educated at Trinity. A captain in the Bedfordshire Yeomanry, John Gore also fought in the war and he was mentioned in despatches. He was both a barrister and a distinguished writer and in 1941, three decades after his father was knighted and his uncle became Bishop of Oxford, he would be made Commander of the Royal Victorian Order and awarded the James Tait Black Memorial Prize for his official biography of King George V.

*

In 1911, Sir Algernon Firth donated a park and a drinking fountain to the people of Bailiff Bridge near Brighouse in West Yorkshire. He did so in recognition of the king's recent accession, both to the crown and to the Emperorship of India. But that was neither the first nor the last of his generous public benefactions.

Algernon Firth had been born in 1856, the son of Yorkshire carpet manufacturer Thomas Freeman Firth and his wife, Hannah Mariah Willans. He was educated privately and then entered the family business, which was wool. T. F. Firth and Company had been founded when Algernon was four years of age, and it would come to own the enormous Heckmondwike Woollen Flush Mills and also Clifton Mills in Brighouse. In 1909, the year after Joseph Blackburn married Jessie Bennett, Algernon Firth succeeded to the baronetcy that had been created for his father only a short time before. The second Baronet Firth of the Flush, as he was styled, would come to occupy Scriven Park, a stately pile near Knaresborough in North Yorkshire that had existed since at least the 14th century.

When, on his father's death, Sir Algernon also took control of the family company, he began developing its foreign business and turning it into a true, and early, multinational concern. The company specialised in heavy-duty carpets, in particular for hotels, trains and ships, and for many years it would operate not only in Yorkshire, but also across the Atlantic, in Cornwall, a town on the Hudson River some fifty miles from New York City. For a while, the company employed around six hundred workers at Firthcliffe, the name given not only to its factory in the town, but also to the model lodgings the company built nearby in order to house its workers and their families.

Sir Algernon and his wife, Lady Janet, were for many years generous patrons of good causes across the West Riding and beyond. In 1917, for example, they allowed one of their properties, Holroyd House in Halifax, to be used as a hospital and convalescent home for injured servicemen, while three years later, they would fund the building of a cenotaph and memorial garden, again in Bailiff Bridge. In the years that followed, on land in Heckmondwike that Sir Algernon had donated for the purpose, a new estate was built so as to accommodate workers from the Flush Mills. That estate, too, would be named Firthcliffe and, as its creator had stipulated, it would command spectacular views of the surrounding countryside. In 1933, Sir Algernon would commission the building in Leeds that would for seventy-five years house the Institute of Pathology at the city's university, and that now provides a home for many of its students.

Holroyd House had previously served as a home for Sir Algernon and Lady Janet's only child, their daughter, Dorothy Gertrude Firth. She married Michael Bruce Urquhart Dewar in 1910. He was the son of a housemaster at Rugby School and was educated there and at Trinity College, Cambridge. An engineer by training, Michael Dewar had been a director of the T. F. Firth Company and he would serve in the Royal Engineers. In 1916, after he was transferred to the Ministry of Munitions, he began a rapid ascent that would within two years see him appointed Director of National Projectile Factories and Assistant Controller of Shell Manufacture. At the close of hostilities, Michael Dewar would be awarded the OBE for his services. He would become an eminent figure in British engineering and, during the Second World War, the leader of the nation's tank mission to the United States of America. It was in that capacity that he would become intimately involved in the design of the Sherman tank.

Sir Algernon Firth would die in 1936, at the age of eighty years, when, because he had no male issue, the baronetcy created for his father would become extinct. He is the subject of a portrait that is now in the collection of the University of Leeds and that is notable not only for the many shades of brown in which it is rendered, but also for the black of its subject's capacious morning coat.

Done in 1933, the painting is the work of George Fiddes Watt, the Scottish artist and engraver, whose many other works encompass a familiar company of marquesses and viscounts, of industrialists, senior academics and eminent surgeons, and of aldermen, county council chairmen and – given their creator's origins – provosts. G. F. Watt was also the painter of a celebrated portrait of H. H. Asquith, the Liberal politician who was once the longest continuously serving Prime Minister of the United Kingdom. Mr Asquith's mother, Emily Willans, was the sister of Sir Algernon's mother, Hannah, and the two men were therefore cousins.

18

The appeal tribunal which sat in Preston had eight members, including its illustrious chairman. That was fewer than the Salford and West Derby tribunals, but more than the Lonsdale one. Those members all came from within Lancashire, even if some of them lived or worked on the county's fringes, but if they were geographically diverse, many of them shared similar social, economic or political backgrounds.

In the records of the Lancashire tribunal, James T. Travis-Clegg is another man who is said to have no occupation. Once again, that is far from the whole story and the records go on to state that he *does much public work*. Mr Travis-Clegg (whose middle name was also Travis) was by now the chairman of the cotton-spinning company founded by his father. He had been educated at Eton College having first attended a preparatory school within sight of the grand old windmill at Lytham on the Fylde coast. For years a local politician, he was an officer of the Oldham Conservative Association when Winston Churchill was the town's MP. Since 1898, Mr Travis-Clegg had also been a member of the Lancashire County Council, of which he would eventually become chairman, and he was an alderman of the county.

At one time, James Travis-Clegg had entertained hopes of entering national politics and he unsuccessfully sought election to Parliament in 1905 and also the following year. He was now a Justice of the Peace and an Income Tax Commissioner and he sat on numerous public committees, including those charged with arranging care for Lancashire's inebriates and its tuberculars. He was also a member of the

Carlton Club and of several Masonic lodges, and for a while he had served as honorary treasurer of the North of England Society for Women's Suffrage.

Mr Travis-Clegg's home was Whalley Abbey, a country house built in the ruins of a 13th century Cistercian monastery, whose last abbot had been executed for refusing to accept King Henry as the head of the English church. The abbey was drawn by J. M. W. Turner in 1799 and it came into Mr Travis-Clegg's hands a century later.

*

It was in March 1537 that the aged abbot, John Paslew, met his end, convicted of high treason at Lancaster Castle and swiftly hanged, drawn and quartered. His remains were then taken to Whalley, to a grove of oaks close to the place where the seventh Earl of Derby would be routed barely a century later. There, beside an ancient stone circle, the remains were put on public display. Abbot John's grievous offence had been revealed, and his death sentence pronounced, by a special tribunal appointed by the king. The tribunal's president was Edward Stanley, the third Earl of Derby.

The earl had already served Henry well, not least as an emissary to the Holy See, where he told the Pope about the king's divorce from Catherine of Aragon, and years later, he would also preside over the trial of Lady Jane Grey. For many years, Lord Derby kept a minstrel of his own: Richard Searle, a harper and balladeer from Staffordshire, who is said to have been the creator of *The Famous History of Flodden Field*. It is likely that Mr Searle's works also include the *Stanley Poem*, a 1,300-line epic that lauds the valour of several generations of the family's men.

On 21st June 1916, just after Joseph Blackburn was given his first exemption from military service and just before the seventeenth Earl of Derby became Minister for War, labourers felled an ancient tree in a field near Whalley. The tree had for many years been known as the 'Paslew Oak', in recognition of the part it reputedly played in the murder of Abbot John.

*

Among his many other public appointments, Mr Travis-Clegg was a member of the Committee of Visitors of the County Asylum at Whalley. Originally intended to house people who were then called 'imbeciles', and also those called 'moral imbeciles', 'idiots' and the 'feeble-minded', that institution opened in April 1915 and was immediately given over to a different and more pressing purpose, becoming Queen Mary's Military Hospital. Sir James, as he would become, was chairman of the Extra Comforts and Entertainments Fund there, and he was also a director of a company that made artillery shells in the village where the hospital stood.

A short distance away lies Brockhall, which was itself once the place of an asylum. The Lancashire Inebriates Reformatory was erected there in 1904 by one of the county council committees on which Sir James Travis-Clegg sat. In that year, a third asylum – the Langho Colony for Sane Pauper Epileptics – also opened in the area. The villages of Whalley, Brockhall and Langho stand together in the Ribble Valley and none of the three asylums was more than two miles from the others.

Unsurprisingly, perhaps, Sir James Travis-Clegg is also commemorated in oils. His is a splendid three-quarter-length portrait, which – like those of his colleagues on the Lancashire tribunal, Sir James Openshaw and Sir Peter Peacock – was painted by John A. A. Berrie. Done in the usual discreet tones – in his case of beige, claret and grey – that portrait now hangs in County Hall in Preston, only a few steps from the room in which countless military service appeals were heard.

In time, Whalley Abbey would return to ecclesiastical use, with its new owners reflecting the divisions of Abbot Paslew's time and the accommodations that subsequent centuries would bring. In 1919, Mr Travis-Clegg would sell part of the abbey to the local Roman Catholic church and three years later, he would sell the remainder to the Anglicans.

*

There were other, similar men on the Preston tribunal, including Mr Rowland Rawlinson from Rawtenstall, whose interests were said to include cotton, and Sir Frank Hollins and John Duckworth.

Sir Frank, who was already the first Baronet of Greyfriars, was head of Horrockses, Crewdson & Co, a long-established and celebrated cotton concern based in Preston. At his instigation, and with great success, the company had moved from the wholesale to the retail trade and by 1913, it was said to be the largest in the land. In the summer of that year, Horrockses received a great honour. On the afternoon of Tuesday 8th July, its factory played host to King George and Queen Mary, whose motorcade swept into the yard under an arch of cotton bales. The royal couple had come into the town by train, past a banner proclaiming *A Gradely Welcome To the King And Queen Is Offered By Proud and Loyal Preston*. In the market square, they had been serenaded by a choir of eight hundred primary school children and by the band of the 4th Battalion of the Loyal North Lancashire Regiment – the very one to which, little more than two years later, Joseph Blackburn would be assigned.

The visit was part of a tour of north-west England that would be as comprehensive as it will have been exhausting. Over eight days, the royal couple covered more than two hundred miles, much of it by motor car, and visited almost forty towns and cities. Three days after they were in Preston, they travelled to

Liverpool, where they opened the new Gladstone Dock, which had been built where Seaforth Hall used to stand.

Throughout the tour, the royal couple were accompanied by Edward Stanley, the seventeenth Earl of Derby, who also found them board and lodging at Knowsley Hall. And it was there that, at the end of the first day of the tour, a special Royal Command performance was held, featuring some of the most celebrated music hall artists of the day. The performers included George Formby Senior, the father of the more celebrated son, who proclaimed himself the 'Lancashire Torreador' and took the stage with his famous 'Plink-Plonk' song, *The Skin of a Spanish Onion*, which he sang to the tune of Bizet's march.

The other performers that evening included Tom Edwards, 'The Huntsman Ventriloquist', who would appear on stage in riding gear and was about to find himself embroiled in a suit for desertion brought by his wife. They also included Neil Kenyon, who wore a kilt and performed monologues in a broad Scottish dialect, and the suave conjurer, David Devant, who was said once to have made Queen Alexandra laugh out loud.

The bill was completed by Olga, Elgar and Eli Hudson, a trio that combined Eli's piccolo, and also his flute, with the soprano voice and piano his wife and sister provided. Elijah Rennison Hudson had played on Skegness pier and performed for the Kaiser even before he studied at the Royal College of Music, and he would eventually join the LSO. The trio toured the land, claiming to be *the most refined turn on the music-halls today*, and they performed in full concert dress on a stage decked out as a Victorian parlour, replete with standard lamps and bearskin rugs.

The performance that evening was given to honour the king and queen, of course, but also to celebrate the nineteenth birthday of Edward, Lord Stanley – the son of the seventeenth earl, who would before long become the baby of the House of Commons.

While he, too, had cotton interests as the head of his family company, John Duckworth was also a Liberal party politician. In 1923, he would be elected as Member of Parliament for Blackburn, a seat he would hold for six years. The town was then a two-member constituency, for which the Liberals and the Conservatives each put up but a single candidate so as not to split the anti-Labour vote. In January 1924, Mr Duckworth was one of only a few Liberal MPs to defy his party's whip and vote with the Conservatives in an – unsuccessful – attempt to prevent the country's first Labour government.

On 11th July 1913, John Duckworth, too, received his royal visit when, during their whistle-stop tour, the king and queen called at his factory in Blackburn. There, one of the weaving rooms sported a banner proclaiming, *We workers loyally greet your majesties*. The royal couple had already laid the foundation stone of the King George's Hall in the town and later, they would officially open a recreation ground, on land close to his factory that Mr Duckworth had donated for the purpose. For their trouble, they were presented with monogrammed handkerchiefs and a pair of miniature clogs.

The Preston appeal tribunal also included as a member Sir Reginald Arthur Tatton, who owned Astley Hall in Chorley and also Cuerden Hall near Preston, which was currently being used as a military hospital. The membership was completed by His Honour Judge Hugh Murray Sturges, who often sat in the county court in Blackpool, and Mr Fred Thomas of Burnley, the only acknowledged representative of labour, whose description in the surviving documents reads simply, *Weavers unions*. Mr Thomas was, in fact, a senior official in the Burnley Weavers' Association and he is now remembered as a fierce opponent not only of his association's rivals, but also of socialism itself.

There was someone else connected to the Lancashire

tribunal who received a royal visit in the summer of 1913. In recent weeks, Harcourt Clare, the tribunal's clerk, had not been particularly well and on Tuesday 8th July, in between trips to Blackpool and Preston and nearby Southport, King George and Queen Mary stopped at the gates of Bank Hall to enquire after his health.

19

On 27th February 1917, the Thornton tribunal held its only session of the month and the members were handed a sheaf of letters together with another seven circulars from the Local Government Board. One letter came from a Mr Edwards, indicating that he had started working for a Mr Dier, while another came from a Mr Dier, confirming that he had recently taken on a Mr Edwards. This correspondence seems to have been solicited by the tribunal itself, for in a note sent to Mr Edwards the week before, the clerk, Richard Bowman had told him:

> *The Tribunal will be meeting on Tuesday afternoon next the 27th inst. and if you are not yet in a position to report that you have taken up work of national importance, it would be better if you could attend at the Tribunal or send any correspondence that you have had with anyone respecting the same.*

Like that of Joseph Blackburn, the case of William James Edwards had come up in Thornton on 9th January, when the man was awarded an exemption and ordered to join the VTC. His name was also among those mentioned in the letter Mr Bowman then sent to Captain Musgrave of the Blackpool Corps. In his case, however, although the exemption was made conditional upon his taking up work of national importance, it was not limited in time.

It seems that Mr Dier provided, or that William Edwards hoped to convince the tribunal that he provided, precisely that kind of work. Mr Dier was a market gardener and he, too, had gained exemption from military service, his claim having been considered at Four Lane Ends eight months before. The surviving records do not say why the latitude he and his new employee were given couldn't also have been afforded to Joseph Blackburn.

At the February session, the Thornton tribunal also received letters concerning two men, William Nicholson and William Beahan, indicating that they too had found work, with the United Alkali Company. The letters helpfully enclosed certificates to that effect provided by the company itself. The final missive was from Mr Hughes, the clerk to the Lancaster local tribunal, *enclosing anonymous letter.*

The correspondence dealt with, Mr Bowman had some interesting news to impart. It concerned Joseph Blackburn, to whom the tribunal had recently given an exemption that was not only conditional but also temporary. The clerk announced that in Joseph's case, the county tribunal in Preston had now considered the military representative's appeal and decided to dismiss it. The representative in question was not Captain Booth, with whom the Thornton members were familiar, but one Captain Hayman. It was doubtless to him that the task fell of attending sessions at County Hall.

In the weeks and months to come, Councillor Dewhurst and his colleagues would have reason to think and speak at length about the decision the appeal tribunal made. From what they said, it seems that the decision was the same as the one they themselves had made: the Preston tribunal was satisfied that Joseph's principal occupation was that of market gardener. Given what the regulations said, the tribunal must also have decided that his personal labour or superintendence was indispensable for the proper cultivation of his holding and that such cultivation was expedient in the national interest.

As Richard Bowman will have explained, however, this was

not the end of the matter, for in its wisdom, the Preston tribunal had granted the military representative a significant indulgence – he would be permitted to make one further appeal. That would be to the Central Tribunal, which adjudicated upon points of law or principle and was the ultimate authority on matters of this kind. In giving permission for Joseph's case to be taken to Westminster, the Preston tribunal also posed a tricky question: in the case of a man with a market garden, how large would his holding have to be for him to gain exemption from military service?

*

The question of size is one that had exercised the Central Tribunal from the outset, and as early as its third session the tribunal had found itself considering the position of farmers. Under the regulations then in force, such men weren't entitled to be 'starred' and couldn't be regarded as exempt from military service, at least on grounds of their occupation.

On 4th January 1916, as Allen Clarke's *Windmill Land* found its first readers, the members of the tribunal considered two letters they had received; one from the local tribunal for Tutbury & Atcham in Shropshire and the other, concerning the equivalent position of crofters, from the tribunal for Ross & Cromarty in the Highlands of Scotland. They concluded that *misunderstanding and difficulty is already arising with regard to the position of farmers, who are not starred as such.*

The problem, the tribunal decided, was that *farmers may not be regarded as starred, even when they act as their own shepherds or cowmen, and may be indispensable to the continued working of the farm.* The solution was clear:

> *It may be necessary that 'working farmers' should be included in the list of 'reserved occupations'... The*

discrimination should be based upon whether or not the
man is necessary to the cultivation of the land.

This was a yardstick the Central Tribunal would have cause to
wield again in the months that followed.

It is plain that the precise number of men required to work
the land was a subject of discussion throughout Westminster.
The subject had come up at the tribunal's meeting on 1st March
1916, which was the day before the first claims from conscripted
men were heard at Four Lane Ends. The minutes of that meeting
include a memorandum written by the tribunal's secretary, Mr
I. G. Gibbon.

Ioan Gwilym – later Sir Gwilym – Gibbon was a senior
civil servant, who also served the War Cabinet, together with
the Ministry of Health and several others. The author of a
number of renowned works on public administration and an
expert on social insurance and on town and country planning,
I. G. Gibbon was also a noted historian of the London County
Council and in 1913 – the year Joseph Blackburn's daughter,
Elizabeth, was born – he had produced a study of schemes to
reduce child mortality. In that study, he wrote about infant
welfare centres and the possibility that fathers as well as mothers
might be encouraged to venture through their doors. It was
one he did not favour, because, he explained, *The better type of*
father will probably keep away. He regards the whole thing as the
wife's business.

In his Central Tribunal memorandum, Mr Gibbon wrote:

I have talked over with Mr Cheney of the Board of
Agriculture the number of men required for agriculture.
He said that it was extremely difficult to lay down any
rule. The circumstances differed so greatly in different
parts of the country, and on individual farms in the same
district... With regard to market gardens and fruit farms

it was difficult to make any suggestion, but it might be
said that one man would be required for every two farm
horses.

Mr Cheney looms large in the tribunal's deliberations on this
issue. It seems, for example, that he was present in person at the
session on 31st March, when, the minutes note:

The Tribunal proceeded to discuss the scale of labour
required on farms in order to maintain the full
productivity of the land. It was felt that some scale was
desirable as a guide to the Central Tribunal when dealing
with cases.

Mr Cheney proceeded to advise the Tribunal with
regard to the suggested scale, but pointed out that owing
to the varying conditions, even in the case of farms in the
same parish, it is difficult to do more than to suggest very
generally the amount of labour required to keep the land
in cultivation and to maintain the stock upon it.

At that session, Mr Cheney made one particular
recommendation:

One man, with the assistance of unskilled labour, may
be expected to cultivate 3 acres of land cultivated as a
market garden. In the case of field market gardens one
man with the assistance of unskilled labour would be able
to cultivate 8 acres. In both cases, the assistance might be
afforded by members of the market gardener's family or
by female labour.

The influence of Mr Cheney can be discerned in the tribunal's
approach to the case of a Mr Wilson. A conscripted man, he,
like Joseph Blackburn, was both a market gardener and from

Lancashire. Unlike Joseph, however, it seems that the Preston tribunal had found against him. On 7th November 1916, the Central Tribunal dismissed Mr Wilson's appeal and decided he should not be exempt from military service. In words no doubt drafted, or at least suggested, by its clerk, the tribunal decreed:

> *The Central Tribunal do not feel that they can properly lay down any general rule as to the size of a holding in respect of which exemption may be granted. Each case must be decided on its own circumstances. The principles applicable to such cases are indicated in the list of certified occupations R.94 (page 11, paragraph (b), under 'Farmer').*

This would not be the last time the tribunal offered such an explanation.

*

One reason the size of a holding was considered important was what had already come to be known as 'the allotment question'. It was perhaps the most significant reason and it is easy to see why it might have loomed so large in Joseph Blackburn's case. The question is one to which, in January 1917, at least one of the newspapers covering the Thornton area was giving some thought. At precisely the time Joseph's case was being considered afresh at Four Lane Ends, the newspaper asked, *The allotment question: what of military age men?*

> *Suppose a man of military age gets a good big allotment of land and grows a large supply of potatoes or other vegetables. Will he be allowed to urge this before the Tribunal as a reason for exemption from serving in the Army or Navy?*

Having posed the question, the newspaper did not hesitate to provide an answer:

It should be clearly defined that men of military age, unless rejected on medical grounds, cannot be granted allotments.

It seems that what Joseph had, while plainly both good and big, was something more than a mere allotment. His market garden covered a sizeable patch of land and he had worked it, at one time with his father but now alone, for a good many years.

*

In the Thornton local tribunal, the session held on the afternoon of 27th February 1917 ended on a celebratory note when, according to the minutes, *the Chairman congratulated Major Booth on his promotion from the rank of Captain.*

Captain Booth had been present at that session, together with his assistant, Mr Robinson, and Mr Walsh, the agricultural representative, who must by now have been restored to health. It seems, however, that there was a consequence of Captain Booth's elevation that he did not reveal that Tuesday afternoon. It is one of which he might not have been aware at the time, but that he would communicate to the Thornton tribunal in writing in the next few days.

On 15th March 1917, in a letter the Thornton copy of which is handwritten, Richard Bowman, the clerk, wrote to Major Booth:

I read your letter of the 6th inst. to the Tribunal at their meeting today and they desired me to express, on their behalf, their regret that you had relinquished your appointment as Military Representative.

They hope that your new sphere of work will prove congenial and will always look with pleasure to the time they were officially connected with you.

Although the work of the Tribunal is at times unpleasant in its character they recognise that your unfailing courtesy and tact has been of the greatest assistance to them.

May I also add my personal regret at the severance of our association and my best wishes for your future success.

The Thornton tribunal's relationship with Major Booth's successor would not always accord with the sentiments expressed here.

On 3rd March 1917, Richard Bowman sent a letter to the Central Tribunal, in response, it is plain, to one the Thornton tribunal had recently received. He wrote:

I enclose herewith papers relating to JS Blackburn, Case No 17923, the answers appear to be in order.

Mr Bowman's letter concludes, *The delay in replying is owing to the envelope being insufficiently addressed.*

20

Sir John

John Fowler Leece Brunner was a Member of Parliament and also of the Liberal party.

Born on 24th May 1865 – the same year as Joseph Blackburn's mother-in-law and Edward Stanley, the future Lord Derby – he was the eldest son of John Tomlinson Brunner. In 1919, he would succeed to the baronetcy of Druids Cross in Lancashire, which had been created for his father fourteen years before. He would also become chairman of Brunner, Mond & Co, the company of which his father had been one of the founders.

Sir John's father was born in Liverpool, one of five children of the Reverend John Brunner, a schoolmaster of Swiss origin. Having begun his working life as an office boy, he became, with Ludwig Mond, the proprietor of the wealthiest British chemical company of the late 19th century and, according to a title given to him by *The Times*, the 'Chemical Croesus'. As an employer, he was paternalistic, introducing shorter working hours, sickness and injury insurance and paid holidays.

Politics occupied a large part of John Tomlinson Brunner's life and he was first elected to Parliament in 1885, for the Northwich constituency in Cheshire. Having lost that seat after a year, he regained it twelve months later, on both occasions against opposition from the new Liberal Unionist party. He held the seat in 1906, gaining his largest ever majority at the general election of that year, and he would retain it until he left Parliament four years later. At Westminster, J. T. Brunner supported his party's leader, W. E. Gladstone, in his support for Irish Home Rule. He was also in favour of Free Trade, trade unions, disestablishment of the Church of England and, as war approached, a more sympathetic stance towards Germany. He had opposed the Boer War and campaigned for compensation for people whose homes had been damaged by the pumping of brine, an activity that was for a time as common in Northwich as in Thornton.

A prominent Freemason, J. T. Brunner was also a noted philanthropist. His benefactions helped found a public library in Northwich and fund schools both there and elsewhere in Cheshire; he paid for a guildhall in Winsford and in Runcorn, where he also bought a disused chapel so that it could be used by friendly societies; he gave large sums of money to build the Runcorn and Widnes Transporter Bridge; and at Liverpool University, he endowed chairs in economic science, physical chemistry and Egyptology. He would also decline a peerage.

Like his father, John Fowler Leece Brunner was a member of the Liberal party. At the 1906 general election, when his father retained Northwich, he was elected MP for Leigh in south Lancashire. He was the successor in that seat to C. P. Scott, the editor and later proprietor of the *Manchester Guardian*, and for a few years he was therefore a parliamentary neighbour of Stephen Walsh.

The two Brunners sat together on the Liberal benches until 1910, when, at the first general election that year, the son succeeded his father as MP for Northwich. That was also when Max Muspratt began his short parliamentary career in Liverpool, but unlike Mr Muspratt, John F. L. Brunner was also successful at the year's second general election. He would retain his seat until 1918 and represent the town of Southport for a short while thereafter.

From his marriage to Lucy Marianne Vaughan Morgan, Sir John had a son, Felix, who served in the Royal Field Artillery during the First World War and would marry Dorothea Irving, the granddaughter of the actor Sir Henry Irving. Sir John also had a daughter, Joyce Morgan Brunner, whose own daughter, Katharine, would marry Prince Edward, the Duke of Kent and become the Duchess of Kent.

There would also be tragedy and scandal in the Brunner family, for in 1926, Harold Roscoe Brunner, the brother of John F. L. Brunner, would murder his own wife, Ethel, and then kill himself. He would do so at the London home the couple's daughter, Shelagh, shared with her husband, Prince Ferdinand de Lichtenstein. Roscoe Brunner had resigned as chairman of Brunner Mond only months before. He was in poor health and had opposed the recent merger with the United Alkali Company and the consequent creation of ICI.

One of John F. L. Brunner's cousins, Cecil Heywood Brunner, served with the Royal Horse Artillery and the Royal Field Artillery in the First World War. Cecil's son was named Clive Muspratt Brunner. Clive's mother (and Cecil's wife) was Ricarda Molesworth Muspratt, and one of her many cousins was Max Muspratt. In 1917, Mr Muspratt was chairman of the United Alkali Company, a competitor of Brunner Mond, and he was also a member of the appeal tribunal for Lancashire. Another Brunner cousin was Kate, and her son, William Ronald Oulton, also saw service in the war, first in the Cheshire Regiment and then in the Royal Flying Corps and the Royal Air Force.

John F. L. Brunner's first recorded contribution in Parliament came in February 1906, just a fortnight after the general election. On the 22nd of the month, he asked the Undersecretary of State for the Colonies, Winston Churchill, whether he was aware that 'natives' of Northern Nigeria had "been selling their children as slaves, and that the prices at which they were sold represented normally one shilling and nine-pence-worth of corn and ten shillings in salt".

In his long parliamentary career, John Brunner would go on

to make well over a hundred such contributions, but it seems that, in the chamber at least, he was less exercised than Lord Salisbury by the exigencies of the Great War. Shortly before the two men joined in the Central Tribunal's decision about Joseph Blackburn – as the last Russian czar abdicated, the United States entered the fray, the Germans retreated to the Hindenburg Line and the second Battle of Arras began – Mr Brunner rose in the House of Commons to put a question to the president of the Board of Trade:

"Has he considered the case of blind piano-tuners who in the course of their business are obliged to travel by railway and pay the increased fares; and can some concession be made in their case?"

The answer, it seems, was that no concession could be made.

17,923

21

Throughout its life, from early 1916 until the end of hostilities and beyond, the Central Tribunal could be found in Westminster. At first that was on Broadway, but from the beginning of 1917, the tribunal was based at 16 Queen Anne's Gate.

That is a street, close to Westminster Abbey and the Houses of Parliament, at one end of which is a statue of the monarch who gave it its name. It is only a short stroll from the church where Lord Louis Mountbatten would one day marry Edwina, the daughter of Colonel Wilfred Ashley. During the Restoration – and like the rough, rum-soaked quayside at Skippool at the same time – the lane from which the street would later be formed was the site of a notorious cockpit. This one, though, might have been put there by King Charles himself.

The dwelling at number 16 sits in the middle of a terrace of four-storey, brick and stucco-fronted town houses built in 1775. It was to there that the Thornton tribunal's letters about Joseph Blackburn were sent.

As with the Lancashire Appeal Tribunal and its coevals, the work of the Central Tribunal would be governed by the Military Service Act 1916. Unlike the county appeal tribunals, however, the Westminster one had enjoyed a previous existence. It convened for the first time on 22nd November 1915, four days after the death of Joseph Blackburn's mother, and for several weeks thereafter it heard appeals made by men who had attested under the Derby scheme.

Once the new Act came into effect, the tribunal also dealt with appeals from conscripted men. In either case, its powers were equivalent to those of inferior tribunals and, again, it would not be constrained by what they had either found or decided. The job of the Central Tribunal was not simply to review a decision made by the relevant appeal tribunal or local tribunal. In Westminster, a man's case could be looked at afresh and the original decision remade. That was a power the tribunal would use repeatedly in the three years and more of its existence.

On 21st March 1916, two months after the new Act was introduced, a notice in the *London Gazette* announced that among the Central Tribunal's members would now be the Marquess of Salisbury, Sir Algernon Freeman Firth, Sir Francis Charles Gore, Sir Robert Warrand Carlyle and Mr George John Talbot. It was these men, alongside John Fowler Leece Brunner, who would consider the appeal made in Joseph Blackburn's case. All of them except Lord Salisbury and Sir Robert Carlyle had served on the tribunal since its inception.

Among other members of the Central Tribunal announced in March 1916 were Lord Sydenham of Combe, Sir Osmond Williams, Sir George Younger and Cyril Jackson, and they would in time be joined by Evan Charteris.

*

George Sydenham Clarke, the first Baron Sydenham of Combe, would be the first chairman of the Central Tribunal. Born in 1848, the son of a Lincolnshire vicar, he had been a soldier, serving with the Royal Engineers and rising to the rank of major general, and also a military journalist. Subsequently, Mr Clarke entered public life. Knighted in 1893, the year Francis Gore became Recorder of Canterbury, he was Governor of the State of Victoria in Australia for two years until 1903 and of Bombay for six years from 1907. His time in India therefore coincided with the latter part of Robert Carlyle's service there. It was in 1913 that Sir George Clarke became a peer. He had been a member of the committee that recommended significant reform of the British Army and he had subsequently chaired a royal commission on venereal disease.

Originally a Liberal, Lord Sydenham would in his later years become prominent in his support of far-right political groups. He would join The Britons, an anti-Semitic organisation active between the two world wars, which disseminated a version of *The Protocols of the Elders of Zion*. The organisation's founder, Henry Hamilton Beamish, had left Britain after losing a libel case brought by Sir Alfred Mond, the noted industrialist, Liberal turned Conservative politician and, latterly, Zionist. Sir Alfred was the son of Ludwig Mond, the man who had founded the mighty chemical company with the father of Lord Sydenham's tribunal colleague Sir John Brunner. Henry Beamish claimed to have tutored Adolf Hitler and in December 1936, in Berlin, he was an honoured guest of the Nazi foreign minister, Joachim von Ribbentrop. Even as the work of the Central Tribunal was coming to an end, his colleague, Lord Sydenham, was working on perhaps his most controversial work – a book entitled *The Jewish World Problem*.

It was in the Australia of the very early 20th century that Cyril Jackson, too, performed at least some of his public service, as the senior inspector of schools in the state of Western Australia. Born in 1863, the year after Jessie Blackburn's father, Mr Jackson was the son of a stockbroker and, having acquired a large private income, he was able to devote himself to good works and to politics. After studying at New College, Oxford, he undertook social work in the East End of London and, from 1885 – the year J. T. Brunner was first elected to Parliament – he lived at Toynbee Hall, the university settlement in Whitechapel that had been founded the year before. Cyril Jackson ran a boys' club there, at a school that would be renamed in his honour and that survives to this day. In 1891, he became a member of the London School Board and for six years until 1913, while George Clarke was in Bombay, he sat on the London County Council. He was leader of the Municipal

Reform party, a grouping allied to the Conservatives that aimed to overturn Labour party control of local government in the capital. Cyril Jackson was for a while the chairman of the council, although he had relinquished that post by the time he was appointed to the Central Tribunal. He was knighted in August 1917.

Born in 1849, Arthur Osmond Williams was a Welsh landowner and, in 1917, the serving Lord Lieutenant of Merionethshire. Educated at Eton College, he was the son of David Williams, who had been a Liberal Member of Parliament for that county. Osmond Williams shared his father's politics and in 1900, he also acquired his parliamentary seat. It was one he would hold for a decade, leaving Westminster when he became a baronet. Sir Osmond was married with six children. One of his sons, Osmond Trahaearn Deudraeth Williams, of the newly formed Welsh Guards, was killed on 30th September 1915 at the Battle of Loos. He was thirty-two years of age. Captain Williams is buried in Lapugnoy Military Cemetery, which lies close to the town of Béthune in the very north of France and is another of those designed by Edwin Lutyens. Like Joseph Blackburn, Osmond Williams left a wife and two small children, including a daughter, also named Elizabeth, who was only a month old when her father died.

Evan Charteris, too, was educated at Eton College. The youngest child of the tenth Earl of Wemyss, he studied at Balliol College, Oxford and then embarked upon a career at the Parliamentary bar, taking silk in 1919. Originally a member of the Coldstream Guards, he rejoined the Army when hostilities broke out and, even though he was past fifty years of age, served as a captain first in the Royal Flying Corps and then in the Tank Corps. He would become chairman of the trustees of the National Portrait Gallery in 1928 and of the board of the Tate Gallery six years later. The biographer of the artist John Singer Sargent, who was his friend, and of the writer Edmund Gosse, he would in 1932 become Sir Evan Charteris.

Sir George Younger was also a Member of Parliament, having represented the constituency of Ayr in Scotland since 1906 – the same year that saw his tribunal colleague John F. L. Brunner, and also Stephen Walsh of the Lancashire Appeal Tribunal, returned to Westminster. Sir George did so, however, in the Unionist cause, and in 1916, he became chairman of that party. Born in 1851, the oldest son of James Younger, George was a scion of the famous brewing family and became chairman of the company in 1897. He was a Clackmannanshire councillor from 1890 until he entered Parliament and Deputy Lieutenant of that county from 1901. Like Francis Gore, his colleague on the Central Tribunal, he had been knighted in 1911. Of Sir George's three sons, the second was killed in the Boer War and the third in the First World War. Charles Frearson Younger, a lieutenant in the Lothians and Border Horse, died on 21st March 1917 at the village of St Léger in Picardy. He was thirty-one years of age.

22

The members of the Central Tribunal also included George Nicoll Barnes, who was present from the outset, and James O'Grady, Robert Tootill and Viscount Hambleden, who joined the tribunal subsequently.

Like Sir George Younger, James O'Grady entered Parliament in 1906, when he was elected to represent the Leeds East constituency. Unlike Sir George, however, he would do so in the Labour interest. It was at the general election held that year that the party's first Members of Parliament were returned.

Born in Bristol, the son of Irish immigrants, Mr O'Grady had left school at the age of ten years, trained as a cabinetmaker and become active in trade unionism. A member first of the Social Democratic Federation and then of the Independent Labour Party, he also served as president of the Trades Union Congress in 1898, the same year that James Travis-Clegg became a member of the Lancashire County Council. James O'Grady would hold his parliamentary seat until 1918, when it was abolished and he, like Colonel Wilfred Ashley, moved to a newly-created seat. That seat was Leeds South East, for which he was returned unopposed.

At Westminster, where he was for a time Labour's only Roman Catholic MP, James O'Grady spoke frequently on foreign affairs. A staunch supporter of the Great War, he made several visits to the Western Front and was a vigorous participant in recruitment campaigns both in Britain and in Ireland. Mr O'Grady was also interested in Russian affairs and in 1917, shortly after Joseph Blackburn's case was considered by the Central Tribunal, he travelled to Moscow to meet Alexander

Kerensky, the leader of the new provisional government. After the October Revolution, however, Mr O'Grady would describe Lenin as a "great statesman" and argue for recognition of the Bolshevik government and against international attempts to defeat it by military force. In addition – and like his fellow Labour MP and fellow tribunalist Stephen Walsh – he served for a time as vice president of the British Workers' League. James O'Grady would leave the House of Commons in 1924, when he was knighted and began a new career in colonial administration, as governor first of Tasmania and then of the Falkland Islands.

Like James O'Grady and also Sir George Younger, George Nicoll Barnes was a Member of Parliament who had first been elected in 1906, and like Mr O'Grady, he was a member of the Labour party. In 1917, he was, in fact, Minister for Pensions and a member of the War Cabinet of David Lloyd George. Born in Dundee in 1859, the same year as his Central Tribunal colleague and fellow Scotsman Robert Carlyle, Mr Barnes was the son of a Yorkshire engineer who had moved north for work. He followed his father's calling and in 1896 became the general secretary of the Amalgamated Society of Engineers. Like Sir George Younger, Mr Barnes represented a Scottish constituency – that of Glasgow Blackfriars and Hutchesontown – but although he had been one of the first two Labour members to be elected in Scotland, that hadn't been his first attempt to win a parliamentary berth. In 1895, he had unsuccessfully contested the Rochdale seat for which, five years later, the writer and *Windmill Land* creator Allen Clarke would fight with the same lack of success.

Although, for twelve months from February 1910, George Barnes served as his party's leader at Westminster, he would find himself opposed by an official Labour candidate at the general election of 1918. That is because, like Stephen Walsh, his fellow Member of Parliament and junior minister, Mr Barnes refused to disavow the coalition government in which he had served.

Having therefore been expelled from the Labour party, and with support from the British Workers' League of Mr Walsh and James O'Grady, he would found the National Democratic and Labour party and stand in the election on a 'Coalition Labour' ticket. George Barnes would leave Parliament in 1922 and thereafter devote himself to the International Labour Organisation and to writing.

Like Sir Osmond Williams and Sir George Younger, George Barnes, too, lost a son on the Western Front. In September 1915, five days before the death of Captain Williams, Henry Barnes, a second lieutenant, was killed in action while serving with the Seaforth Highlanders. He, too, died at the Battle of Loos, in his case on the first day. He was twenty-six years of age.

Robert Tootill was also a Labour MP, having represented the constituency of Bolton since a by-election held in 1914. He had first come to prominence nearly thirty years before, when, in the aftermath of a six-month-long engineers' strike, he had been one of eight Labour representatives elected to the town's council. That strike, which at one point saw hussars ride into the town to keep the peace, was both controversial and divisive. It also made a deep impression on another Bolton resident, Allen Clarke, who used it as the backdrop for his celebrated novel *The Knob-Stick: a Story of Love and Labour*. In his newspaper, *Teddy Ashton's Northern Weekly*, Clarke described Tootill as *a powerful speaker, though at times carried to rashness by his own eloquence*. Like James O'Grady, his colleague on the Central Tribunal, and like Stephen Walsh of the Lancashire Appeal Tribunal, Robert Tootill served as vice president of the British Workers' League. His connections with that organisation would in fact lead to his being asked to resign from the National Executive Committee of the Labour party.

William Frederick Danvers Smith, the second Viscount Hambleden, would be chairman of the Central Tribunal from October 1917 until the end of its life. He had succeeded not his father, but his mother to the title in 1913, the same year George Clarke became a peer. Emily Danvers Smith had been made Viscountess of Hambleden in 1891, in honour of her newly deceased husband, the newsagent and Conservative politician William Henry (W. H.) Smith. It was in that same year that W. F. D. Smith inherited from his father both control of the family business and the parliamentary seat of The Strand. He would hold that seat until 1910, when he was succeeded by Walter Hume Long, the two-time President of the Local Government Board.

Born in 1868 and educated at Eton College and then at New College, Oxford, Frederick Smith would serve in the Royal First Devon Yeomanry, gaining the rank of lieutenant colonel and seeing service in Egypt and at Gallipoli. His wife, Esther, was the daughter of the fifth Earl of Arran and the sister of Lady Cicely Gore, and through her, Viscount Hambleden was therefore related to her brother-in-law, and his own colleague on the Central Tribunal, Sir Francis Gore.

On Saturday 26th July 1913, a fortnight after their tour of the North-West had come to an end, Viscount Hambleden attended the opening by King George V and Queen Mary of the new King's College Hospital in south London. The site had been donated by him ten years before and he would now be chairman of the hospital's board of managers.

*

The Victoria and Albert Museum is but a short stroll from Westminster, and among the four million objects for which it now provides a home is a set of bath taps, made in 1900 by the celebrated artist and craftsman Nelson Dawson. Done in copper and silver in the Arts and Crafts style, the taps were made for Greenlands, the riverside house near Henley-on-Thames that Viscount Hambleden bought for himself in 1868. The house was disparaged by Jerome K. Jerome in *Three Men in a Boat* and now houses a business school.

It is comforting to know that although the Smiths are long gone – and with them the British Workers' League, Cyril Jackson's Municipal Reform party and the cockpits that might have stood in Skippool and in what is now Queen Anne's Gate – some of the family's taps, at least, remain.

23

Lord James

James Edward Hubert Gascoyne-Cecil, the fourth Marquess of Salisbury, attended his first Central Tribunal meeting on 23rd March 1916 and his last just over eighteen months later. Although to his intimates he was 'Jem', the marquess was known at Queen Anne's Gate as Lord Salisbury and he frequently took the chair at meetings of the tribunal. He did so, for example, at the 297th meeting, when the case of Joseph Blackburn was among those discussed.

James Gascoyne-Cecil was a British statesman and a Conservative politician. Born in 1861, he was a contemporary of George Talbot, his colleague on the tribunal, and of Jessie Blackburn's father. His own father, Robert Gascoyne-Cecil, was the third Marquess of Salisbury and Prime Minister of Great Britain on three separate occasions between 1885 and 1902. On the first two occasions, Lord Robert Cecil, as he was styled, was both preceded and succeeded by W. E. Gladstone, while on the final occasion, he was succeeded by Arthur Balfour, his own nephew.

The Cecil family was and remains one of the most prominent in the land. It rose to favour under Queen Elizabeth I, whose chief minister was William Cecil, the first Baron Burghley. His younger son, Robert Cecil, was a leading minister not only under Elizabeth, but also under her successor, King James I. It was the latter who, in 1605, made Robert Cecil the first Earl of Salisbury. The sixth earl was made a marquess by King George III.

It was the first earl who, in the early 17th century, built Hatfield House, the splendid pile in Hertfordshire that has been the seat of the Cecil family ever since. The house was created from the old Palace of Hatfield, which had belonged to John Morton. Under King Henry VII, he had simultaneously held the offices of Lord Chancellor and Archbishop of Canterbury. Like the old Cistercian abbey at Whalley, the palace and its surrounding park were seized by the next King Henry and they were then used by him as a home for his children. It was at Hatfield that Henry's daughter, Elizabeth, learned that she had become queen and held her first Council of State, and it was Queen Elizabeth's successor, King James, who gave the old palace to the first earl.

*

Viscount Cranborne – as James was styled in his younger years – was educated at Eton College and then at University College, Oxford. He began his political career at the general election of 1885 with a five-vote victory in the Lancashire constituency of Darwen. He first entered Parliament, then, at the same time as the father of John F. L. Brunner, his future colleague on the Central Tribunal. Viscount Cranborne retained his seat in 1886 by a greater margin, but he lost it six years later. He returned to Parliament in 1893, when he was elected unopposed for the Kent constituency of Rochester, and he would occupy that seat until, upon his father's death in 1903, he moved to a new one in the House of Lords.

He had also been a soldier. Ultimately reaching the rank of lieutenant colonel, Viscount Cranborne commanded the 4th Battalion of the Bedfordshire Regiment from 1892 until January 1915, and he fought in the Boer War. He would remain aide-de-camp to King George V until 1929 and a committed member of the Territorials thereafter.

Viscount Cranborne's ministerial career began in 1900, when, during the Conservative-Liberal Unionist coalition that had already governed Britain for several years, he was appointed by his father to serve as a minister in the Foreign Office. That was something he would continue to do under his cousin, Mr Balfour. In 1903, the viscount became a marquess and in October of that year, he joined the Cabinet as Lord Privy Seal. Two years later, he was made President of the Board of Trade.

Lord Salisbury was a prominent Anglican and a zealous defender of the Established Church. He was one of the leading opponents both of Lloyd George's 'People's Budget' and of the Parliament Bill, which aimed to limit the power of the House of Lords. It was the success of that bill which ended any hopes his tribunal colleague, Richard Cavendish, might have had of becoming a peer.

Although he was out of office during the First World War, Lord Salisbury would come to assume informal leadership of the Conservatives in opposition. In government again, under Prime Ministers Andrew Bonar Law and Stanley Baldwin, he would, in 1922, be appointed Chancellor of the Duchy of Lancaster and Lord President of the Council, holding those posts for a year and two years respectively. In 1924, he would become Lord Privy Seal again and the year after, he would become Leader of the House of Lords, holding each post until 1929.

Ultimately, Lord Salisbury would become alienated by what was sometimes seen as Mr Baldwin's liberalism, and he would choose not to serve in the National Government formed in October 1931. Thereafter, he would devote himself to strengthening the House of Lords and opposing self-government for India. He would also be a strong opponent of appeasement and, with Winston Churchill, he would help organise British defences against Nazi Germany. In 1937, he would be Lord High Steward at the coronation of King George VI and Queen Elizabeth. The fourth Marquess of Salisbury died in April 1947 at the age of eighty-five years.

*

Lord Salisbury had married in 1887, the year Joseph Blackburn's wife, Jessie, was born. His wife was Lady Cicely Gore, the second daughter of Arthur Gore, the fifth Earl of Arran. It was through her that he was related both to Sir Francis Gore, the fifth earl's son, and to Viscount Hambleden, who had married her sister. Lady Cicely was also a descendant of William Lamb, the second Viscount Melbourne, the Whig statesman, who was Prime Minister in 1834 and who until 1841 served as mentor to the young Queen Victoria.

Lord Salisbury's eldest son was Robert Gascoyne-Cecil, who, upon his father's death, would become the fifth Marquess of Salisbury. Also a Conservative politician, Robert – or 'Bobbety' – would, like his father, be a Member of Parliament and he would ultimately become Leader of the House of Lords under Sir Winston Churchill. He would also be Lord President of the Council under both Churchill and his successor, Anthony Eden. Lord Robert, too, was educated at Eton College and then at Christ Church College, Oxford, which he left for war service without completing his degree. Commissioned as a lieutenant in the Grenadier Guards, he saw action in France and was awarded the Croix de Guerre. He was invalided home in September 1915 and in 1916, he served as personal military secretary to the seventeenth Earl of Derby, who was then the Undersecretary of State for War and the progenitor of the scheme that had recently seen Joseph Blackburn attest his willingness to serve.

*

Of Lord Salisbury's brothers, one was Edgar Algernon Robert Gascoyne-Cecil, a lawyer, politician and diplomat who, during the First World War, served as a minister in the Foreign Office and sat in the Cabinet as Minister of Blockade. An internationalist, a negotiator at the Paris Peace Conference in 1919 and a key progenitor of the League of Nations, Lord Robert Cecil was, in 1937, awarded the Nobel Peace Prize.

Another of Lord Salisbury's brothers was Edward Gascoyne-Cecil, a distinguished and highly decorated soldier, a colonial administrator and, latterly, a politician. He served in the Grenadier Guards, rising to the brevet rank of lieutenant colonel, and was an advisor to King Menelik of Abyssinia and then aide-de-camp to Lord Kitchener in Egypt. Mentioned in dispatches on several occasions, he fought at the Battle of Omdurman and, like Viscount Cranborne, in the Boer War. Afterwards, Lord Edward Cecil served as a government minister, both in the War Office and in the Treasury. His only son, George Edward Gascoyne-Cecil – who, like his father, was a Grenadier Guardsman – was killed in action on the Western Front on 1st September 1914 at the age of eighteen years. He is buried in what has become known as the Guards' Grave, which lies in forest at the edge of the town of Villers-Cotterêts. Captain Cecil is commemorated, together with the comrades who fell with him, in a stone memorial, placed next to the grave by his mother.

The third of Lord Salisbury's brothers was Rupert Ernest William Gascoyne-Cecil. Known as Lord William Cecil, he was Bishop of Exeter for two decades from 1916 and had four sons who fought in the First World War. The oldest son, Victor, was wounded twice but survived the conflict. Educated at Westminster School and the Royal Military College at Sandhurst, he would become a major in the Hampshire Regiment and the Tank Corps and would go on to fight on the North-West Frontier and in the Second World War.

The last of Lord William Cecil's sons, Rupert, was killed in action on 11th July 1915 at the age of twenty years. He was a lieutenant in the 4th Battalion of the Bedfordshire Regiment and his death, closely followed by those of Gilbert Talbot, George John Talbot's cousin, and of Frederick Lascelles, Sir Francis Gore's nephew, meant that in the single month of July 1915, three men who would shortly become members of the Central Tribunal lost a close relative.

Lord William's middle two sons, Randle and John, were, respectively, a lieutenant and a captain in the Royal Horse Artillery, and the latter also served in the Royal Field Artillery.

Lord Salisbury's youngest brother, Lord Hugh Cecil, was for a time one of the two Members of Parliament for the Oxford University constituency. A member of the Conservative party, he was first elected to that seat in 1910. He was, therefore, the immediate successor to John Talbot, the father of George Talbot, who was a colleague of Lord Salisbury on the Central Tribunal.

On 21st January 1916, the day after the Thornton local tribunal heard from its first claimant, Robert Stafford Arthur Palmer died of wounds he had sustained at the Battle of Umm-el-Hannah in Iraq. A soldier in the 6th Battalion of the Hampshire Regiment, Captain Palmer was the son of William Waldegrave Palmer, the second Viscount Selborne, and his wife, Lady Beatrix Maud Gascoyne-Cecil. She was Lord Salisbury's elder sister and Captain Palmer was therefore his nephew.

*

In early 1916, the Hatfield estate was the venue for a military experiment that would have significant consequences. There had for some months been considerable official concern about the stalemate which trench warfare had created and the desire to break that stalemate had yielded plans for a new, robust and versatile armoured vehicle. Initially known as the 'landship', what would for reasons of secrecy come to be called the 'tank' had first been seen in the autumn of 1915.

On 26th January 1916, the very day the first Military Service Act came into effect, an early prototype tank called *Mother* was brought to Hertfordshire under cover of darkness. Over the next few days, on parkland outside Hatfield House that had been turned into a facsimile of the Western Front, *Mother* was put through its paces. The manoeuvres that took place on 2nd February were observed by a particularly distinguished group, which included the Prime Minister, H. H. Asquith; David Lloyd George, the Minister of Munitions; and Earl Kitchener, who was Secretary of State for War. Also present was Lord Salisbury's cousin, Arthur Balfour, who had already served as Prime Minister and was now the First Lord of the Admiralty. Six days later, King George V arrived at Hatfield and, having watched *Mother* do the rounds one more time, actually took a ride in the vehicle himself. British tanks would first see combat seven months later, during intense fighting on the Somme.

*

Lord Salisbury was a lean man, in both his physique and his face, and each was set off perfectly by the winged collars and cinched frock coats he chose to wear. To the caricaturists who often made him their subject, his high, pronounced forehead was a particular gift, as were his large ears. He had a long, strong nose and lines around the corner of his mouth that suggested there had been some laughter. He also sported – and this, too, figured prominently in drawings of him – a particularly fine 'paintbrush' moustache.

In parliamentary speeches during the First World War, Lord Salisbury addressed subjects such as the military service legislation, recruitment and the treatment of conscientious objectors. It was his suggestion, made in the House of Lords on 22nd May 1916, that many married men who were prevailed upon to enlist under the Derby scheme did so because they were persuaded that it offered their only chance of going before a local tribunal.

That same month, in debates on the second Military Service Bill, Lord Salisbury spoke about the relationship between the county appeal tribunals and the Local Government Board, and about the possibility, which he deplored, that the latter might seek to overturn decisions of the former. What he said would find an echo in public sentiments expressed by Sir Harcourt Clare the following year.

During those debates, Lord Salisbury also raised the possibility that a county appeal tribunal might refuse a man permission to appeal to the Central Tribunal, and he warned of the "very serious effect" of such refusals "in the case of a great many agricultural districts, in which men have been taken unreasonably from the farms".

*

It seems that Lord Salisbury attended the very first meeting at Queen Anne's Gate for which he was eligible, for the letter appointing him to the Central Tribunal had been sent out only the day before. The author of the letter was Walter Tapper Jerred, who was then the assistant secretary to the Local Government Board. Things must have moved very swiftly to that point, for less than a week before he heard from Mr Jerred, Lord Salisbury had received a letter from Lord Sydenham, the chairman of the tribunal. He wrote:

> Dear Lord Salisbury,
> Hearing that you would like to serve on the Central Appeal Tribunal, I ventured to mention it to Mr Long. It will be a great help to have your assistance and I shall be grateful for it.

The Mr Long referred to will be Walter Hume Long, who was then the President of the Local Government Board. In fact, on the day that Lord Sydenham wrote to Lord Salisbury, Mr Long did the same:

> *My dear Lord Salisbury,*
> *As the work of the existing Central Appeal Tribunal will be largely increased under the Military Service Act, it is considered desirable to add one or two additional members.*
> *Your name has been suggested to me by Lord Sydenham, the Chairman, and I write to ask if you could see your way to accept membership. I hope you will be able to do so.*
> *Perhaps you wouldn't mind letting me know your decision by return.*

Two days before that, the subject of Lord Salisbury had come up for discussion at Queen Anne's Gate. The minutes of its twenty-fourth meeting state:

> *The Tribunal decided that the chairman should write to the President of the Local Government Board suggesting that Lord Salisbury and Sir Robert Carlyle should be added to the Tribunal.*

It is possible that Lord Salisbury had some misgivings about a role with the tribunal and even that he considered it insubstantial, for on 18th March 1916, Lord Sydenham wrote to him again:

> *Dear Lord Salisbury,*
> *Many thanks for your letter. I shall be most glad of your help for so long as you can give it and you need not feel tied if more useful work offers itself.*

Lord Salisbury was plainly keen to find himself meaningful employment. In the last fortnight, he had received a letter from Sir Frederick Robb, who was then the military secretary to the Secretary of State for War and therefore responsible for staffing issues within the British Army. The contents of Sir Frederick's letter suggest that what its recipient hoped to be given was not necessarily a desk job:

> Dear Lord Salisbury,
> I wish I were in a position to find an immediate appointment for you. Unfortunately, vacancies so seldom occur now. At one time there were plenty.
> I will, however, put your name on the list of officers desirous of commanding battalions in the field.

In fact, it is clear that Lord Salisbury had been making enquiries of this kind for some time, and at least since *Mother* came rolling into Hatfield House. On 26th January 1916, he was sent a letter written by Colonel O. Fitzgerald of York House:

> Dear Lord Salisbury,
> Forgive me for not answering your letter before but the difficulty is to obtain definite information.
> From all the inquiries I have made there is every intention of employing you again, although at the moment there is nothing available, the decision will really be with Lord K.
> You are going away for a short holiday now and before you come back I will get the Military Secretary to put your name up before Lord K so that you know how you stand.
> I quite understand that you want to take up your Parliamentary work if you are not to be employed in a military capacity.

I am so sorry to hear you have been laid up the last few days and am sure you will be all the better for a holiday.

The 'Lord K' referred to will be Earl Kitchener, who was at the time the Secretary of State for War and to whom, for a while, Lord Salisbury's brother had been aide-de-camp. York House is part of St James' Palace and it would be home to Lord Kitchener until his sudden, tragic death at sea later that same year.

24

On 6th January 1917, three days before the Thornton local tribunal considered Joseph Blackburn's case for the final time, Lord Richard Cavendish joined the Central Tribunal. He was already chairman both of the Lancashire Appeal Tribunal and of the discrete tribunal that heard appeals from the Lonsdale division of that county. Now, he would have additional judicial responsibilities in Westminster.

A prominent figure in the Cavendish family, Lord Richard was a younger son of Lord Edward Cavendish. The seventh Duke of Devonshire was his grandfather, the eighth was his uncle and the ninth was his elder brother. Lord Richard was also related by marriage to Sir Francis Gore, who already sat on the Central Tribunal – one of his uncles was married to Sir Francis' sister.

And there was another, rather more direct link between Lord Richard and Queen Anne's Gate. On 8th December 1915, his daughter, Elizabeth, had married Robert 'Bobbety' Gascoyne-Cecil, Lord Salisbury's son, who was convalescing from injuries he had sustained on the Western Front. The wedding was held at Holker Hall, the seat of the Cavendish family, which stands near Cartmel, a village that was then in the very north of Lancashire. It took place only two days before Joseph Blackburn went to Poulton and attested his willingness to serve in the British Army. Shortly before that, in a letter to Lord Salisbury, whom he addressed as *Mr dear Jem*, Lord Richard wrote:

> *I am afraid that you will think this a very remote spot for the wedding but both Bobbety and Betty wish to have it here and it is certainly nicer than London.*

Lord Richard Cavendish is one of nine members of the Central Tribunal to be remembered in the National Photographic Record. That is a collection of images of eminent people that was begun in 1917. Housed in the National Portrait Gallery in London, it now embraces more than ten thousand subjects.

The collection was the idea, and up to the eve of the 1960s the sole work, of the photographer Walter Stoneman. It focused on political and military figures and its sitters included five monarchs, nine Prime Ministers, a dozen Lord Chancellors, eighty admirals and a hundred generals. Mr Stoneman's original intention was that the portraits he made should not be seen publically. In time, however, they came to be exhibited and, as postcards, distributed much more widely.

The other members of the Central Tribunal to be remembered in this way are Evan Charteris, Lord Salisbury, Mr Barnes and Mr Jackson, who were photographed in 1916 and 1917; Sir Robert Carlyle, who sat the following year; and Lord Sydenham, Viscount Hambleden and Mr Talbot. John Fowler Leece Brunner does not appear in the collection, but his father, Sir John Tomlinson Brunner, does.

Sir George Younger and Sir Osmond Williams are also absent from the National Photographic Record, but the National Portrait Gallery holds images of them both, taken by Sir Benjamin Stone and by Bassano Ltd in 1907 and November 1916 respectively. The gallery also holds a portrait Sir Benjamin made of Lord Richard Cavendish in 1897.

Sir Benjamin Stone was himself a Conservative politician, as well as a celebrated traveller and writer. In 1906, he held the seat of Birmingham East that he had won at the general election of 1895, the same election that had seen Lord Richard Cavendish enter Parliament for the first time. Sir Benjamin was the first president of the National Photographic Record, and in 1911, he was the official photographer at the coronation of King George V.

The National Photographic Record also includes photographs of Walter Hume Long, the two-time President of the Local Government Board and (by now) the first Viscount Long of Wraxall; Walter Jerred, the board's functionary, who had become Sir Walter by the time Walter Stoneman got round to him; and Sir Edwin Lutyens, the architect not least of a plethora of military cemeteries. And the collection also embraces Wilfred William Ashley, the first Baron Mount Temple, who had been Joseph Blackburn's MP. The images of him were made in December 1927, by which time their subject had moved on to a new constituency and joined the Cabinet of Stanley Baldwin.

The National Portrait Gallery holds several other photographs of Baron Mount Temple. They too were the work of Bassano Limited and they show their subject resplendent in his ermine robes, his hair and moustache impressively dark – even though he was now approaching his eighth decade – and contrasting sharply with his pale skin. The photographs were taken a matter of weeks after his lordship, just like Baron Sydenham of Combe, had been an honoured guest of Nazi high command.

*

The Central Tribunal considered Joseph Blackburn's case on Thursday 17th May 1917, when its proceedings were led by Lord Salisbury, and Mr Brunner, Sir Robert Carlyle, Sir Algernon Firth, Sir Francis Gore and Mr Talbot also took part. From the minutes, and from what members of the Thornton tribunal said later, it seems that Joseph did not attend those proceedings. It is possible that he found the cost of travelling to Westminster prohibitive, or that he simply couldn't spare the time now that spring had come to the Fylde coast.

If Joseph Blackburn did choose to absent himself that would not have been unusual, for few appellants seem to have turned up at Queen Anne's Gate. The Central Tribunal had set out with the best of intentions, decreeing at its very first meeting:

> *That in every case which came before the Tribunal an opportunity should be given to the man or his employer, as the case may be, to attend when a claim or application was considered. Notice should be sent to him of the date and place where the case was to be considered and he should be told that he can be heard in person or that he may submit written representations.*

Those good intentions soon wavered, however, and only two meetings later, the tribunal reversed its position, stating:

> *On the general question whether the appellant or applicant should be afforded an opportunity of being heard in person, it was decided that the decision of the meeting of the 22 November should be varied, and that for the present, unless otherwise expressly decided, parties should not be heard but should be given the opportunity of submitting written representations, which must be furnished within seven days.*

The procedure the tribunal came to adopt would give rise to real concerns, for it was felt that if a man was not present when his appeal was considered, the result might well be injustice. Those concerns reached the House of Commons, where they were taken up by Edmund Harvey. A Liberal, a Quaker and a pacifist, Mr Harvey, like Cyril Jackson, had long been associated with Toynbee Hall, having served as a warden there for eight years. Since 1910, Mr Harvey had, like James O'Grady, been a Member of Parliament for Leeds, in his case for the city's West constituency. He had also helped draft provisions in the first Military Service Act that allowed conscientious objectors who wished to be exempt from service to perform work of national importance instead.

On 6th April 1916, Mr Harvey asked a question of Walter Long, who was then still the president of the Local Government Board:

> *Mr Edmund Harvey – To ask the President of the Local Government Board whether the Central Tribunal does not intend as a rule to see appellants in person; and if so, whether, in cases where the appellant is not heard in person, the military representative will also not be heard in person, in order that the two parties to the case shall be on an equal footing.*
>
> *Mr Long – It is for the Central Tribunal to determine their own procedure. I will communicate with them on the subject to which the Hon. Member refers.*

It seems, then, that concern about injustice in the proceedings at Queen Anne's Gate arose from the possibility that the tribunal might not hear from the man concerned, but also that it might choose to take evidence from the military representative notwithstanding the man's absence.

The tribunal's minutes rarely say which of the parties was present at the hearing of an appeal and it is therefore unclear whether concern about the second possibility was justified. That concern had, however, reached Parliament and there is strong evidence to support it in the Westminster documents and, in particular, in the case of Joseph Blackburn.

It also seems, however, that there were some cases in which the tribunal did hear from the men at the centre of the appeals it considered.

In a debate in the House of Lords on 4th May 1916, the

Bishop of Oxford spoke of the tribunal having "decided not to hear the men individually, but only to receive their papers".

Lord Salisbury, who must have had some personal knowledge of the situation, replied, "That is not universal. Some cases are heard orally."

The bishop in question was Charles Gore, the younger brother of Sir Francis Gore, Lord Salisbury's relative by marriage and his colleague on the Central Tribunal. What Lord Salisbury told Bishop Charles was demonstrably true, even if only infrequently so.

25

There is evidence to support Edmund Harvey's fears, for it is clear that when it considered appeals, the Central Tribunal was willing to hear from the military and sometimes did so in the absence of the man concerned.

It was evident from the very first meeting, in November 1915, that the tribunal was not to be left to its own devices. On that occasion, the minutes state that *by leave of the Tribunal, Captain Seymour Lloyd attended on behalf of Lord Derby.* The seventeenth Earl of Derby was newly appointed as Director General of Recruiting and though his own status became ever more elevated as the months rolled by, Mr Seymour Lloyd would continue to make regular trips to Queen Anne's Gate. The minutes for the tribunal's second meeting, held a month later, confirm that *the chairman read a letter from the War Office appointing Captain Seymour Lloyd as Assessor for the War Office.*

It is plain that the good captain busied himself with tribunal business even from the outset. At the third meeting, on 4th January 1916, he:

> *...Briefly described the arrangements made in the City of London by the military representative with regard to the calling up of attested men employed in banks. It was thought that an extension of the scheme to the whole country was necessary, but the tribunal considered that they could not at present make a definite proposal in the matter.*

Nine days later, meanwhile:

> *Captain Seymour Lloyd informed the Tribunal that Lord Derby was prepared to meet the case of the 'working farmer' provided a satisfactory arrangement could be reached.*

In one case, that of a Mr Martin, the minutes state that as well as the man and his own representatives, there were in attendance Colonel Seymour Lloyd and *Mr Jervis (the Military Representative)*. This suggests that where the services of a military representative were required, they were provided by someone other than Colonel Seymour Lloyd, and also that where a military representative attended the meeting, his presence was deemed worthy of being noted.

Something similar happened eight months later, when the Central Tribunal heard appeals from men employed by two friendly societies in the Cumberland town of Workington. By that time, the military representative had become the 'national service representative' and the minutes tell us that the men were represented by Mr May, from the Co-operative movement, and that *the National Service Representative to the Appeal Tribunal and a representative of the National Service Department were also present.*

*

John Hall Seymour Lloyd was a barrister and a member of the Parliamentary bar. In that capacity, he occupied a seat in the House of Lords close to the royal throne. For more than thirty years, Mr Seymour Lloyd was legal adviser to the Independent Peers Association and he was, in particular, the close confidant of those who, in 1909 and 1910, opposed the 'People's Budget' of Mr Asquith's Liberal government. The budget was championed by the Chancellor of the Exchequer, David Lloyd George, and his then-Liberal colleague Winston Churchill. It sought to redistribute wealth among the British people and it would see the introduction of unprecedented taxes on the rich, and of a radical programme of social welfare spending.

Among the most prominent of the many peers who opposed the budget was the fourth Marquess of Salisbury and by the time Captain Seymour Lloyd began appearing at Queen Anne's Gate, the two men will have known each other very well. They also had another close connection, in the form of the Carlton Club. Both men were members of that venerable institution, as indeed were Lord Salisbury's father and son and also Walter Long and Lord Derby and James Travis-Clegg.

Appointed a temporary lieutenant colonel in May 1916, when the Thornton tribunal first considered Joseph Blackburn, Mr Seymour Lloyd was made Lord Derby's deputy the following February. And when, in the autumn of 1917, the task of recruiting was transferred to the Ministry of National Service, he was appointed Director General and his military rank was made substantive.

*

Whatever the appeal of Mr Martin and those from Workington might suggest, it is plain that at Queen Anne's Gate, Colonel Seymour Lloyd sometimes put forward *a* – if not *the* – military case, and that sometimes when he did so, the man was nowhere to be seen. On 31st July 1917, for example, the colonel is noted as having attended before the Central Tribunal *to present the views of the War Office with regard to the provisional decision in the case of AE Harrison and it was decided to adjourn further consideration of the case.*

The Harrison matter had first been discussed five days before. It concerned an exemption granted to an employer in respect of its employee. That exemption had come from the City of London local tribunal, which was the one for the area in which the employer had its headquarters. When he sought to challenge the exemption, however, the military representative made his application not in London, but to the local tribunal for the quite different area in which the employee worked. That tribunal, and also its county appeal tribunal, ruled that this was an incorrect course and, both in a provisional decision and subsequently, after it had heard from Colonel Seymour Lloyd, the Central Tribunal concurred. There is no evidence that Mr Harrison ever attended at Queen Anne's Gate or that he was told what the colonel had to say.

The position was clearly the same a year later, for the minutes of a meeting held on 11th September 1918 state that Sir – as he had since the beginning of the year been – John Seymour Lloyd:

> ...Attended the meeting of the tribunal and submitted the views of the Ministry of National Service on the decision of the Central Tribunal in cases 19,850 and 19,851 proposed for circulation for the information of tribunals.

Those cases concerned a Mr Waterman and a Mr Payne, who were respectively a milk carrier and car-man and a cork manufacturer. The issue in each case was whether, when a local tribunal came to consider a man's request to extend an exemption he had already been given, it was able to consider all the facts of the case or only those arising since the earlier decision. Neither man seems to have been present to hear that issue debated.

*

John Seymour Lloyd had at one time sought election to the House of Commons. He contested the seat of Dundee at both general elections of 1910, when Max Muspratt and John Fowler Leece Brunner were among those returned to Parliament. On each occasion, however, Mr Seymour Lloyd was defeated by the Labour candidate, Alexander Wilkie, and also by the Liberal candidate, who happened to be Winston Churchill. (On the second occasion, indeed, he was also defeated by the Liberal Unionist candidate.) With George Nicoll Barnes, Mr Wilkie had been the first Labour MP elected in Scotland and like him – and Stephen Walsh, James O'Grady and Robert Tootill – he was a staunch supporter of his country's involvement in the Great War.

After Dundee, Mr Seymour Lloyd did not seek elected office again and he returned to his parliamentary legal practice and to writing. Among his works is *Elections and How to Fight Them*, a book not, presumably, based solely upon his own experience. Three portraits of Sir John Seymour-Lloyd now form part of the National Photographic Record. They were made by Walter Stoneman in 1921, by which time their subject had chosen to hyphenate his surname.

*

Sometimes, as the Waterman and Payne cases make clear, the role Colonel Seymour Lloyd played in proceedings before the Central Tribunal was indistinguishable from that of the military representative. And that was so even before 1918. On 6th March of the previous year, for example, when it considered the case of a Mr Southwick, the tribunal heard from the man and his solicitor and, the minutes note, *the military authorities were represented by Colonel Seymour Lloyd and Mr Scriven*. It is plain from this that the good colonel represented the military authorities, in the eyes of the tribunal at least, and that he took an active part in the proceedings. Just how active that part could be is evident from an even earlier hearing, held on 12th July 1916 in the case of Ernest Sydney. He was the manager of a London hat factory and chose to attend the proceedings in person. There, according to the minutes, Mr Sydney was examined by his own representative, but he was also cross-examined by Colonel Seymour Lloyd. No other advocate, and certainly no military representative, is said to have been present at the time.

26

When, on Thursday 17th May 1917, the Central Tribunal considered the case of Joseph Blackburn, almost a year had passed since the day upon which, under the old Derby scheme, he had been due to go to the Colours. In that time, Joseph had made two claims to the local tribunal in Thornton and the second of them had also been considered by the county appeal tribunal in Preston. He had been successful on each occasion and been granted limited exemptions from military service, but now, his case would receive an altogether different response.

The minutes of the Westminster tribunal's meeting record all the appeals dealt with that day, but they occupy little more than a single, closely typed sheet of paper. They also record the names of the members who were present, but they mention no one else and certainly say nothing about a military representative.

We are first given Joseph's name and the fact that he is an attested man and then we are told that he is a *market gardener, vegetable and fruit hawker*. Joseph had for some time described himself as a market gardener and we know, if only from the local newspaper report, that at Four Lane Ends, he had conceded that he was also a hawker. Noting that the appeal had been made by the military representative, the minutes then state that it is upheld and that there shall be *no exemption*. By way of explanation, the minutes add:

The Central Tribunal do not feel that they can properly lay down any general rule as to the size of the holding in respect of which exemption may be granted. Each case must be decided on its own circumstances. The

principles applicable to such cases are indicated in the list
of certified occupations R.117 (page 15, paragraph (ii)
under 'Farmer').

In so saying, the tribunal was simply following a course it had set some time before – the one suggested in discussions between its clerk, I. G. Gibbon, and Mr Cheney of the Board of Agriculture. That course had been taken most recently in November 1916, when the tribunal dismissed the appeal of another Lancashire market gardener, Mr Wilson, and the words it used then were precisely the ones it chose to use now.

The list of certified occupations to which the minutes refer in fact came into effect only on 1st February 1917. That was almost a month after Joseph had last been before the Thornton tribunal, when the relevant list was R.105. This reminds us that in Westminster, his case would be considered afresh. In his circumstances, however, the two lists would have precisely the same effect.

The minutes conclude with the following observation:

In this particular case the man appears to be employed
principally in the hawking of fruit and vegetables and
the Tribunal are not satisfied that the holding would go
out of cultivation if the man were called up for military
service.

There had already been occasion at Queen Anne's Gate to consider what this might mean. On 17th August 1916, the tribunal heard the case of John James Spence, a crofter from Caithness, and it ruled:

The list of certified occupations provides that if a 'farmer'
is partly occupied in another occupation he is not in
a certified occupation unless his personal labour or

superintendence is indispensable for the proper cultivation
of his holding and such cultivation is expedient in the
national interest.

Whether these conditions are fulfilled, the tribunal continued,
will depend on a number of circumstances such as the amount
and kind of produce.

It seems, because it did not say otherwise, that the tribunal
was satisfied that Joseph's cultivation of his market garden was
expedient in the national interest. In that respect, therefore,
the Westminster decision echoed the Thornton one. It is also
relevant that for its part, the local tribunal did not say that
market gardener was Joseph's sole occupation.

The only issue then, and the only point of difference
between the first tribunal to consider Joseph's case and the
last, was whether his personal labour or superintendence
was indispensable for the proper cultivation of his holding.
Thornton was satisfied that it was, while Westminster seems to
have concluded that it was not.

If we are to take its very brief statement of reasons at face
value, the Central Tribunal's decision was based upon the
finding that Joseph was employed principally in the hawking
of fruit and vegetables. And it seems to have been that finding
which led the tribunal to conclude that – given the presumably
brief time his hawking allowed him to devote to it – Joseph's
agricultural holding would not go out of cultivation if he were
called up for military service.

But that conclusion is contentious, not least because it
contradicts one the local tribunal made. It is clear that in
January 1917, the members convened at Four Lane Ends were
satisfied that, as their chairman would later state, Joseph was
"not hawking most of his time" and was "engaged mostly
in his garden". As we know from the newspaper report, that
conclusion was based upon Joseph's own oral evidence. When

cross-examined by Captain Booth, he said that although it was his practice to hawk his produce, together with other fruit he bought, he did that on only two days a week. Joseph said that he worked fully four days on the land.

It is difficult to account for this discrepancy between the findings of the two tribunals. The Central Tribunal would not, of course, be bound to reach the same conclusion as a local tribunal, even where each was presented with precisely the same evidence. Law and the appellate process do not work like that.

In Westminster, Joseph's hearing will have taken longer than the five minutes allocated to it in Thornton. It could hardly have taken or been given less time. But while Joseph was present for the hearing at Four Lane Ends, he did not attend Queen Anne's Gate. No matter how thorough its approach, therefore, the Central Tribunal will have been deprived of an opportunity of which its inferior was able to take full advantage: to assess the man's evidence by looking him straight in the eye. As the Thornton tribunal would later tell them, that fact should have given Lord Salisbury and his colleagues pause and made them reluctant to overturn the earlier decision.

There is, however, a further possibility and it is one that might help explain the Westminster decision. When it considered the appeal in Joseph's case, the Central Tribunal might have had the benefit of evidence that had not been available to the local tribunal. That evidence would have come in the form of a statement from the military representative, and Councillor Dewhurst and his colleagues plainly suspected that such a document had been sent.

The statement would have been to the effect that Joseph was mainly a hawker, but while its existence might explain the Westminster decision, it would not alleviate concern about the tribunal's conduct. There is nothing to suggest that a statement of that kind was ever vouchsafed to Joseph. As we shall see, however, there is something to suggest that it was received at Queen Anne's Gate.

Though brief, the explanation the Central Tribunal gave in Joseph's case was longer than it might have been. Like the question of size, the subject of reasons had come up before. As early as 14th March 1916, when recording deliberations in a case from Fordingbridge in Hampshire, the Westminster minutes state:

> *The letter from the Local Tribunal respecting the decision of the Central Tribunal was considered, and it was decided to reply in general terms without stating reasons. It was considered that it was inadvisable to give reasons in any case decided by the Tribunal.*

Lord Salisbury and his colleagues would soon have reason to rue the breaking of that self-denying ordinance.

*

There is evidence that the Westminster tribunal was less indulgent than the local tribunals towards the men at the heart of the appeals it heard. On the day the tribunal considered Joseph's case, for example, it dealt with thirteen appeals and concluded twelve of them. (One appeal, concerning a tailor's cutter named Mr Polikoff, was referred back to the appeal tribunal from which it had come.) Of those twelve appeals, nine were decided against the man.

Of the thirteen appeals, six are said to have been brought by the military representative and of those, five were decided in his favour and only one in favour of the man. Even in that one case, the successful appellant, a colliery engineman named Mr Norman, was exempted only from combatant service. Three of the appeals concerned men working on the land. They were from the Fife, the Lancashire and the Northumberland appeal tribunals and all three were decided in favour of the military.

*

On Wednesday 6th June 1917, less than a month after the Central Tribunal took his exemption away, Joseph Blackburn was finally mobilised for military service. When, eighteen months before, he had attested his willingness to serve under the Derby scheme, Joseph had been assigned to the Loyal North Lancashire Regiment. A note was now made of that fact, and of the regimental number Joseph had been given, and he was posted to the regiment's 4th Battalion. The following day, at Lancaster, he was examined by an army doctor.

It is from the recordings made at his examination that we learn more or less the only personal details about Joseph that are preserved in the public record. He stood 5' 5½" tall, which was around the average for British soldiers of the time, and he weighed 128 pounds and had a 39½-inch chest.

It seems that Joseph passed his medical, for on the same day, again in Lancaster, he was formally appointed to his battalion. That deed was done when a colonel completed the form begun in Poulton in December 1915:

> *I certify that this Attestation of the above-named Recruit is correct, and properly filled up, and that the required forms appear to have been complied with. I accordingly approve and appoint him to the 4th Loyal North Lancs.*

Though unquestionably elegant, the colonel's signature is, sadly, indecipherable.

27

Whatever we think of the decision the Central Tribunal made, there is one conclusion that is hard to escape – before deciding his appeal, the tribunal should have allowed Joseph Blackburn to comment upon any new allegations made against him and any fresh evidence that was relevant to his case.

That would certainly be the expectation today. In legal proceedings in England and Wales, and particularly in judicial tribunals that deal with such things as employment or tax disputes, mental health detention and claims for welfare benefits, there are clear rules of procedure – rules intended to ensure that cases are dealt with fairly and justly. Those rules require that the parties are on an equal footing and every appellant knows exactly what case he will have to meet.

That requirement is not, however, unique to the present day. It dates back many decades, if not a century or two. In fact, it was a key element of the practice the tribunal itself had already chosen to adopt.

*

The way the Central Tribunal dealt with appeals was determined by its members themselves, chiefly at their sixteenth meeting, held in Queen Anne's Gate on Tuesday 29th February 1916. That was around the time the first Military Service Act came into effect, and a matter of days after the session that produced the first Thornton cases for the new appeal tribunal in Preston.

In deciding how they would conduct their business, the members plainly had one eye on the changes the Act would bring, for the minutes of their Leap Day meeting state that the new procedure was to be used in *cases received under the old instructions*. Joseph Blackburn's was one such case, and the procedure would therefore apply to him.

The tribunal decided that at each meeting, and in each case, it would be for the members then convened to consider the evidence available to them. If they were satisfied that it was sufficient, they would proceed with the appeal, but if they were not, they could ask for further evidence to be supplied. They might also refer a case for comment by a government department or recommend that it be decided in the tribunal by other means.

Where the evidence was insufficient, the final possibilities agreed in February 1916 were that the Central Tribunal might send cases back to the local tribunal or *require opportunity to be given to the applicant or appellant to make further representations*. It is this last possibility that is of particular interest in Joseph's case, for that man was given no such opportunity.

*

There are several occasions upon which the Westminster tribunal can be seen to have sought further evidence about the man who was the subject of one of its appeals.

It did so, for example, in the case of Mr McNaughton, who came from Berkshire and said he was "in charge of stallions".

Consideration of Mr McNaughton's case was adjourned because the tribunal was not satisfied with the information it had received. That suggests that the man was not present to give evidence himself, and the minutes state, starkly:

Local Tribunal to be informed that Central Tribunal understand the Military Representative states that it was ascertained that McNaughton was never engaged in agricultural work except at harvest time.

Crucially, the minutes conclude:

Local Tribunal to be asked for their observations on the statement and also for information as to whether the man does in fact act as bailiff of the farm and what proportion of his time he devotes to this work.

There is nothing to indicate how the new statement was made; whether the military representative had simply provided a written submission or appeared in person before the members of the tribunal. What is plain, however, is that what the representative said was not to be allowed to go by default.

The case of Mr McNaughton is interesting, not least because, like that of Joseph Blackburn, it raises two uncomfortable possibilities: first, that the man concerned pursued a different trade from the one he claimed; and second, that the military representative gave information to the Central Tribunal that the man himself was not allowed to see. Here, however, the local tribunal, at least, would be given that information and also invited to comment upon it.

What is particularly interesting about the case is the date it was first considered: 5th July 1917. As we shall see, that is only a few days after a significant letter was received at Queen Anne's Gate. The letter came from Four Lane Ends and it expressed for the first time the Thornton tribunal's great dissatisfaction with the outcome of Joseph's appeal. The Central Tribunal probably treated Mr McNaughton as it did because of the controversy which the appeal had created and the Thornton letter had now confirmed.

*

If the course adopted by the Central Tribunal on 5th July 1917 suggested that it might now seek out the views of others, it seems those others included only the local tribunal which an

176

appeal concerned. What is striking about Mr McNaughton's case is that the Westminster tribunal did not require that the man himself be told what the military representative had said about him, or that he be given an opportunity to comment upon that evidence or provide further evidence of his own.

That course was not, in any event, entirely novel. There had been other cases, before that of Mr McNaughton, in which the Central Tribunal, finding itself short of essential evidence, had chosen to defer its decision so that such evidence might be obtained. In doing so now, the tribunal was simply following a procedure it had itself laid down almost eighteen months before.

We can, for example, see the tribunal taking precisely that course the previous month in the case of Mr Hollands, a coal and coke merchant from East Sussex. Consideration of his appeal was adjourned so that further enquiries might be made of the local tribunal, *regarding the statement made by the Military Representative*. Something similar happened a fortnight later, in the case of Mr Longbottom, when the Central Tribunal decided that it could not come to a final decision. The man was the general manager of a colliery and significant allegations had been made about him. According to the minutes:

> *It was decided to send to the Coal Controller (confidentially) a copy of the Military Representative's statement in the case and to ask for his observations thereon and the reasons for his decision.*

The members of the tribunal that dealt with this case were Lord Salisbury, Mr Brunner, Sir Robert Carlyle, Sir Algernon Firth and Mr Talbot. With the addition of Sir Francis Gore, that was the very panel that had determined Joseph Blackburn's case the month before.

At a meeting three weeks later, the tribunal decided to

award Mr Longbottom an exemption from military service, conditional upon his remaining in his present occupation. There is no evidence that he – or, for the matter, the members of the local tribunal – ever saw the Coal Controller's reply or what the military representative said in the first place. In fact, the use in the original direction of the word 'confidentially' suggests very strongly that he, and they, did not.

On a few, rare occasions, however, the Central Tribunal's willingness to solicit further information in connection with an appeal can be seen to have extended to the man in question. Among the cases considered by the tribunal at its meeting on 11th August 1916 was that of Frederick Quick. That day, the minutes state, *It was decided to ask for the appellant's observations on the statement made in the letter of the Local Tribunal.* This was the first time the Westminster tribunal had taken such a course and the statement upon which Mr Quick was invited to comment had been made not by the military representative, but by the local tribunal. The man had, however, been invited to comment and that was significant.

And having taken such a course once, the tribunal quickly did so again. On 1st September, in an appeal concerning James Black, a superintendent for an insurance company, it decided to write to the man, soliciting his comments on the suggestion *that he had served in a volunteer battalion and that he spoke at a meeting held in support of the establishment of a branch of the Volunteer Training Corps.* Save for one other case, this was the last time the Central Tribunal requested a man's comments on allegations about him before it received news of the Thornton strike.

*

Whatever its decisions about Messrs Hollands, Longbottom, Quick and Black might suggest, it is plain that the Central

Tribunal was not always keen to solicit the opinions of the men whose cases came before it. As late as 8th March 1917, for example, in the case of Mr Wragg, a butcher's manager from Derbyshire, the tribunal upheld the appeal of the military representative and denied the man exemption. In doing so, it stated:

> *On the further facts now disclosed the Central Tribunal see no reason for differing from the decision of the Local Tribunal.*

There is nothing to suggest that those further facts were ever disclosed to Mr Wragg.

It is intriguing to note that here, the Westminster tribunal was happy to uphold the decision of a local tribunal and to cite the fresh facts it had received as a reason for doing so. It may be significant that the result was that the man would go to the Colours. The members of the tribunal in this case included Mr Brunner, Sir Robert Carlyle, Sir Algernon Firth and Mr Talbot – four of the men who, a little over two months later, would decide the appeal in the case of Joseph Blackburn.

28

From the case of Mr McNaughton, the Berkshire man who might or might not have been in charge of stallions, the evidence seems clear: after the letter of protest was received from Thornton there was a distinct change of procedure at Queen Anne's Gate. There would now be much greater disclosure of evidence in military service appeals.

There is another case, however, that suggests a rather different possibility. That case concerned Mr J. M. Martin and much of it took place before the Thornton letter had even been written. There too we see the Westminster tribunal giving an appellant the opportunity to comment upon what had been said about him, and we also see the tribunal going to great lengths to ensure that the man's comments could be taken into account.

Mr Martin came from East Suffolk and the tribunal considered his case on Wednesday 16th May 1917. That was the day before Joseph Blackburn's case was heard and the members who convened then – Lord Salisbury, Mr Brunner, Sir Robert Carlyle, Sir Algernon Firth and Mr Talbot – made up five sixths of the panel that would sit the following day. (Only Sir Francis Gore was missing.)

The subject of Mr Martin had come up in Queen Anne's Gate before. On 4th April, the tribunal gave him a temporary exemption, but it also directed that the exemption should not be renewed. According to the minutes, that was because *the Central Tribunal are not satisfied that every effort has been made to obtain a substitute by the offer of substantial remuneration.* In other words, it might be possible to find someone else to do what Mr Martin did and, therefore, to free him up for military service.

Six weeks later, however, the tribunal took a rather different approach. Faced with the man again, it decided to rehear his case and to give the military representative an opportunity to make further representations. It seems that Mr Martin had provided new evidence – conceivably as to the efforts he had made, and the remuneration he had offered, in order to obtain a substitute – and it was that evidence which any further representations would address. The military representative plainly accepted the opportunity he had been given and when, on 6th June, the tribunal considered the case again, its members decided to revert to Mr Martin. The minutes state:

The man to be asked for his observations on the statement of the Military Representative – Consent of the Military Representative to be obtained.

The approach taken that Wednesday afternoon was novel. The minutes of previous meetings suggest that the tribunal had not previously sought the views of a man upon comments made by the military representative. But while the approach might have been novel, and though it was adopted only after the tribunal had dealt with Joseph Blackburn, it cannot have been influenced by the controversy caused by that case. The timing simply isn't right. On 6th June 1917, the day the Central Tribunal again considered Mr Martin, the Thornton tribunal's letter had not yet been dispatched by its clerk, much less received in Westminster. In fact, almost three weeks would elapse before the clerk was even instructed to write that letter.

On 21st June, having presumably discovered what Mr Martin wished to say, the Central Tribunal decided to hear from him in person and also to hear from the military representative. That decision was again taken by five sixths of the tribunal that dealt with Joseph Blackburn's case. (Only Sir Robert Carlyle was missing.) Mr Martin's evidence was taken six days later, when the tribunal granted him an exemption from military service, conditional upon his remaining in his present occupation. His name does not appear again in the tribunal's records.

The approach taken in the Martin case – and, in particular, the decision to allow the man to comment upon what the military representative had said – seems to anticipate the one taken after the Blackburn case had been heard and the letter of protest from the Thornton tribunal had been received. There is, however, good reason to treat it with caution.

Mr Martin was an unusual appellant and that is for at least two reasons: first, he was by profession a solicitor, and not a man employed on the land, in a colliery, in a butcher's shop or a tailor's or in commerce. The second reason is that throughout his appeal, Mr Martin had a solicitor of his own and, at least when he finally gave oral evidence, he was also represented by a barrister. That makes him very unusual indeed and it would not be surprising if the Central Tribunal chose to act circumspectly in his case.

It should also be borne in mind that the comments to which Mr Martin was invited to respond had been made in response to further evidence he had himself supplied, and that too was rare. Finally, it is plain that the approach taken here was very different from the one more often taken by the Central Tribunal. That is another reason for treating Mr Martin's case with caution.

The different approach the tribunal took is evident from other cases it heard; from other cases it heard, in fact, at the very same meeting.

On 16th May 1917, having decided to rehear Mr Martin's case, the Central Tribunal turned its attention to Mr Cartwright, a conscripted man from Warwickshire who claimed both to be a haulier and to keep a beer-house. The tribunal dismissed the man's appeal, although it went on to state that this would be only a provisional decision and that the papers were *to be submitted to the Ministry of Munitions for observations*. If the ministry did ever volunteer any observations, they do not appear to have been shared with Mr Cartwright. That fact didn't damage his cause, however, for a month later, the tribunal cancelled its provisional decision and gave him an exemption from military service conditional only upon his remaining in his present occupation.

The meeting on 16th May saw the Westminster tribunal make a second provisional decision. It came in the case of Mr McKearney, who was from Perthshire and said he was a china, rag and metal merchant. The man had enlisted for military service under the Derby scheme and now the tribunal dismissed his appeal. Although the Ministry of Munitions was to be invited to provide its observations, there is no other similarity with the case of Mr Cartwright, for on 26th June, the tribunal made its provisional decision final and it refused Mr McKearney the exemption he had sought. There is nothing to suggest that he ever found out what the ministry said.

On 6th June 1917, when it decided to invite Mr Martin to comment on what had been said about him, the Central Tribunal had also adjourned the case of Mr Hollands, the merchant from East Sussex. It seems that by 21st June, the purpose of the adjournment had been fulfilled and the local tribunal had responded to the military representative's allegations, for on that date, the tribunal dismissed the man's appeal and refused him exemption from military service. There is no evidence that Mr Holland was ever afforded the opportunity extended to the local tribunal, or, again, that he ever got to see what the military representative had said. The meeting at which his appeal was dismissed was the one at which the Central Tribunal decided to take oral evidence from the solicitor, Mr Martin.

*

If, therefore, the procedure of the Central Tribunal changed in the middle of 1917, that is more likely to have been because of the letter it received from the Thornton tribunal than because of concerns raised by the wholly uncommon case of Mr Martin. From that point on, the tribunal often chose to inform men of allegations made against them during an appeal and it did so, in particular, where the allegations came from a military representative.

On Tuesday 11th September 1917, the tribunal adopted a decidedly transparent approach in the case of Mr Tulloch, a conscripted man from Orkney who said he was a shop assistant. Having looked at the papers, the tribunal directed:

> *The Military Representative's letter of 16th August to be submitted to the man for information as to his occupation as a letter carrier.*

If he were to turn out not to be a letter carrier, the minutes add, *the Central Tribunal are of opinion that man should be sent to a Special Medical Board.* A fortnight later, a similar course was taken in the case of Mr Morris, another conscript, who came from Montgomeryshire. Although the man said he was a butcher, it seems he might have had colleagues who could deputise for him. That suggestion had not, however, come from the military representative. Mr Morris was given an opportunity to provide observations *upon the letter of 18th September from the Appeal Tribunal.* Furthermore, the minutes direct:

> *Local Tribunal to be asked for particulars as to the nature of the employment of the third butcher referred to by the Appeal Tribunal and whether he would be available as a substitute.*

The Central Tribunal can also be seen to have used this more transparent approach with men who worked on the land. Mr

G. F. Smith, a conscript from East Sussex, was one such man. On 29th May 1918, the tribunal adjourned his case *in order that full information regarding the staff of the brother-in-law's farm may be furnished.* By that time, the Ministry of National Service had assumed responsibility for military recruitment and the National Service Representative had replaced the Military Representative in proceedings before the various military service tribunals. Now, the tribunal decided that both Mr Smith and the national service representative were:

> *...To be asked to forward further representations (through the Local Tribunal) on the latter's suggestion that the farm could be managed by the brother-in-law who is a tenant of an adjoining farm.*

That approach was still being taken as late as 9th October 1918, when the Central Tribunal considered the case of Mr W. Jenkins, an attested man from Cardiganshire who claimed to be a coal, lime, wood and oil merchant, a haulier and a contractor. Consideration of his appeal was adjourned, specifically so that he might comment upon representations made by the national service representative. In addition, Mr Jenkins was to be invited to give *particulars of the amount of hauling, coal hawking, and hackney carriage driving he has done in the last six months.* And the adjournment would serve other purposes, for the tribunal also directed:

> *Local Tribunal to be asked whether there is a shortage of hauliers in the district and whether they think this man is required for hauling timber.*

Finally, the tribunal directed:

> *National Service Representative to be asked whether the man was offered work in accordance with the decision of*

185

the Appeal Tribunal dated 13th April 1917, and if so the nature of the work.

The procedure the Central Tribunal followed in the case of Joseph Blackburn was, then, different both from the one it would follow in many subsequent cases and also from the one it had already committed itself to following. The tribunal would come to regret changing its procedure, and it would even resort to expressing that regret openly.

29

There is another way in which what happened to Joseph Blackburn was unusual. When it came to deal with his case, the Westminster tribunal didn't just depart from a procedure to which it had pledged itself and would soon return. The tribunal also departed from a procedure it had already followed in a good many cases.

We have seen how, with Messrs Hollands, Morris and Jenkins, appeals were adjourned so that the comments of the local tribunal could be obtained. That was in fact an approach the Central Tribunal often took. Sometimes, the local tribunal was used as a source of further information or even as a means of bringing that information to light. In the case of Mr Wix, for example, Lord Salisbury and his colleagues:

> ...Decided to enquire of the Local Tribunal whether, if the man is called up for service, it would be possible in the present circumstances to obtain another tenant and also whether the man would obtain a reasonable return for his fixtures etc.

In January 1917, the tribunal was equally inquisitive in the case of Mr Fly, a conscript from East Sussex who worked as a pig-keeper. The members who convened that day included not only Lord Salisbury, but also Mr Brunner, Sir Robert Carlyle and Sir Algernon Firth. They were two thirds of the tribunal that would determine Joseph Blackburn's case and now, they directed:

*Local Tribunal to be requested to inform the Central
Tribunal as to the means of the mother of the man and
also whether the other son, Edwin, is available for looking
after the pigs.*

Sometimes, the local tribunal was not the source of the
information required, but merely a conduit through which it
might be conveyed to Queen Anne's Gate. In March 1918, for
example, in the case of Mr Duthie, who worked in dentistry, the
tribunal directed:

*Local Tribunal to be informed that the Central Tribunal
would be glad to receive the opinion of the Medical
Officer of Health on the statements made in the man's
representations regarding the present facilities in the
district and whether in his opinion the man is actually
needed in the district. If the Medical Officer of Health
is of opinion that the man is not required, the Central
Tribunal decided to refuse exemption.*

There are at least two interesting aspects of this decision. The
first is the willingness of the Westminster tribunal to seek
information not just from a local tribunal, but from other
parties, including ones not directly affected by an appeal. Here,
in fact, what was being sought was not merely information, but
an opinion, and the tribunal's clear intention was to defer to
that opinion and decide the case in accordance with the medical
officer's view. The deference that suggests is rarely found in
cases decided before Joseph Blackburn's was.

The second interesting aspect of the decision about Mr Duthie
is the courtesy the Central Tribunal sought to display, and maybe
wanted to be seen to display, in its dealings with the local tribunal.
That too could have been influenced by Joseph's case, which
had been decided nearly ten months before, and by Thornton's

vehement protest against the way Westminster had behaved.

Sometimes when they were approached from Queen Anne's Gate, local tribunals were asked not merely to provide further evidence, but actually to volunteer an opinion of their own. On 5th July 1917, for example, attention turned to the case of Mr Robinson from West Sussex and it was directed:

> *Local Tribunal to be asked to inform the Central Tribunal whether they are satisfied that the man is the manager of his father's business.*

A fortnight later, in a case concerning Mr Worsley, the request for an opinion was combined with one for further information:

> *Local Tribunal to be asked (1) whether facts now reported are correct, (2) whether they can state the probable duration of Mr Singleton's illness, (3) for their observations on the present conditions under which the mills are being carried on during Mr Singleton's absence.*

This sensitivity to local opinion, and the Central Tribunal's apparent willingness to accord that opinion some weight, is again striking. It is surely no coincidence that the cases in which it was most openly exhibited were heard in Westminster as the controversy surrounding Joseph Blackburn began to grow. It might also be relevant that Mr Robinson worked in a market garden and Mr Worsley came from Lancashire.

Whatever its cause, this newly solicitous approach continued throughout 1917. On 19th September, in the case of Mr Showell, a baker and confectioner, the tribunal directed, comprehensively:

> *Man and Local Tribunal to be informed that the Central Tribunal learn that the man has made arrangements*

for the carrying on of his business, has offered his whole time for substitution work, and has been offered by the Ministry of Munitions a position as inspector of small tools. The Central Tribunal to be informed whether these statements are correct, and, if so, whether he has taken up such work. If the reply shows that the man has not arranged for the carrying on of his business and has not taken up substitution work, the Central Tribunal decide to grant exemption for a time on condition that he endeavours to obtain a substitute but he must offer not less than £300 a year.

It is clear that by now, the Central Tribunal was not only willing to seek further information from a local tribunal, together with its opinion on the facts of a case. It was also willing to give the man concerned a chance to see, and to comment upon, the things that had been said about him.

Mr Showell's case was the first of two dealt with on the same day in the same manner. The other one concerned Mr Pugh, another solicitor and one who, unlike Mr Martin, appears to have represented himself. In that case, it was to the appeal tribunal that the Westminster one had recourse. It directed:

Letter to be addressed to the Appeal Tribunal stating that the Central Tribunal could not grant exemption on the ground that the man assists his partner, but on the point of national interest they will be prepared to give the case further consideration if they are informed whether the requirements of the district would be met by the other solicitors in Stamford if his business is very much restricted or even closed down.

The case came up again on 9th October, when Mr Pugh was given a two-month exemption, in order that efforts might be made to find a suitable substitute. This was, however, to be the end of the line, for if Mr Pugh was minded to request a further exemption, he was warned:

> *The Central Tribunal will not consider that sufficient efforts have been made to find a suitable substitute unless the applicant is prepared to offer as much as £500 per annum in order to secure a manager.*

And so the Central Tribunal went on, seeking further information both from those who were involved in an appeal and from those who might have thought they were not. Towards the end of 1917, in the case of Mr Perry, the hearing was adjourned *in order that the Local Tribunal may have an opportunity of commenting on the capabilities of the two former managers.* In addition, the tribunal directed, *Case to be referred to the Local Government Board Inspector.*

An adjournment was also granted in March 1918, in the case of Mr Duncan, a builder and contractor from Aberdeen. That was so that further enquiries might be made of the man *respecting the land under cultivation and the exact nature of the building repairs now in hand,* and also so that *full particulars respecting the staff available* might be supplied. In addition, the Central Tribunal directed:

> *Local Tribunal to be asked to forward their observations on the replies and to favour the Central Tribunal with their opinion whether the man's services are essential for the cultivation of the holding.*

An opinion of that kind offered by a tribunal of that sort was not something to which Westminster had always been sensitive.

30

From the middle of 1917, then, a distinct change can be seen in the attitude of the Central Tribunal towards its inferiors. All of a sudden, it began to display much greater courtesy in its dealings with them. In fact, the tribunal also seemed keen to ensure that its decisions were properly understood, or at least that they were perceived to have been properly explained.

On 24th July 1917, the tribunal dismissed the appeal of a Mr Cohen and it denied him the exemption from military service he had sought. In doing so, however, the tribunal attempted to explain itself more fully than it ever had before. It seems that the appeal tribunal had allowed Mr Cohen to go to Westminster because it was exercised by a particular aspect of his case. Now, according to the minutes, the Central Tribunal stated:

> *With regard to the special point on which leave to appeal was granted the Local Tribunal having stated that the case was decided entirely on merits and that the offer made by the man as to the use of a motor car was not taken into account in arriving at their decision, the Central Tribunal have not thought it necessary to express any opinion in the matter.*

Although it is not clear what use Mr Cohen, a jeweller, had proposed be made of his motor car, the decision in his case is revealing. It suggests that the Central Tribunal was willing to defer both to the local tribunal's findings of fact and to the conclusions it had drawn from them. It is surely significant that Mr Cohen's case was heard in Queen Anne's Gate the month after the Thornton tribunal's letter of protest will have arrived there. And it may not be merely coincidental that Mr Cohen was also a man from Lancashire whose appeal had been heard at County Hall.

This apparently novel respect for facts found and for the interests of absolute clarity is demonstrated in a second case heard that day. In the appeal of a Cumberland schoolmaster named Lowes, the tribunal directed:

> *Further enquiry to be made of the Appeal Tribunal as to whether they found as a fact and are fully satisfied that the school would close if Mr Lowes is refused exemption.*

And:

> *Appeal Tribunal to be informed that Central Tribunal are reluctant to grant exemption as it is thought that the school might be carried on under female teachers.*

Three weeks later, a tribunal that was five sixths of the one that had dealt with Joseph Blackburn dismissed the appeal of Mr Cooksley, an insurance agent from Devon. (Only Sir Francis Gore was missing.) In doing so, and apparently for the benefit of others, the tribunal stated:

> *Appeal Tribunal and Local Tribunal to be informed that the Central Tribunal have fully considered the case of hardship and that the Central Tribunal are of opinion that the circumstances do not warrant the granting of exemption.*

There was a similar result when, a week later, the tribunal considered the case of Mr Bailey, a cow-keeper from the West Riding of Yorkshire. In that case, the appeal of the military representative was dismissed, the tribunal explaining:

Appeal Tribunal to be informed that the Central Tribunal think it of importance that the business should be maintained but that it should be maintained by a man of over military age. In the meantime they dismiss the appeal so that the Appeal Tribunal may reconsider the case when it comes up before them again. It is, however, with great reluctance that the Central Tribunal grant exemption to a man age 22 and in medical category A.

On 5th September 1917, the Central Tribunal took the same thorough course in appeals concerning Mr Ingram and Mr Dunkerley. They were considered together and the minutes state:

Special letter to be addressed to the Local Tribunal asking whether they are of opinion that it is in the national interest to retain these men in civil employment, particularly in view of the alteration of the age limits in the List of Certified Occupations and the regulations of the Board of Trade under which a percentage of the machinery is stopped. Local Tribunal to be asked to forward their reply through the Appeal Tribunal.

It is not clear what would make the letter to the local tribunal special. What is clear, however, and what might be of significance, is that – again – both men came from Lancashire and each, like Joseph Blackburn, had already had his case dealt with by the appeal tribunal for that county.

Aside from Joseph's case, however, and from any sensitivity to cases from Lancashire or those concerning market gardeners, there is another reason why the Central Tribunal should have treated its inferiors with respect; why, indeed, it should have been extremely reluctant to overturn their decisions or even to disagree with the facts they had found.

When, on Leap Day 1916, the members of the tribunal set out to agree the procedure they would follow in military service appeals, they did more than provide for the mutual exchange of evidence. They also set out a number of 'general principles' that would govern their tribunal's relationships with others. In particular, the members decided that:

> Decisions of the Local Tribunal are to be confirmed unless there is a good reason to the contrary.

Little more than a month later, this approach was enshrined in a draft letter the Central Tribunal's secretary, Mr Gibbon, submitted to its members. That draft, prepared now the first Military Service Act had come into effect, sought to establish the types of case in which a man might be permitted to appeal from the county appeal tribunal to the Central Tribunal. Once approved, the letter would be sent to Walter Long, the President of the Local Government Board, and it had something particular to say about *cases which turn on questions of fact.* (Joseph Blackburn's was, of course, such a case.)

> Cases of this kind should have been fully elucidated at the time that they have been heard a second time, and therefore, unless there are special reasons, an appeal would not appear necessary.

In other words, the Central Tribunal should accord considerable, and usually decisive, weight to the facts found and the conclusions reached by the local tribunals, and also by the county appeal tribunals.

There are some Westminster cases that make this seem more than a hollow promise. They include the cases of Messrs Robinson, Showell, Cohen, Lowes, Ingram and Dunkerley, but they are not confined to those ones. On a number of occasions, the Central Tribunal demonstrated that it was willing, and even keen, to defer to one of its inferiors. That was especially so in areas in which those tribunals were thought to have developed particular expertise. The tribunal can, in fact, be seen to have elevated that approach to a point of principle.

On 28th November 1916, the case was considered in Queen Anne's Gate of Mr Shire, a leather stainer from Somerset, who had attested under the Derby scheme. The members of the tribunal that day included Lord Salisbury, Sir Robert Carlyle and Mr Talbot and they refused the man the exemption he had sought. In doing so, they upheld not only the appeal of the military representative, but also, it seems, the decision of the local tribunal. The minutes state:

> *The Central Tribunal agree with the opinion expressed by the Appeal Tribunal that when a Local Tribunal has dealt with a large number of cases connected with an important local industry on general lines, adopted after careful consideration of the requirements of that industry and after consultation with the local representative of that industry and the Military Representative, the Appeal Tribunal should not interfere with that decision in one or two isolated cases which involve hardship on particular firms and in which the general lines have not been strictly adhered to, unless they are satisfied either that a real injustice has been done to those firms or that the national interests have been prejudiced by the decision.*

So, in matters in which it had achieved particular expertise, the decision of a local tribunal was not to be put aside lightly by an appellate tribunal. That wasn't, of course, what happened when Joseph Blackburn's case reached Westminster. Then, the decision of the Thornton local tribunal, and also that of the Preston appeal tribunal, was very lightly put aside. Perhaps the principle was more easily respected if the decision to which the local tribunal's expertise had led it would see the man being sent to the Colours.

Mystifyingly, we can even see the Central Tribunal deferring to a local tribunal on the specific question of whether a man was fully employed in agriculture. At its 287th meeting, when Lord Salisbury, Sir Robert Carlyle and Mr Talbot were present in Queen Anne's Gate, the tribunal dealt with the case of Mr Clemoes, a general draper from Essex who had been conscripted into the Army. The appeal had been made by the military representative and it was promptly dismissed:

> *The Central Tribunal have been informed that the man is fully employed in agricultural work, viz., from 6am until 5.30pm daily and they decided to grant exemption conditionally upon the man's being fully employed in agriculture to the satisfaction of the Local Tribunal.*

The meeting at which this case was considered took place on 1st May 1917, barely a fortnight before the case of Joseph Blackburn came up, and the panel that considered it included half of the members that would also deal with him.

31

There was one other thing the Central Tribunal could do if it found itself lacking significant information. It wasn't required to turn only to the man who was the subject of the appeal, or to the inferior tribunals that had already considered his case. According to the practice it had chosen for itself, the tribunal could make enquiries in other quarters.

Quite often, the tribunal can be seen to have sought information from another party to an appeal. Sometimes, that party was the military representative or his successor, the national service representative. That is what happened on 28th November 1916, in the case of Mr Lamerton, a conscripted man from Middlesex who said he was a furniture dealer. On that occasion, proceedings seem to have taken place in the absence not only of the man, but also of the military representative. When the Westminster tribunal concluded that the evidence was insufficient, there was only one course it felt able to take. The minutes state:

> *Further enquiries to be sent to the man as to hardship and to the Military Representative as to the statements made by the man regarding his income.*

On other occasions when the tribunal called upon the military representative, it did so in a way that suggests he was seen not as a party to the proceedings, but as an independent judicial investigator. Earlier in November 1916, for example, in the case of Mr Jellis, a farmer from Huntingdonshire, the tribunal had given a broad direction to the local military representative:

Mr Mager to be requested to arrange for a local investigation of this case as the Tribunal are of opinion that the man should not be exempt provided the farm could be carried on with the aid of a foreman or under the supervision of the man's brother and father.

As this case and others demonstrate, the enquiries the military representative might be required to undertake were broad but also, sometimes, elaborate. On 5th January 1917, for example, when it considered the case of Mr Dedman of East Suffolk, the tribunal directed:

Enquiry to be made by Captain James as to the importance of the work on which the man is employed; the facilities in the district for the upkeep of farm buildings and other property; and also whether the man's wife is capable of undertaking other work by which the income of the family could be supplemented.

This approach has an equivalent in one adopted, if only briefly, at Four Lane Ends. On 13th August 1917, the Thornton local tribunal adjourned proceedings in the cases of three men in order that the military representative might make enquiries of the United Alkali Company. At the same session, the same man was also directed to enquire as to the results of a medical examination performed on another Thornton claimant, James Lupton. (Several months later, Mr Lupton would be declared *medically unfit*.) These examples are, however, unusual and there appears to have been no other occasion upon which the Thornton tribunal gave the military representative a similar direction.

There are several appeals in which, though the Westminster minutes specify the enquiries that are to be made, it is not clear precisely who will be expected to make them. That is so, for example, in the case of Mr Hockey, which was considered by the Central Tribunal on 18th January 1917. The man came from Cambridge, where he was an auctioneer, but it seems that the full nature and extent of his business had not been revealed. The minutes direct:

Further enquiries to be made as to the man's full income and whether arrangements could not be made for the carrying on of the business by persons similarly engaged who are not eligible for military service.

There was a similar result on 12th September 1917, in the case of Mr Hiner, who came from West Suffolk and said he was a tailor's cutter. Before determining his appeal, the tribunal directed that further enquiries should be made *in reference to the persons dependent upon the firm and that the usual business questions be sent.*

The result of these changes in the approach of the Central Tribunal can be seen in the case of Mr Hattersley, a tailor and outfitter from Lancashire, who had attested for service under the Derby scheme. The tribunal first considered the man's appeal on 30th January 1918, by which time it had begun routinely to call upon military representatives, or their successors, to solicit the observations of local tribunals and to give men the opportunity to have their further observations heard. The tribunal was clearly intrigued by written comments about Mr Hattersley that had been submitted by a third party. The result was a complex, if by now familiar, series of investigations, disclosures and further representations. The minutes state:

It was decided to ask the National Service Representative to obtain from Mrs Marsden, the wife of Mr Hattersley's partner, a joint statutory declaration by herself and the three witnesses whom she named, confirming the

statements contained in her letter to the National Service
Representative, such declaration when received to be
communicated to Mr Hattersley. Any comments which
Mr Hattersley wishes to make on the statutory declaration
to be forwarded to the Central Tribunal through the
Local Tribunal who should be asked to forward their
observations on the case.

It seems that a decision was subsequently made by the tribunal, that the decision went against the man and that the man did not feel able simply to accept it. Mr Hattersley appears to have requested a rehearing of his case, for at its meeting on 6th March 1918, we find the tribunal refusing to order such a thing. In addition, however, the tribunal seems to feel compelled to explain its decision more fully, for the minutes go on to direct:

Man to be informed that the matter referred to in Mrs
Marsden's letter had no weight with the Central Tribunal
and it did not influence their decision.

There are many cases in the minutes of the Central Tribunal in which the evidence the tribunal required could only be obtained from an independent person or body. Often, that is the man's employer. At its meeting on 17th August 1916, for example, the tribunal considered the case of Alfred Smith, an attested man from East Suffolk who said he worked on the railway. The tribunal directed:

The Great Eastern Railway Company to be asked
whether Mr A Smith, Senr, is in fact engaged as a cartage
contractor in connection with the Company. If the reply
is in the affirmative the man is in a certified occupation
and the man is to be exempt so long as he continues in his
present occupation.

Something similar happened in two appeals considered in the spring of 1917. The first of them concerned Mr Watts, a conscript who was employed by the Oakley Explosives Company. That company was based in the Essex village of Great Oakley, which resembled Preesall in that it had ancient salt reserves that were now being exploited in the manufacture of munitions. On 27th March, the tribunal directed:

> Letter to be written to the Company as to products of the firm, the man's duties, the uses to which the products of the firm are applied, and whether this man handles any explosives used for the purposes of the war.

The second case was heard on 12th April and concerned Mr Benson, about whom, it is plain, the tribunal had some reservations. The minutes direct:

> Firm to be invited to make observations as to the nature of the man's work in the mill, and to be informed that it is only in exceptional circumstances that the Central Tribunal could grant exemption to a man who does not come within the terms of the Regulations relating to certified [occupation]. The Central Tribunal will be prepared to consider any statement by the firm as to the nature and importance of the man's work.

Often, however, the information in question could not be provided by the man's employer and the tribunal found itself compelled to cast its net more widely. The independent bodies, or people, to whom it can be seen to have had recourse were many and various. They included other military institutions or representatives, such as the Admiralty, the Territorial Forces Association, the Army Medical Department (and its advisory body), and the War Office (and its Separation Allowance Department) and, gnomically, 'Colonel Galloway'.

In addition, the tribunal often found itself posing questions to official organisations, such as the Ministries of Labour, National Service and Munitions; the Boards of Education, Control and Trade, the Local Government Board and the Board of Agriculture; the Coal Controller, the Postmaster General and the War Trade Department; the Reserved Occupations, Local Pensions, Dental Service, District Agricultural, Home Grown Timber and War Pensions Statutory Committees; and the police and *one of the high officials of the Metropolitan Police*. The Central Tribunal can also be seen to have requested information from the Ministry of Food, the Food Production Department and the Chief Food Commissioner, Northern Division.

The tribunal also had recourse to a variety of non-state bodies, including the Birmingham Law Society, the Leyton Old Age Pensions Committee, the Society of Accountants and the Institute of Accountants and Actuaries of Glasgow. In one case, that of Mr Spring of Lancashire, the tribunal deferred a final decision so that it might receive a deputation from the Cinematograph Exhibitors' Association, while in another case, the tribunal contacted a local authority, requesting *a report on the question whether this is a suitable man for delivering milk.*

In the case of one appellant, Mr Brown, representatives of the Board of Agriculture, the Ministry of Food and the Ministry of National Service were summoned before the Central Tribunal to answer a single, key question:

> ...*Whether it is in the national interest that men of military age should be exempted from Army Service for the purpose of managing poultry farms.*

From time to time, and as they often did in Thornton, agricultural cases occupied the time of the Westminster tribunal. In order the better to deal with those cases, the tribunal on 29th November 1917 received a deputation comprising representatives of the Ministry of Food and of the Food Production Department, who were required to speak *on the value and importance of tomatoes as food, and on the labour required for cultivation*. The meeting resulted in the following decision on the general question of growing tomatoes:

> *The Central Tribunal are of opinion that the production of tomatoes is of national importance, and therefore a specially skilled man, engaged in growing tomatoes on a substantial scale, should prima facie be exempted. Such a man would be able efficiently to supervise the work of a considerable number of unskilled or comparatively unskilled workpeople, and exemption would as a general rule only be justified where this is done.*

32

There was, then, a significant difference between the way Joseph Blackburn was treated in Queen Anne's Gate and the way other men were treated there. That difference was not, however, confined to the steps the Central Tribunal took to obtain further information about those men or to solicit their comments once such information had been received. It extended to the results of the cases themselves. Put simply, the tribunal treated Joseph more harshly than other appellants, whose circumstances were similar to his own.

On a number of occasions, the Westminster tribunal found itself able to grant exemption to men who followed Joseph's trade or calling. It did so, for example, on 8th February 1917, in the case of Mr Warner, a conscripted man from Worcestershire whom the tribunal seems to have had no doubt was a market gardener. The members of the tribunal who convened that day included Lord Salisbury, Mr Brunner, Sir Robert Carlyle and Sir Francis Gore. They were four of the six members who would, in little more than three months, consider Joseph's case and they decided that Mr Warner should be exempt from military service as long as he remained in his present occupation. There was a similar outcome two months later, in two cases from Gloucestershire that were considered together. Those cases concerned a market gardener's foreman and his assistant, and the tribunal granted each man an exemption from service, conditional only upon his continuing to work the land.

Later in February 1917, on a day when it once again had two thirds of the members that would determine the Blackburn case, the Central Tribunal considered the case of Mr Moll, who came from East Suffolk. The tribunal accepted that he was a market gardener and it once again granted him exemption from military service, this time on condition only that he perform some national service.

It is plain from the minutes that at times, the tribunal was receptive to the arguments of men engaged in agriculture, even where that was not the only calling the men pursued. That was so both before and after Lord Salisbury and his colleagues dealt with Joseph Blackburn. Towards the end of 1917, for example, the tribunal granted exemption to a Mr Oakley, an insurance broker and farmer from Essex. In doing so, it confirmed the decision of the appeal tribunal and required only that the man work *four days a week on some neighbouring farm*. That was not a novel solution.

On 7th July 1916, the Central Tribunal had considered the case of another market gardener, a Mr Brown from Gloucestershire. Having done so, Lord Salisbury, Sir Robert Carlyle and Mr Talbot among others granted the man exemption while ever he remained in his present occupation. That exemption was also said to be:

> ...Subject to the proviso that if within twenty-one days he undertakes, under the direction of the Committee on Work of National Importance, work which is of national importance and under conditions approved by the Tribunal.

In Mr Brown's case, the minutes continue:

> The work proposed to be reported to the Tribunal for approval. Power is reserved to the Tribunal to extend the period of twenty-one days or to vary the order if the appellant establishes to their satisfaction that he has done his best but has failed to comply with the condition.

It was in the following month that the tribunal considered the case of the Caithness crofter, John James Spence. That was the case in which the military representative had questioned the amount of time the man concerned actually spent on the land. The minutes state:

> *In this case the Tribunal decided that having regard to the facts as to the man's employment and his domestic circumstances he should be exempt from military service so long as he continues to be employed in an agricultural occupation.*

The position of crofters was, of course, a particularly sensitive one and it would continue to be so for some time yet. What is interesting about Mr Spence's case, however, is that the facts the Central Tribunal referred to, and that proved decisive, appear first to have been found by the local tribunal. It seems that here at least, the Westminster tribunal was perfectly content to accept the judgment of its inferior.

A similar issue arose on 22nd December 1916, in the case of Mr Kerslake, a smallholder from Somerset. In that case, the tribunal proved equally indulgent. It awarded the man a temporary exemption, until 1st April 1917, conditional upon him demonstrating *that he devotes his spare time in giving assistance to other occupiers of land.* The minutes state:

> *In the case of a small holding which does not occupy the holder's full time a Tribunal would be justified, if the other circumstances of the case make such a decision appropriate, in granting exemption subject to the condition that the holder devotes his spare time to other agricultural work to the satisfaction of the Tribunal.*

Crucially, it was to the satisfaction not of the Central Tribunal itself, but of the Somerset appeal tribunal that Mr Kerslake was to demonstrate that fact.

There are even cases in which the body to whose opinion the tribunal was happy to defer was a non-judicial one. When, on 11th July 1917, two thirds of the tribunal that had dealt with Joseph's case again came together at Queen Anne's Gate, the appeals they considered included that of Mr Shorthouse, who came from Glamorgan and was a china and hardware merchant, a cinema proprietor and a farmer. The exemption the man sought was granted on two conditions: that he remain in his present occupation and that he devote *full-time to cultivating his present holding and the additional 22 acres of land adjoining.* Mr Shorthouse's compliance with the second condition was to be judged not by the local tribunal or the appeal tribunal, but by the County War Agricultural Committee.

We do not know how much time the Central Tribunal decided Joseph Blackburn gave to tending his market garden. It seems that in Queen Anne's Gate, little credence was given to what Joseph had said at Four Lane Ends. What we do know is that the tribunal concluded that he gave more time to the 'hawking' of fruit and vegetables. This assumes, of course, that the two are wholly discrete tasks and that it is not properly the function of a market gardener to sell the product of his labours. It is possible that neither the Thornton local tribunal nor the Preston appeal tribunal was willing to make such a distinction. That, certainly, would explain the conclusion they both reached that Joseph was wholly engaged on the land.

We can see, in any case, that in granting exemption to some men on condition that they work on the land, the Westminster tribunal was content for them to do so for less than the whole of their working week. There is nothing in the documents it has left behind to indicate why the tribunal could not have afforded Joseph Blackburn that modest indulgence.

On Tuesday 27th March 1917, a tribunal that included Lord Salisbury, Mr Brunner and Sir Robert Carlyle among its members considered a case that closely resembles that of Joseph Blackburn. The case concerned a Mr Livingstone, who came from Lanarkshire and was acknowledged to be a market gardener. Crucially – and as, six weeks later, it would do in Joseph's case – the tribunal concluded that the man was *not fully occupied in his holding*. That fact was not, however, seen as fatal to Mr Livingstone's claim and it was certainly not used as a reason to send him to the Colours. The tribunal granted the man the exemption he had sought, conditional only upon his submitting himself for national service within fourteen days.

It is possible, of course, that the three members of the Central Tribunal involved both in Mr Livingstone's case and in Joseph Blackburn's case had forgotten the former before they came to consider the latter. That on discrete occasions the same tribunal could have reached opposing conclusions on essentially the same facts is an outcome that is to be deplored. It is not, however, one that is confined to the Central Tribunal, or to the administrative justice of only the 20th century. If, however, we do the tribunal the courtesy of assuming that it was consistent in its approach to appeals, the only possible difference between the two cases is that we know that in the later one, Joseph was found to be a hawker. But that creates a further problem. It is difficult to see how that fact alone could have made a difference, and difficult to fathom how it might have persuaded the tribunal to deny Joseph the relief it had already granted to another part-time market gardener.

33

It is also the case that, even when they could lay no claim to working on the land, other men who came before the Central Tribunal were given considerable licence.

On 20th March 1918, the tribunal seems to have been in a particularly indulgent mood. It first considered the case of Mr Jenkins, a monumental mason from Cardigan, who had plainly given little thought to what he wished to achieve through his appeal. That did not, however, mean that he would have to be sent for military service. The minutes state:

> *Man to be informed that the Central Tribunal can hold out no hope that the man will be granted exemption unless he submits to the Central Tribunal some proposal for taking up full time work of national importance to the satisfaction of the Local Tribunal. The Central Tribunal will expect to receive such proposal within a month.*

The mere possibility that he might do some work of national importance was therefore sufficient to ensure, for the moment at least, that Mr Jenkins was not committed to the Colours.

At the same meeting, the tribunal considered the case of another man from Wales: Mr Stainton, who came from Denbigh and was a taxi proprietor. In adjourning his case, the tribunal was indulgent once again. The man was to be informed:

> *…That the Central Tribunal will be willing to consider the question of granting him exemption on condition that he takes up some work of driving in connection with*

Army work or some other work of national importance;
and to be asked to make some proposal in the matter.

In case Mr Stainton was as short of ideas as Mr Jenkins seems to
have been, the tribunal further directed:

National Service Representative to be asked to suggest to
the man some work of national importance which he can
take up.

Mr Stainton's case was considered again on 1st May, when the
tribunal gave him a temporary exemption for a further three
months. That exemption would, however, also be subject to the
condition that he engage:

…Three days each week in agriculture to the satisfaction
of the Denbighshire War Agricultural Executive
Committee and upon his producing each month to the
National Service Representative to the Appeal Tribunal a
time book signed by his employer.

There were other cases in which men whose cases came before
the Central Tribunal were thought to require, and were duly
given, some prompting. On 10th April 1918, for example, in the
case of Mr Evans, a verger and caretaker who also came from
Denbigh, the man was told:

Central Tribunal will be prepared to consider the question
of granting exemption provided he submits some proposal
for taking up full time work of national importance – e.g.
work in an aeroplane and munitions factory.

Any such work was *to be carried out to the satisfaction of the*
Local Tribunal.

On 9th May, a Derby scheme man named Mr Sill had his case adjourned:

> *...In order that the employer may make a suggestion as to work of national importance the man can do on three days a week as a condition of exemption.*

Mr Sill was, however, warned:

> *If no suggestion can be made, Central Tribunal will refuse exemption.*

Later in March 1918, on the 26th of the month, the tribunal considered for the first time two cases to which it would in time have cause to return. The first of those cases concerned Mr Flanders, a conscripted man who came from Huntingdon and was a hairdresser. He, it seems, had given as little thought to his future as Mr Jenkins and Mr Stainton had to theirs. In adjourning Mr Flanders' case, the tribunal gave him some firm advice:

> *Man to be informed that the Central Tribunal will be willing to consider the question of granting exemption on condition that he takes up work of national importance for at least three days a week or obtains work which would release a fit man for service. On receipt of a proposal from the man the Central Tribunal will reconsider the case.*

In addition, the tribunal directed:

> *Local Tribunal to be asked whether the man can be utilised as a substitute for a fit man.*

This request for further information would, at the adjourned hearing, become something close to a ceding of judicial responsibility, for the tribunal then directed:

> *Temporary exemption to 1st November 1918, conditionally upon his being employed three days per week in agriculture to the satisfaction of the Local Tribunal.*

The second of the cases considered on 26th March 1918 would come before the Central Tribunal more than twice. The case concerned Mr Ricketts, an attested man from West Sussex who was *part proprietor and manager of goods agents and carriers.* At the first hearing of his appeal, the man was given a by-now-familiar prompt:

> *Man to be informed that the Central Tribunal will be willing to consider the question of granting exemption on condition that he takes up work of national importance (e.g., agriculture) for at least three days per week, and on receipt of any proposals from him the Central Tribunal will give further consideration to the case.*

Here, we see again that in some cases at least, the tribunal regarded even part-time work on the land as a suitable cause for a man's exemption from military service. It seems that Mr Ricketts responded to the tribunal's prompt, for on 8th May, the hearing of his case was adjourned again, this time so that further information could be obtained. The minutes state:

> *Man's proposals as regards undertaking farm work to be submitted to the Local Tribunal and their opinion asked on the question whether the farm is already sufficiently staffed without Ricketts.*

It may be that the local tribunal took an unfavourable view of Mr Ricketts' proposals, for when his case was next considered, the Central Tribunal directed:

> *Man to be informed that the Central Tribunal do not approve of the work proposed but they will be prepared to grant exemption provided they receive, within seven days, a further proposal to take up work for three days a week on a farm where his services are required owing to the shortage of staff. Inform man Local Tribunal may be able to assist him with advice as to a farm where his services are required. Local Tribunal to be informed.*

It is interesting to note not only the indulgence the Central Tribunal was willing to afford Mr Ricketts, but also the tribunal's courtesy towards its inferior, whose expertise it had already acknowledged and which it was keen to keep informed, and to be seen to keep informed, of all developments.

These themes re-emerged when the tribunal considered Mr Ricketts' case for the final time. That was on 12th June 1918, almost three months after the tribunal had first done so. On that occasion, the man was given a temporary exemption that would not expire for six months and that would be conditional upon his *taking up agricultural work for three days per week.* That work was to be done *to the satisfaction of the Local Tribunal.*

STRIKE

34

It was on 26th June 1917 that members of the Thornton local tribunal learned what had happened in Queen Anne's Gate. The session held that day was the first for two months and it seems to have been convened for only one purpose. The members present to hear the news were joined by Richard Bowman, the clerk, and the agricultural representative, Mr Walsh. Also attending Four Lane Ends that Tuesday afternoon was the new military representative, and he would waste no time in making his presence felt.

*

Thomas Pym Williamson had been the secretary of the Royal Lytham & St Annes Golf Club since 1903, the year Viscount Cranborne became Lord Salisbury and joined the House of Lords. He was a mere thirty-three years of age then and by way of salary had been promised £175 a year, *plus lunch, but not including liquor.*

In his even younger days, Thomas – or 'Tom', or 'Pym' – Williamson had been an actor and had appeared in the West End and even toured South Africa with Owen Nares. He had also been part of the theatrical company assembled by Lillie Langtry for her later tours of the United States of America. The winter of 1894, for example, had seen them both performing on the East Coast and in the Midwest.

Born in 1869, just before Wilfred Ashley and just after Lord Richard Cavendish, Pym Williamson had broken with the tradition of at least five generations of his family by eschewing the Church. As far back as the late 17th century, his ancestors had been ordained ministers in towns across the north of England. Pym shared his name with three of those men and like at least four of them he had attended Cambridge University. Unlike them, however, he had not been awarded a degree.

On stage, back in Britain, Pym Williamson had forged a successful career. In May 1899, for example, he had appeared alongside Brandon Thomas, already famous for his *Charley's Aunt*. While in July of the following year, as Lord Salisbury prepared to take up his first ministerial post, Pym was in the cast of *English Nell*, a new play that had been written for Miss – later Dame – Marie Tempest and now starred her in the title role. The cast also included Granville Barker, who would drive a Red Cross ambulance on the Western Front and produce a compelling memoir of his experiences.

Pym Williamson was part of the Lillie Langtry company as late as the autumn of 1901, when they both performed at the Imperial Theatre in Westminster. That theatre, which had been bought by Ms Langtry the year before, was part of the old Royal Aquarium and Winter Garden and stood where the Methodist Central Hall does today. It was but a short stroll from Queen Anne's Gate.

Of all his theatrical roles, perhaps the most fêted is one Pym Williamson performed in 1900, in productions of Cecil Raleigh's play *Hearts are Trumps* at the Grand Theatre in Islington and the Broadway Theatre in New Cross. Of his performance, one reviewer wrote, *Mr Pym Williamson gives a manly and unaffected interpretation of the part of the Reverend John Thorold*. As his stage career drew to a close, it seems that Pym finally got to play the role for which his heritage best qualified him.

Lillie Langtree and Marie Tempest, and Brandon Thomas and Granville Barker, were not the only celebrated actors with whom Pym Williamson shared a stage. The first production of *English Nell* also featured Fuller Mellish, who would subsequently make a successful transition to the screen. In 1915, indeed, as Joseph Blackburn prepared to attest his willingness to serve, Mellish played a starring role in the first, silent film version of A. E. W. Mason's novel *The Four Feathers*.

*

The session on 26th June would be the last at Four Lane Ends for several months. Having welcomed Mr Williamson, the members of the tribunal learned that the Central Tribunal had effectively sent Joseph Blackburn off to war. The minute book states:

> *Read letter of 22nd May 1917 from the Central Tribunal re: Case No. 164 advising that 'they do not feel that they can properly lay down any general rule as to the size of holding in respect of which exemption may be granted. Each case must be decided on its own circumstances' and had decided that the man be not exempt.*
>
> *As the exemption had been granted by a local Tribunal and confirmed by the Appeal Tribunal, and only referred to the Central Tribunal to settle the point as to the size of the holding in respect of which exemption might be granted, it was felt that protest should be made against the calling of the man to the Army and after full discussion.*

The minutes tell us nothing more about any discussion that took place, but it is clear that Councillor Dewhurst and his colleagues were disappointed with what Mr Bowman told them. So disappointed, in fact, that they decided to take action:

> *It was Resolved:*
> *That the Thornton Local Tribunal protest against the*

decision of the Central Tribunal in Case No. 164 and that the Clerk be instructed to communicate with the Central Tribunal thereon and that this meeting stand adjourned until the man has been released from the Army or a satisfactory explanation is forthcoming.

Though it would subsequently reject the word, the only reasonable conclusion is that from now on, the Thornton local tribunal was on strike. Although the official minutes were restrained, the local press was a good deal less so.

*

TRIBUNAL ANGRY
Indignant protest at Thornton
CENTRAL BOARD'S ACTION RESENTED
SOME PLAIN TALKING

The Thornton tribunal met on Tuesday afternoon, in the Council Chamber, after an interval of two months. There were thirty-two cases, all military reviews, down for hearing, and included in the list were several officials and workmen in the employ of the Urban District Council.

The chair was taken by Councillor T. Dewhurst, and there were also present Councillors T. Waring, J. Titherington, T. R. Strickland and W. Betney, the clerk (Mr R. Bowman), the military representative (Mr T. 'Pym' Williamson), his assistant (Mr Robinson) and the agricultural representative (Mr Walsh).

At the outset, the clerk read a letter from the Central Tribunal with reference to the case of a local market gardener and hawker, who had been granted conditional exemption by the local tribunal. This decision had been confirmed by the Preston tribunal, but on the application of the military representative the case had been taken to the Central Tribunal, with a view to

220

deciding the point of what constituted the quantity of land to justify the exemption of a market gardener.

The Central Tribunal now wrote stating that they could not lay down any general rule as to the size of the holding, and each case would have to be decided on its merits. In this case, they were of opinion that the man spent most of his time hawking, and their decision was that he would have to join up, and he was now in the Army.

Councillor Titherington said this particular case had been treated on its merits, and the local tribunal were well acquainted with the circumstances.

He objected to the local tribunal being treated in this shameful manner, and added, "I don't feel like sitting on the tribunal any longer."

Councillor Betney said the man came before them, and they decided that he was actually a market gardener, and was employed on the land. The Preston tribunal confirmed their decision to give him conditional exemption, and now the Central Tribunal, who did not know anything of the facts, had overruled these decisions. In their letter, they said such cases ought to be tried on their merits. That was just what the local tribunal had done in arriving at their decision. He would like the public to say which body were the right persons to judge in such a case. They were told they must not take men off the land, and yet men were being taken off the land. About twelve months ago, the local tribunal decided that a man who was employed on the land must go to the Army, but he was still in Thornton. The military were asking for men, and when the tribunal sent them they would not take them.

The Chairman – If I remember rightly, when this man was before us, he said he was not hawking most of his time, but that he was engaged mostly in his garden. According to the letter from the Central Tribunal, they think he was engaged

221

hawking most of his time. His place is not a big one, but he works hard on it, and produces two crops a year.

Councillor Titherington – The man has lost both his father and his mother. He spent over £30 in seeds. You cannot find anything like it within a radius of twenty miles, and in the face of what we have considered, knowing what the man produces, the military take him to Preston, and after our decision has been confirmed they go further to the Central Tribunal.

A Member – If he had been an expert rose grower, he would have got off.

Councillor Betney – We ought to raise a protest against the Central Tribunal's decision.

Councillor Titherington – I feel inclined to leave the Tribunal today, and I ask the other members to do the same, until this man is brought back. To come here, wasting our time, and then to be treated in this way by someone who knows nothing of the circumstances is simply abominable. This man had not the money to go to London before the Central Tribunal, and he was frightened into the Army. What are we here for?

Mr Pym Williamson – May I ask what you have a Central Tribunal for?

Councillor Titherington – The Preston Tribunal upheld our decision. The young man told us he had not the money to go to London to defend his case before the Central Tribunal. He was frightened into the army.

Mr Pym Williamson said the Preston tribunal must have given the military leave to appeal. He had heard a good many cases tried before the Preston tribunal, and it was a very unusual thing indeed for them to give permission to take a case to the Central Tribunal. He did not know, but he thought the appeal tribunal were not in agreement in this case.

The clerk said he was not at the appeal tribunal at Preston when the case was heard, and the only information he had with regards to what took place was from Major Booth. Leave to appeal was given to Major Booth, so that the point might be settled as to what quantity of land constituted a market garden for the purpose of granting exemption. That was the only point on which there was any doubt, so far as the Preston tribunal were concerned, otherwise they would have refused consent to take the case to the Central Tribunal. That point the Central Tribunal had not settled yet.

Councillor Betney – Mr Williamson has said it is very rare they send these cases for further trial.

Mr Williamson – What is the reason? Because the military representative in most cases is satisfied that the Preston Tribunal has settled the case, and he thinks it is not worthwhile to go to the Central Tribunal.

Councillor Titherington – He is not right there.

The Chairman – If he had had another acre of land, but had not cultivated it, I suppose he might have been left off?

Mr Pym Williamson – I don't think so.

Councillor Betney – We have a case of a man who was before this Tribunal last February, and he went to Preston and was told he must join up. Then his family or someone else moved heaven and earth, and he went to Lancaster and was sent back again.

Mr Pym Williamson – What was he sent back for?

Councillor Betney – To go on the land.

Mr Pym Williamson – Why?

Councillor Betney – Because he was on the land.

Mr Pym Williamson – Or because he was rejected by the Medical Board?

Councillor Betney – That is what we want to know.

223

The Chairman – I think we have had a fair discussion on this point, and I suggest we adjourn the hearing of the other cases.

Councillor Betney – There has been a lot of shenanigans with regard to these military men. If you read the papers, you don't know what to do and think.

The Chairman – I suggest the Clerk should write a letter and get some understanding, if that falls in with the views of the Tribunal. We can adjourn these cases down for hearing until we get an understanding on this particular case. We want to know the reason why the Central Tribunal arrived at their decision.

Councillor Titherington – I cannot see anything else for it, unless we are going to be treated differently.

The Chairman – Do you approve of it?

Councillor Betney and other members – I do.

The Chairman – Then please show.

All the members put up their hands, and the chairman said the vote was unanimous.

Mr Walsh (the agricultural representative) – I'm off back. I've work of national importance to do.

Mr Pym Williamson – I would like to express my opinion…

35

Following the tribunal session held on 26th June, and the significant decision the members took that Tuesday afternoon, the clerk acted decisively. A letter of protest was dispatched to Queen Anne's Gate in a matter of hours:

Sir,

> *Thornton Local Tribunal*
> *JS Blackburn 17923. Lancashire (Preston)*
> *Your communication of the 22nd May 1917 conveying the decision of the Central Tribunal in the above case was considered by the Thornton Local Tribunal at their meeting today.*
>
> *The Local Tribunal granted additional exemption with a full knowledge of the local circumstances and the Preston Appeal Tribunal refused the appeal of the Military Representative but gave leave to appeal to the Central Tribunal for their decision as to the size of holding in respect of which exemption may be granted.*
>
> *As the Central Tribunal have not decided the point on which their decision was sought the Local Tribunal are of opinion that their decision as confirmed by the Appeal Tribunal should have stood.*
>
> *They find however that the man has been called to the Army and as a protest they have adjourned the consideration of any further cases until the man has been released from the Army or a satisfactory explanation is forthcoming.*
>
> *I am, Sir,*

At the same time, the clerk also wrote to the secretary of the Local Government Board, enclosing copies of the Westminster letter and the Thornton reply:

As intimated in the latter letter the Tribunal have adjourned the hearing of any further cases until the man referred to is released from the Army or a satisfactory explanation is forthcoming.

*

The decision to adjourn seems to have come easily to the tribunal, and the thinking behind it had certainly been rehearsed before.

Over the preceding winter, and at the request of the government, the tribunal had deferred hearing cases about agricultural men, only to find that they had been taken to the appeal tribunal in Preston. When, in the New Year, the tribunal remonstrated with the military representative concerned, Councillor Titherington expressed his particular displeasure. He said he did not think it was any use the members of the tribunal sitting there if their decisions were going to be opposed in this way. It was totally wrong, after gentlemen had given their services to try to do the best they could for their king and country, that their decisions should be overruled. They might just as well stay at home and if that kind of thing was going to occur, he was not venturing out these cold evenings and wasting his time.

Those words were very similar to the ones he would use the following June.

*

It seems that a response was soon received at Four Lane Ends, for on the last day of the month, Richard Bowman wrote to the board again, acknowledging receipt of the reply and promising to lay it before the tribunal. On the same day, Mr Bowman notified the members of the tribunal that a further meeting would take place on the evening of the following Tuesday. The business of that meeting was, he wrote:

(a) *Letter from Local Government Board.*
(b) *Letter from the Military Representative enclosing*
    appeals in connection with adjourned cases.
(c) *Any other business that may arise.*

On 2nd July 1917, Mr Bowman sent out another letter. This one was addressed to a Mr Elias at 36 Falkner Street, Liverpool.

Built – like 16 Queen Anne's Gate in Westminster – during the second half of the Georgian era, the two-storey house at number 36 is made of brick, stone and slate and stands on land once owned by Edward Falkner. A former soldier and High Sheriff of Lancashire, he was a slave trader who had seen the wisdom of diversifying his business interests. He was also responsible for a feat that resembles Lord Derby's more than a century later. In the space of a single day in 1797, or maybe even a single hour, Falkner mustered a thousand men to defend the city of Liverpool against a rumoured – if improbable – invasion by the French. Much later, the house was owned by Brian Epstein, the manager of the Beatles, and in the autumn of 1962, it was briefly the home of John Lennon and his new wife, Cynthia.

Mr Bowman's letter notified Mr Elias of the meeting that was to take place the following day. It did so tersely – *Meeting called tomorrow 6.30 to consider matter* – and it was handwritten, which suggests that its purpose was simply to confirm a conversation that had already taken place. William

Elias, as those members of the Thornton tribunal who did not know him would soon discover, was a representative of the Local Government Board. He was, of course, one of the board's redoubtable inspectors.

*

Mr Elias had recently had cause to return to a familiar subject, that of the feeding of the poor, and it seems he was still exercised by the question of bread. At a meeting of the Ormskirk guardians he told them they should:

> *...Pay special attention to recipients of outdoor relief who might find the food problem difficult of solution. For such a purpose lady relieving officers and lady children inspectors might visit the house and prove of great value.*

He went on to explain:

> *Where the provision of food substitutes involved additional cost, allowances of money might be raised accordingly by way of encouragement to the thrifty. The simplest solution of the bread problem would probably be in some combination of barley, oats, maize, or rye with wheat flour.*

Although some of the guardians thought this a sensible idea, others did not. One, for example, said that "probably some of the women whom the lady inspector went to visit would be able to instruct her in household duties", while another remarked "that the poor were the best bakers". On a vote being taken, however, the motion was carried by a large majority and Mr Elias' culinary advice was once again taken on board.

*

Mr Elias did not attend the meeting in Thornton on 3rd July. It would not be long, however, before he made the journey to Four Lane Ends.

The tribunal had a wealth of correspondence to consider that evening. From the Westminster tribunal there were two letters, dated 22nd May and 2nd July. Intriguingly, the second of those letters appears to have been a reply to Mr Bowman's letter of 26th June. No trace remains either of that letter or of any further response the Thornton tribunal might have sent. From subsequent events, however, it is clear that whatever was said by the Central Tribunal, its letter contained neither an explanation nor an apology.

There was also another letter from the Local Government Board, sandwiched between the Thornton tribunal's own to that body of 26th and 30th June, and another from its inspector – presumably Mr Elias – of 30th June. Finally, there was a – no doubt weighty – package from the military representative, Mr Williamson, submitting appeals in thirty-three cases.

Its discussion over, the Thornton tribunal resolved:

That a further communication be sent to the Local Government Board restating the position of the Local Tribunal and asking for an explanation and assuring them that as hitherto the Tribunal were desirable to carry out the work of the Tribunal on the lines set out in the Regulations issued by the LGB.

The position referred to was the one the Thornton tribunal had adopted in the case of Joseph Blackburn.

The letter the tribunal had resolved to send to the Local Government Board is dated 4th July 1917. It is in the name of the clerk, Richard Bowman, and addressed, as always, to the secretary of the board. At first, the letter simply repeats the history of the Blackburn case and restates the tribunal's objections to what had been done in Westminster:

> Your letter of 28th June 1917 has been considered by the Tribunal and they cannot agree that the case referred to has been decided by the Central Tribunal in accordance with the merits of the case.
>
> The case was carefully considered by the Local Tribunal and in granting Conditional Exemption so long as the man remained a Market Gardener (one of the Certified Occupations) they were satisfied that this was his principal occupation which is shown by the reasons for their decision endorsed on the form of appeal.
>
> This decision was confirmed by the Preston Appeal Tribunal but permission was given to the Military Representative to carry the case to the Central Tribunal so that their ruling could be on the quantity of land which justified an exemption being granted.
>
> This the Central Tribunal (after four months' consideration) as stated in their letter to me of 22nd May 1917 have not decided but have cancelled the exemption on the ground that the principal occupation of the man is hawking which is contrary to the facts elicited by the Local Tribunal and set out in the reasons for their decision referred to above.
>
> The Local Tribunal are and always have been very desirous to comply with the Regulations issued by your Board, and have refrained from making protests in other matters which have arisen and which would have been justified but did not involve important matters of principle.

At this point, however, the letter turns to a number of other, less directly relevant issues. In reciting those issues, Mr Bowman might have hoped to gain the sympathy of the Local Government Board. He also, however, provides a fascinating summary of the first eighteen months of the Thornton tribunal's work.

We learn, for example, that the population of the area the tribunal served was 5,500, of whom seventy-one men – *only seventy-one men*, as the letter puts it – were currently exempt in some way from military service. We also learn that of those men, thirty-eight worked on the land or in market gardens; that of that number, twenty-nine were married and nine single; and that of the remainder, eleven were in other certified occupations, five had been exempted upon taking up work of national importance, two were engaged in munitions and two were *mentally and physically unfit*.

Then, alluding to the contents of Mr Williamson's recent postal package, the letter concludes:

> *The Tribunal have to consider 33 claims by the Military Representative for review of Certificates which will require very careful consideration having regard to the Instructions issued by your Board but they feel that the arbitrary decision of the Central Tribunal, if allowed to stand, opens the door to unfair persecution of individuals who are entitled to consideration in the national interest.*

Not only is Mr Bowman's letter of 4th July intriguing for its content, it is also revelatory. It demonstrates, for example, that the Thornton tribunal thought it worthy of praise – or thought the Local Government Board might think it worthy of praise – that only a small number of exemptions had been granted. In fact, the number of exemptions awarded at Four Lane Ends is less meaningful than the proportion of appeals in which they came. As we have seen, that proportion was actually quite large.

Once again, the Thornton tribunal received a swift response to its letter, for in a further note, dated 11th July 1917, the clerk informed members that another meeting would be held the following day. The purpose of that meeting, he said, would be to *consider letter received from the Local Government Board.* A copy of that letter was helpfully enclosed.

In the late afternoon of 12th July, and with the exception of Councillor Strickland, all members of the tribunal convened once again at Four Lane Ends. Mr Bowman read to them the latest correspondence concerning Joseph Blackburn. After hearing what he said, the members resolved:

> *That as the explanation asked for is not given in the reply of the Local Government Board, the Clerk be instructed to communicate further with them thereon and to ask for the return of the papers connected with Case No. 164.*

Although no copy of any such letter remains, it is plain that further attempts were made to resolve this matter and that those attempts involved the Local Government Board. At least at first, they also involved an unfamiliar person from, it seems, the military. On 17th July, the Thornton clerk wrote to Mr Elias, of the board:

> *In reply to your telephone message nothing resulted from the interview I had with Mr Williamson (Military Representative) who was accompanied by Mr Metson.*
>
> *The matter upon which we wrote to the Central Tribunal was not one which Captain Metson could settle.*

We know from an acknowledgement sent by Richard Bowman that the reply the Thornton tribunal received from the Local Government Board was dated 19th July. Five days later, Mr

Bowman wrote to his members again. He had urgent and intriguing news to impart:

I have had intimation that the Local Government Board Inspector will attend the meeting tonight, please endeavour to attend.

36

The meeting with William Elias, the Local Government Board inspector, took place as planned on Tuesday 24th July 1917. All members of the tribunal were present in the Thornton council chamber that evening, together with their clerk, Richard Bowman.

It is likely that Mr Elias found his way from Falkner Street to Four Lane Ends without much difficulty, for, to him, the north of the Fylde was familiar ground. Before going up to Oxford University, the young William had attended Rossall School. He had, in fact, been a pupil there when Lord Salisbury first entered Parliament, when Joseph Blackburn and his future wife were born and when the new chemical works began to rise up from the salt marshes beside the River Wyre.

The school at Rossall stands in the settlement of that name, which is now on the edge of the town of Fleetwood but was once at the heart of the Hesketh-Fleetwood estate. The school was founded by the Church of England in 1844, just after Joseph's parents were born, as a northern equivalent of Marlborough College in Wiltshire. The building and land it at first comprised were acquired when the debts Sir Peter had incurred finally threatened to overwhelm his family. Rossall is barely two miles west of Four Lane Ends in Thornton and, the land between being flat and unobstructed, the school is within sight of Marsh Mill.

After the usual pleasantries had been exchanged, Richard Bowman read aloud the letter the tribunal had recently received from the Local Government Board. It will have served as a suitable introduction to the board's inspector, for the minutes tell us that he spoke next:

> *Mr Elias pointed out that nothing further could be done in the matter, the Local Tribunal not being entitled to any explanation, but it did not warrant the holding up of cases.*

We can only guess how this statement was received by Councillor Dewhurst and his colleagues. What Mr Elias said suggests that the priority, at least of the Local Government Board, was the hearing of cases in general and not the case of Joseph Blackburn in particular. And in stating that no explanation was due, he was repeating an assertion the Central Tribunal itself had made more than eighteen months before. It was not, of course, one to which that tribunal had scrupulously adhered in the intervening months.

Regrettably, and save for the brief note Mr Bowman made, no record remains of the meeting that July evening. What we do know, however, is that Mr Elias' statement was far from the end of the matter, for the minutes say that subsequently, there was *considerable discussion*. From what members of the tribunal said afterwards, it seems that the military representative, his possible presence in Queen Anne's Gate and information he might have given to the Central Tribunal formed at least part of that discussion.

Ultimately, the meeting was adjourned:

> *Mr Elias undertaking to approach the Local Government Board asking if any further explanation could be given.*

That was not, however, before the Thornton tribunal could pass another resolution:

> *That thanks be extended to Mr Elias for his attendance.*

*

Immediately beyond the southern edge of Rossall School stands a group of whitewashed cottages, their window frames, door arches and downspouts picked out starkly in black. Put up in 1901, as Lord Salisbury began his career in government and Pym Williamson prepared his exit from the West End, these cottages have names such as Delph, Mitre and Ivy, and they follow the Arts and Crafts domestic style, with characteristic hipped-and-swept roofs all tiled in red.

Of the same vintage and with the same lineage as the bronze and silver bath taps of the W. H. Smiths, the cottages are all that remains of ambitious plans to develop the former home of the Fleetwood family. They were designed by Edwin – later Sir Edwin – Lutyens, who would achieve much greater prominence in the years to come.

*

What Mr Elias did next is unclear. There is nothing in the Thornton records, however, to suggest that the local tribunal ever received the further explanation he had undertaken to solicit, nor any other account of the decision in Joseph Blackburn's case. In the letter book, however, there is the copy of a note sent by Richard Bowman on 25th July 1917, acknowledging receipt of a package from the Central Tribunal. That package contained not an explanation, but the *application and appeal forms in respect of Joseph Septimus Blackburn.*

On 1st August, Mr Bowman wrote to its secretary, acknowledging receipt of a further letter from the Local Government Board. Although that letter has been lost, it is plain from what happened next that the members of the Thornton tribunal derived little satisfaction from its contents.

A further meeting took place two days later, when, by their own account, members conducted a thorough review of the Blackburn case. They considered their own decision to award

236

Joseph exemption, the decision of the appeal tribunal in Preston, the grounds of appeal lodged by the military representative and the decision of the Central Tribunal.

The Thornton members also considered the recent letter from the Local Government Board, which, it is plain, did not contain the explanation they were hoping for. The minutes of the meeting are again brief. They do, however, confirm that:

After full and careful consideration the Tribunal came to the conclusion that the matter could not usefully be carried further for the present, and instructed the Clerk to write the Local Government Board stating that the papers and correspondence had been carefully considered and the Local Tribunal had been forced to the conclusion that the decision of the Central Tribunal had been based on an ex parte statement by the Military Representative which was contrary to the facts as found by the Local Tribunal and the Appeals Tribunal and therefore contrary to the Regulations issued by the Board and regretting that no explanation had been furnished, and protesting against such a decision being allowed to stand.

The tribunal then resolved:

That the hearing of cases be resumed.

It is intriguing that the tribunal concluded that a military representative had been present when Joseph's case was considered at Queen Anne's Gate, and that he had provided a statement that influenced the decision Lord Salisbury and his colleagues made. That conclusion seems to have been based upon the discussion with Mr Elias and also, possibly, upon the contents of the letter the tribunal subsequently received from the Local Government Board. The surviving records certainly contain no earlier reference to any such conclusion. That the tribunal also formed the impression that the military representative's statement was made ex parte adds weight to the suspicion that Joseph was not present in Queen Anne's Gate at the time.

In a letter dated 4th August 1917, once again addressed to the secretary, Mr Bowman informed the Local Government Board:

> *I am directed by the Local Tribunal to inform you that they have very carefully considered your letter of the 30th July... together with the copy of the papers in the case referred to supplied to them by the Central Tribunal.*
>
> *I am also to state that the Local Tribunal are forced to the conclusion, as a result of such consideration, that the decision of the Central Tribunal has been based on an ex parte statement by the Military Representative which was contrary to the facts as found by the Local Tribunal and the Appeal Tribunal, and therefore contrary to the Regulations issued by your Board.*
>
> *They regret that no explanation has been furnished, but have decided to close the correspondence and to resume the hearing of cases, while protesting against such a decision being allowed to stand.*

The Thornton tribunal's strike was now, therefore, at an end. Although the tribunal concluded only that the protest could not be pursued for the moment, and firmly though the tribunal might have insisted that it should stand, there is no further reference to the protest in the surviving records. The tribunal would soon resume hearing military service claims, something it had not done for more than three months.

37

The next session of the Thornton tribunal, the first after its lengthy adjournment, took place on 13th August 1917. Those present in the council chamber that Monday afternoon included Mr Walsh, the agricultural representative, but also Captain Dixey, an Army man who had come in an official capacity. At the beginning of proceedings, the clerk read a letter from Pym Williamson, who members of the tribunal now knew as the military representative. Mr Williamson wrote that he had appointed Captain Dixey to act as his deputy at the hearing of cases.

The reason for Pym Williamson's absence is unclear. He would attend many of the tribunal's subsequent sessions and although he would sometimes do so alone, there would also be occasions when he did so with Mr Robinson, his assistant. Captain Dixey's face, too, would become familiar at Four Lane Ends, even if his presence now wasn't entirely welcome.

Given what had happened two months before, when the Thornton tribunal last dealt with military service claims – and given Mr Williamson's testy exchanges with Councillors Betney and Titherington – it would be understandable if, on this occasion, he let discretion be the better part of valour. Captain Dixey, however, seems not to have had that option.

Both of those councillors were present at the session, together with all other members of the tribunal. They were told by their clerk that of three recent appeals to the Preston tribunal, one, by the military representative, had been successful. The tribunal then began to consider the many cases its strike had forced it to put to one side.

The tribunal reached a decision in thirty of those cases and in none is there evidence that it acceded to the military representative's request. Of the cases concluded that afternoon, seven were adjourned and eleven withdrawn and in twelve, the man was given an exemption of one kind or another. In fact, the records suggest that the Thornton tribunal never again made an order that would send a man off to fight straight away. It was not, however, the detail of the cases determined by the tribunal, nor even the circumstances of the men concerned, that most excited the interest of the local press.

*

THORNTON TRIBUNAL

The first meeting of the Thornton Tribunal since its abrupt adjournment two months ago was held in the Council Offices, Thornton on Monday afternoon. Mr T Dewhurst presiding. The other members present were Messrs T Waring, J Titherington, W Betney, TR Strickland, with W Walsh (Agricultural Representative), Captain Dixey (Military Representative) and the Clerk, Mr R Bowman. There were 34 cases down for review by the military authorities.

At the outset, the Chairman said that Tribunal had been adjourned six weeks on account of one particular case which was well-known to the Tribunal. However, in the interests of the country and the interests of that particular district the Tribunal had agreed to take the cases, awaiting review by the military, under protest. He felt sure that Tribunal had always tried in every way possible to meet the military authorities. He did not altogether blame the Central Tribunal, who had ruled against them: it was because mis-statements had been made. He considered the high-handed action of the military very wrong.

Mr W Betney said he would like to make comments on remarks made by Captain Dixey at Fleetwood. Captain Dixey was very anxious to let Fleetwood Tribunal know it was not his fault that deadlock had arisen between the Thornton Tribunal and the military. He (Mr Betney) objected to the remarks by Captain Dixey that they were silly and pettish. What right had he to say that, and what right had he to discuss that Tribunal at the Fleetwood Tribunal.

The Chairman – Perhaps Captain Dixey will explain.

Captain Dixey – Were you present at that Tribunal?

Mr Betney – No, but the reporters were, and they are here now. Did you say we were silly and pettish?

Captain Dixey – I did not say you were silly and pettish, but I said the Tribunal were silly and pettish.

Mr Betney (turning to the reporters) – Did Captain Dixey say this or not? He compared us to a Bench of Magistrates who refused to sit because the Sessions had upset their decisions.

Captain Dixey – I have come here at the request of the Military Representative for this district, and what I said at Fleetwood I say again. I am perfectly at liberty to say what I like.

Mr Betney – I don't think you are at liberty to say what you like.

Captain Dixey – I was asked at Fleetwood my opinion, and I gave my opinion and I say again, it is a very silly idea for a Tribunal to strike. It does no good. The notion of striking, to my mind, is silly. It does nobody any good. We were advised to take the case to the Central Appeal Court at the request of the Preston Appeal Court. We did and we won. We have got to do our best for the nation. I say again it is silly and causes friction between people, and if you are going to tell me your decisions must not be upset, then what are the higher authorities for. At Fleetwood last week a gentleman mentioned to me a case of a fish buyer in which the Tribunal there had decided the man must join the army. The Appeal Court at Preston decided the man must be exempted. Now if the Fleetwood Tribunal had struck because Preston Tribunal...

The Chairman (interrupting) – Keep the word Strike out.

Captain Dixey – Well, if Fleetwood Tribunal had adjourned I should have said they were acting silly and I would say that anywhere.

The Chairman – I do think the remarks were very uncalled for, another Military Representative to speak like that at another Tribunal.

Mr John Titherington – The man who uttered these remarks at Fleetwood is the most childish and foolish of the lot.

Captain Dixey – I did not come here to have a row and to be told my duty. I did not come here for the Tribunal to try me on newspaper reports.

Mr Titherington – Mind you don't libel the newspapers.

Mr Strickland – The remarks of Captain Dixey at Fleetwood were very discourteous.

Mr Betney – I would like to have said a few more words, but go on, Mr Chairman...

The proceedings then commenced.

*

The Fleetwood session referred to in this exchange had, in fact, taken place more than a month before, in the early days of July

1917, while the Thornton tribunal stood adjourned. During that session, two men employed by the United Alkali Company said they had already been 'starred' by that tribunal. When Captain Dixey asked if they had the documents to prove their assertion, the Fleetwood clerk was quick to intervene and, as Councillor Betney would note, their exchange, too, was recorded by the local press.

*

CAPT. DIXEY AND THE THORNTON TRIBUNAL

The Clerk – They are in a state of suspension at Thornton.
Captain Dixey – Not through me being there. (Laughter.)
I think it is very silly and petty, because they have prejudiced all the men's cases. All the cases have gone to Preston, and it does not give the men the same chance. It was very wrong, when all is said and done, particularly on such a small point. It is like the magistrates saying they are not going to sit because the Sessions have opposed their decisions.

38

It is plain that in Joseph Blackburn's case, members of the local tribunal believed those of the Central Tribunal to have been the subject of undue influence. On the day the Thornton tribunal's lengthy adjournment came to an end, its chairman expressed particularly trenchant views. As we have heard, Councillor Dewhurst said that mis-statements had been made and the action of the military was both high-handed and very wrong.

The chief difference between the findings of the tribunals in Queen Anne's Gate and at Four Lane Ends was as to the amount of time Joseph spent as a hawker – the former decided it was the greater part of his work while the latter was satisfied that it was not. From where, then, did Lord Salisbury and his colleagues obtain the evidence upon which their conclusion was based?

There is nothing in the surviving records, whether in Kew or Preston or at Hatfield House, to suggest that any such evidence was given in writing. No written submission by the military seems to have been shared with Joseph Blackburn, or with the Thornton tribunal or the county appeal tribunal, and it is unlikely that such a document was received by the Central Tribunal.

There is, however, a further possibility – that the evidence in question was given orally, by a military witness who went to Westminster in person. That is the possibility to which Councillor Dewhurst was alluding.

*

When, in the early days of its existence – in late 1915 and early 1916 – the Westminster tribunal grappled with the thorny question of the procedure it should follow, it produced a series of ever more elaborate schemes.

On Leap Day 1916, as well as deciding how they might remedy deficiencies in the evidence before them, members also considered how the Central Tribunal should be constituted. The arrangement upon which they alighted would have seen the tribunal divided into ten or more sections, each of which concentrated on a particular class of case. (Those involving agriculture were singled out for special mention.) Crucially, though sections would have been led by a member of the tribunal, each would also have included a number of 'assessors', some of whom were legally qualified and one of whom was appointed by the War Office.

Elaborate though this scheme might have been, there is no evidence that it was ever put into operation. When Joseph Blackburn's case came up at Queen Anne's Gate, it was heard not merely by one, but by fully six substantive members of the tribunal. There is, furthermore, no evidence that the case or the people who dealt with it had been allocated to a particular section of the tribunal. The panel was the only one to sit that day and it was no different in its constitution or membership, or in the nature of its work, from others that sat during the lifetime of the Central Tribunal. While it is true that Joseph's case was one of three that day about men who worked on the land, it was soon followed by those of a hairdresser, a butcher's manager, two men who made clothes, a colliery engine-man, two clerks (one to the Commissioners of Income and Land Tax and the other to the Glasgow Stock Exchange) and a missionary pastor.

And even at their most elaborate, these schemes represented nothing more than the development of practices the Westminster tribunal had already begun to adopt. We know that Captain Seymour Lloyd played a significant role in proceedings at Queen Anne's Gate and also that he came from the War Office. As early as the tribunal's second meeting, indeed, he is referred to as an 'assessor' and it is plain that sometimes his role very closely resembled that of the military representative.

Even after that point, and even where there is no mention of Captain Seymour Lloyd or of any intervention he might have made, the minutes continue to record, as a preliminary issue, that whole batches of appeals assented to by the Central Tribunal had first been *agreed to by the War Office Assessor.*

It is certainly true that the Westminster minutes contain no other explicit reference to a War Office assessor beyond the first half of 1916. There is, furthermore, no mention in the note of the meeting at which Joseph's case was considered of the presence of any assessor, whether legally qualified or not and whether from the War Office or any other body.

We should not, however, accord these reservations too much weight. Even in the spring of 1916 – immediately after the Central Tribunal alighted upon its new model procedure and at a time when adherence to that procedure is likely to have been particularly keen – there is no mention of anyone save the substantive members concerned being present at a tribunal hearing. In fact, there is no mention, in the spring of 1916 or at any other time, of a tribunal secretary, even though it is plain, sometimes from the content but always from the fact of the minutes, that such a person was indeed present.

It is, in any case, clear that, whether or not he actually took part, an assessor from the War Office was at least potentially a participant in meetings of the Central Tribunal. At one such meeting, held on 21st March 1916, shortly after the first Military Service Act had come into effect, the members discussed how they should proceed in the case of conscientious objectors. They decided that if, exceptionally, such men were to be heard in person, *the War Office Assessor should be entitled to act as the Military Representative.*

This might, of course, suggest that a War Office assessor did not normally participate in proceedings at Queen Anne's Gate.

If it were otherwise, there would be no need to make this special provision. Furthermore, it is clear that the provision would only apply if the man himself was to be heard. That was not what happened with Joseph Blackburn, who did not, in any case, make any claim to a conscientious objection to military service. It is, however, also possible that what this provision sought to do was ensure not that a War Office assessor attended a meeting at which there would otherwise be no other official participant, but that when he did so it was in substitution for the military representative who would otherwise have attended.

It is not, therefore, impossible that when they came to consider Joseph Blackburn's case, the members of the Central Tribunal had available to them a witness the other, inferior tribunals had not seen – one who gave them evidence that the man himself was unable to challenge and that contradicted specific findings which had already been made. In short, it is conceivable that Councillor Dewhurst was correct.

39

There are many intriguing aspects of the Thornton strike, not least the tribunal's – or Councillor Dewhurst's – aversion to the use of that word. Perhaps the greatest of them, however, is the possibility that the strike was not unique. In June 1917, a local newspaper noted:

> *The Thornton Tribunal is the latest to be added to the list of those who have 'adjourned' on a protest.*

*

Clayton-le-Moors, near Accrington, was another urban district of Lancashire and during the First World War it, like Thornton, had a local tribunal of its own.

That tribunal first convened in December 1915, in the week before Joseph Blackburn and Thomas Hume Dunlop attested for military service, and it heard its first cases early the following year. Ultimately, the tribunal would deal with almost fifty per cent more claims than the Thornton tribunal did. One of those claims was made by Frank Bickerstaff, a book-keeper who lived in Hygiene Place in the town.

In mid-1916, Mr Bickerstaff was twice given an exemption by the Clayton-le-Moors tribunal. Each of those exemptions was said to be final at the time and the second of them expired at the end of August, so when, on 6th February the following year, the man came before the tribunal a third time, his claim was promptly dismissed.

A month later, thoughts tuned to Mr Bickerstaff again, for it seems that after leaving the tribunal, he had managed to obtain a further exemption from military service. That exemption was absolute, in fact, but it had not come from a local tribunal or from the county appeal tribunal in Preston or the Central Tribunal in Westminster. It had been granted by the Ministry of Munitions.

That outcome was neither unlawful nor particularly rare, but it seems to have disappointed members of the Clayton-le-Moors tribunal. According to the minutes of a session held on 6th March 1917, they resolved:

> *That the clerk write the Local Government Board, pointing out the details of the case and the nugatory position in which the Tribunal is placed by the action taken.*
>
> *That a copy of same be forwarded to the Ministry of Munitions.*

Crucially, they also resolved:

> *That the Tribunal adjourn until a reply is received from the Local Government Board.*

So, three months and more before the Thornton local tribunal embarked upon its own, similar action, one of its counterparts in east Lancashire went on strike.

On Saturday 17th March, while Joseph Blackburn was waiting for the appeal in his case to be considered in Westminster, the members at Clayton-le-Moors convened for a special session. The minutes suggest that in preceding days, the tribunal clerk had discussed matters in person with Mr Bickerstaff and sent the necessary letter to the Local Government Board. (No copy of that letter remains.) The clerk now read the response that had been received from the board. It was dated 14th March and was plainly considered inadequate, for the tribunal directed:

That the Clerk reply to the Local Government Board that having regard to the circumstances, we regret that we are not prepared to resume our sittings until a definite reply to the letter sent by the Clerk on the 8th instant is received with respect to the case of Frank Bickerstaff.

A letter in those terms was sent to the board the same day:

In reply to the letter dated 14 March 1917 from the Local Government Board, I am directed by the above-named Tribunal to inform you that at a Special Meeting held this day the case of Frank Bickerstaff was very carefully considered in all its bearings, after which the Resolution was passed of which the following is a copy –

'That the Clerk reply to the Local Government Board that having regard to the circumstances we regret that we are not prepared to resume our sittings until a definite reply to the letter sent by the Clerk on the 8th instant is received with respect to the case of Frank Bickerstaff.'

I am, Sir, Your obedient servant...

Copies of the letter and the resolution were also sent to the recruiting officer in Accrington.

The matter came before the Clayton-le-Moors tribunal again on 21st March, when an Army official was among those present:

The question of the case of Frank Bickerstaff was discussed at some considerable length when Captain Pateson explained the position in which the Recruiting Department was placed with regard to the calling up of men in controlled works.

He then promised to write a letter to the Tribunal giving a statement of the position, and strongly urged

*that the Tribunal might see their way to resume at the
earliest possible opportunity.*

*Resolved: that the Tribunal again meet on Thursday
the 22nd March 1917 at 5pm, to consider the reply from
Captain Pateson.*

The minutes provide the only record of the discussion that took
place that day and we cannot know precisely what Captain
Pateson said. It seems, however, that he acted as quickly as the
members of the tribunal expected him to and that once it was
received, his letter had the desired effect. (It is also conceivable
that at some point, an error had been made, and that the Captain
Pateson encountered here in March 1917 was also the Captain
Metson who would turn up in Thornton four months later.)

At a session held the following day, the good captain's letter
was read by the clerk and the tribunal then resolved:

*That Captain Pateson be thanked for his letter, and that
the Tribunal resume on Tuesday the 27th instant.*

The clerk then wrote to the captain:

*I am directed by the above-named Tribunal to thank you
for your letter of the 21st instant, and to inform you that
the members have decided to resume their sittings.*

*All outstanding cases and reviews... will be dealt
with on Tuesday and Wednesday next week.*

It is plain, however, that interest in this case was not confined
to Clayton-le-Moors, to the local tribunal or to the military
representative. On 22nd March, the tribunal clerk also wrote to
an inspector of the Local Government Board, informing him:

Further to our conversation today, I am directed to

inform you that the Members of the Local Tribunal at a
Meeting held this afternoon 'having received a letter from
Captain Pateson' have decided to resume their sittings
and will deal with all outstanding cases and reviews… on
Tuesday and Wednesday next week.

The inspector in question was William Elias, whose subsequent trip to the Fylde coast would have such a dramatic effect. Further letters were received by the tribunal, both from the board and from its inspector, but their effect was by no means calming. Having convened again on 28th March, the members resolved:

That the Clerk refer those asking for exemption to Mr
Baron, and to the Local Government Board, taking
exception to the terms of the last paragraph.

A letter followed five days later. It was addressed to the secretary of the Local Government Board:

Adverting to the letter dated 27 March 1917 from the
Local Government Board I am directed to state that
Captain Pateson of the Recruiting Department had an
interview with this Tribunal on the 21st ultimo and
after his statement and a confirming letter from him the
Tribunal, while dissatisfied with the waste of time caused
them by the evident misunderstanding and overlapping
of the Recruiting Department and the Department of
the Ministry of Munitions, decided in the interest of the
public and that of the Army to resume the sittings.
  With regard to the last paragraph of the letter, the
statement 'that absolute exemption was granted' was
made by the man referred to, and a member of the firm
when spoken to on the matter refused to forward the

so called letter to the Tribunal, stating that it did not concern the Tribunal.

*

The strike by the Clayton-le-Moors tribunal lasted for only three weeks and its cause was something other than the decision of a superior tribunal. It is possible, in fact, that members of the tribunal were simply misinformed as to the law and unaware that in some respects at least, Whitehall ministries possessed powers that were equivalent to their own.

In other ways, however, the strike resembled the one that would interrupt proceedings in Thornton for almost three months later in the year. It arose out of frustration with a system that allowed significant issues to be determined at some remove from the place in which they arose; it became a matter of interest, and even concern, to the state, not least in the form of the Local Government Board; but it was resolved decisively, albeit with some residual bitterness, after face-to-face discussions. In each case those discussions involved the redoubtable Mr Elias. It seems, however, that in neither case were they brought to the attention of the man concerned.

40

It is perhaps unfair to criticise the Thornton tribunal. It did, after all, grant Joseph Blackburn successive exemptions from military service. Even though he was an attested man, who had already chosen to offer himself up for service, the effect of those exemptions was to keep Joseph away from the Colours, and out of the Great War, for more than a year.

That said, the exemptions the tribunal gave Joseph were a good deal less generous than they might have been. They were certainly less comprehensive and less enduring than ones the tribunal gave to many other men, and that it gave to such men at the time it dealt with him. It is even the case that the tribunal was less generous towards Joseph than towards other men with similar personal circumstances, including those who worked on the land and, indeed, were market gardeners. The short, rancorous protest at Four Lane Ends should be seen in that light.

The tribunal was not oblivious to the national interest and at the end of 1916, it complied with official requests to suspend the hearing of agricultural cases. The result of that compliance might have been the disapproval of Captain Booth, but it was also the retention of Thornton men on the land and in the town. As the events of the following year made plain, that was an objective the tribunal was prepared to use disobedience in order to advance. And the tribunal cannot be considered uncourageous, for we know that its three-month-long strike provoked the state and piqued the interest of the redoubtable Mr Elias.

Ultimately, however, the Thornton tribunal allowed itself

to be persuaded to abandon its strike and, looked at now, that seems curious and unsatisfying. We do not know what William Elias said to the assembled members – whether, on that sultry evening at Four Lane Ends, the Oxford-educated lawyer with a taste for potato bread gave them the explanation they had demanded. From the terse minute left behind, however, it seems that he did not. It is possible that what Mr Elias brought with him was not an explanation but a threat, and that it was one to which Councillor Dewhurst and his colleagues felt obliged to submit. But if a threat was made, it has since been lost.

Whatever was said, it is plain that the man was not released from the Army, either then or subsequently, and that the local tribunal's demands went completely unmet. That state of affairs seems not to have troubled the members, however, or to have done so sufficiently for them to take any further, meaningful action. The Thornton records contain no mention of Joseph Blackburn after that point.

It is possible, of course, that the true cause of the Thornton tribunal's discomfiture was one the Central Tribunal could not remedy. Maybe the real concern at Four Lane Ends was not Joseph and the way he had been treated, but the way the tribunal itself had been treated – and its opinion simply cast aside – in far-off Westminster.

*

The sessions held in Thornton between August 1917, when the tribunal began sitting again, and October of the following year, when it heard its last case, would mark a distinct phase of operations. There were no more strikes and there was little, in fact, in the way of real dispute.

The first session after the long adjournment saw the tribunal consider more than thirty cases and grant exemptions in almost half of them. One of the beneficiaries of this approach was

John Edward Breckell, whose claim would in fact be the first considered on 13th August and, therefore, the first to be heard since the strike. The latest in a line of wheelwrights stretching back at least to the time of Waterloo, Jack Breckell was already into his forties. With a workshop immediately beneath the huge, tapering sails of Marsh Mill, he was the uncle of Jessie Blackburn, Joseph's wife. Now, a conditional exemption granted to him as long ago as June 1916 was confirmed in the face of an application by the military representative.

Subsequently, the tribunal would be a good deal less busy and in each of the six sessions that followed, it dealt with fewer than fifteen claims. From October 1917, the tribunal can be seen to have dismissed three claims and to have granted at least twenty exemptions. Some of its decisions were the subject of appeals and sometimes those decisions were overturned at County Hall. Often, however, they were not and there is no evidence that Thornton business ever again came up at Queen Anne's Gate.

Another notable beneficiary of the largesse of the Thornton tribunal was William Berry. The exemption granted to him was renewed fully seven times and as a result, he was kept out of the army between 25th May 1916 – the day Joseph Blackburn first came before the tribunal – and 31st October 1918. (It is unlikely that Mr Berry went to the Colours thereafter.) And there were other men who received lenient treatment. In the case of George Jackson, for example, a single renewal of his exemption saw him through from 17th August 1916 to at least 31st July 1918, while as a result of orders made by the Thornton tribunal on at least six occasions, John Price Wilson was exempt from military service from May 1916 until the end of hostilities.

We know from the records left behind that exemptions were still being awarded at the final session at Four Lane Ends, which took place on 16th October 1918. On that occasion, and amongst several other men, one Thomas Dewhurst was the recipient of an exemption and it would last for six months.

On Thursday 11th October 1917, in the County Sessions Hall in Preston, a special ceremony took place, the purpose of which was to present Sir Harcourt Clare with the portrait of him that had been painted the year before. The delay was caused by the portrait's having been exhibited in the Royal Academy in the interim, and the ceremony came only days after Lord Salisbury sat in the Central Tribunal for the final time.

At the beginning of the proceedings, Mr James Travis-Clegg gave the apologies of those who had been invited to attend the event but had found themselves unable to do so. They included Lord Richard Cavendish, who will have known Sir Harcourt, at least from the Lancashire Appeal Tribunal, and Lord Derby, who remained the Minister for War and would continue to do so for several months more. Sir Harcourt then gave a gracious speech, which was reported at length in various local newspapers.

He said that the very essence of good local administration was its elasticity and adaptability to meet the special conditions which prevailed in all parts of the country. The control of centralised bureaucracy was the antithesis of that, and he did not believe that one man in ten thousand today appreciated the fact that the true principles of local administration in this country were being undermined and put out of gear by the gradual encroachment of the influences of centralised bureaucracy in London.

Sir Harcourt said he thought it would be wise, therefore, if all who took an interest in local affairs would seriously consider that position before the evil got too big for them to grapple with. That growing power of government departments over the discretion and judgement of local authorities was largely owing to the system of government grants in aid of services of a semi-national character, such as education, police, and so on. Those grants were voted by Parliament and left to be administered by the government departments, and the gentlemen who conducted those administrations, clever, able, and earnest as they were, could hardly help using their power over the purse to enforce their opinions upon the local authorities, and the position practically was that whilst they paid half the piper, they wanted to call all the tune. (Hear, hear.)

He said that if local authorities would fall in with the departmental wishes, would adopt their wishes, and accept absolutely their direction and control, they would get their government grants without any question. The grant was given for the method rather than the result. But let a local authority have the courage to take its own line and produce results infinitely better than those produced by the official method, then there was no grant for them, because they did not conform to governmental requirements.

At the end of the speech, after Sir Harcourt had expressed his thanks to the artist – who, he believed, had well satisfied the numbers of people who had seen the picture – a vote of thanks was proposed by Mr James Openshaw.

41

In May 1916, as the Thornton tribunal heard Joseph Blackburn's first claim for exemption, the Marquess of Salisbury received a letter from someone who signed herself *A Quakeress*. The letter read:

> *My Lord,*
> *Many a Quaker father and mother will give thanks if your suggestion is put into effect substituting civil imprisonment for military. I listened with intense gratitude to your words today and a Liberal said to me as I left, 'The Cecils are trustworthy.'*

The author was Anna Maria Barlow, of Alderley Edge in Cheshire, and she was the wife of John Emmott Barlow, a Baronet and the Member of Parliament for Frome in Somerset. Her husband had won his seat in 1892, the year Edward Stanley, the future Earl of Derby, first entered Parliament, and he would hold it for more than twenty-five years.

Sir John Barlow came from a notable family, which had made its considerable fortune in textiles, tea, coffee and rubber, and in trade with the countries of the Far East. He and his wife were close friends of Sir Henry Campbell-Bannerman, the Liberal who was Prime Minister of the United Kingdom between 1905 and 1908, and between Arthur Balfour and H. H. Asquith, the cousins of Lord Salisbury and Sir Algernon Firth respectively.

Lady Barlow took a keen interest in Free Trade, Temperance and Women's Suffrage. She and her husband also opposed conscription, both before and after it was introduced, and they often took up the cause of conscientious objectors. On that and other issues, Lady Barlow maintained an extensive correspondence with influential figures both at home and abroad. Three photographic portraits of her, done in 1913 by Bassano Limited, are in the collection of the National Portrait Gallery. There is also a single portrait of her husband that was made by Sir Benjamin Stone.

At around the same time, Lord Salisbury received a number of letters expressing similar sentiments. One of those came from a Mr Virgil Boys of Croydon, who wrote:

> *I wish to express my gratitude to you for your protest in the House against the way conscientious objectors are being treated. I know many of them personally and it is not just to put such men in wars and treat them brutally. Surely they could be given useful work under civilian control.*

What prompted these letters was something else Lord Salisbury said during the parliamentary debate on the second Military Service Bill. He was exercised by the position of men whose claim to a conscientious objection had been rejected. Having been taken into the Army, some of those men disobeyed military orders and were, as a result, court-martialled. Lord Salisbury argued that upon conviction, the men should serve any period of imprisonment in a civil prison and not a military one. He argued that, far from offending against the Colours, the man:

> *...Has committed his crime against the community; the community punishes him in the ordinary way in a civil prison; but he is outside the Army altogether, and there is no scope for those scandals which I think are so deplorable and do so much harm to the Army and the whole system of recruiting.*

That was not, however, the military view, and in the course of the debate the Undersecretary of State for War, the Earl of Derby, said:

> *I entirely disagree with and should oppose any such proposal. When such a man is in the Army he is not a conscientious objector. He has put forward a plea that he is a conscientious objector and that plea has been rejected by the Tribunals to whom he has submitted it. Therefore when he is in the Army he is a soldier on exactly the same footing as every other recruit; he is made to go into the Army, and should be treated under military law by the military and detained under military law. I am perfectly certain that if any attempt is made to depart from that procedure it will be subversive of military discipline.*

In the end, it was Lord Salisbury's concerns that prevailed within government. On 26th June 1916, he received a letter from Walter Long, the President of the Local Government Board, asking whether the Central Tribunal would be willing to deal with these cases. Mr Long wrote:

> *It is proposed that if, after the men have been court-martialled and passed to a civil prison, there is good prima facie evidence that they have a genuine conscientious objection based on religious grounds, their case should be investigated by some impartial authority and that, if that authority considers they have made good their cause, they should then be passed to Reserve W and handed over to a special Home Office Committee to be employed in civil work. It is clearly desirable that the 'impartial authority' to sift out the cases should be the Central Tribunal.*

Lord Salisbury put this request before the tribunal at the first opportunity and the minutes of a meeting held the following day state:

> *The Tribunal considered a letter addressed to the Chairman by the President of the Local Government Board, with reference to the Central Tribunal investigating cases in which men had been sentenced by Court Martial but who claimed to have a conscientious objection to military service based on religious grounds. A draft reply, agreeing to undertake the additional work, was approved.*

On 31st July, Lord Derby contacted Lord Salisbury again. In a letter marked *Confidential*, he wrote:

> *Dear Jem,*
>
> *I talked to the Adjutant General on the subject of Conscientious Objectors and found his views coincided with those I gave you as being my own, viz.: that in doubtful cases we do not want the men, they are more trouble than they are worth.*
>
> *At the same time we both feel that if the exemptions were so numerous as to make men think they could easily escape from service, we might take a very different view and ask you to tighten up the examination. But for the present we both agree that it would be better that you give the man the benefit of the doubt.*

Here, Lord Derby appears to do nothing less than warn Lord Salisbury that his tribunal might one day be given official direction on the performance of its duties. That the executive might seek to direct the judiciary, or that it might think it had the right or the ability to do so, would be a matter of significant constitutional concern. In fact, Lord Derby would soon be overtaken by events and his reservations would have to be put to one side. On 27th October, he wrote to 'Dear Jem' again:

I have been into the question of your letter and find that under the present system we are unable to do anything in the direction you urge. I therefore sent your letter over to the Home Secretary, and in order that you may be in possession of the position as it stands, I send you a copy of my letter to him.

The letter Lord Derby copied to Lord Salisbury bears the same date. It is addressed to Herbert Samuel, the Liberal politician whose first, nine-month period as Home Secretary would soon be coming to an end. (Mr Samuel had also been Walter Long's immediate predecessor as President of the Local Government Board.)

In his letter, Lord Derby writes:

Will you please read the enclosed letter from Lord Salisbury, and treat it as Confidential? There is a great deal in what he says, but it really depends on your department rather than on the War Office whether he could be met.

The arrangement arrived at was that where it appeared at the Court Martial of any man for disobeying orders, that the reason for such disobedience was conscientious objection, when sentenced he was sent to the nearest civil prison.

At the Home Office request, in order to facilitate matters, this was altered and instead of being sent to the nearest civil prison, convicted men were sent to Wormwood Scrubs.

If you could consent to these convicted men being sent

to the nearest civil prison, and only sent to Wormwood Scrubs at fixed intervals, and at such times as the Central Tribunal could deal with them, it would probably mean that they would have to undergo a considerable amount of their sentence before they came up for their conscientious scruples to be enquired into.

I am sure Lord Salisbury would willingly come and see you and discuss the matter with you. I am sure there is much in what he says, and if you could meet him it would be in every way satisfactory.

Having at one time opposed the very notion that unwilling conscripts should be held in civil, and not military prisons, Lord Derby was now suggesting that they should in fact be held in those civil prisons for as long as possible before having their cases reviewed by the Central Tribunal.

As Walter Long had explained in his letter of 26th June, one possible result of such a review was that the man concerned would be given civilian work to do and, therefore, that he would be freed from incarceration. The effect of the course Lord Derby now proposed would have been to postpone that undesirable event – and to prolong the man's incarceration – until the latest possible moment. That proposal is unlikely to have found favour among the more judicially minded of his colleagues.

The issue rumbled on into a second year and on 27th September 1917, Lord Derby wrote to Lord Salisbury again:

Many thanks for your letter and your very clear statement with regard to Conscientious Objectors. I agree in the main to what you say, and I think the present position is an intolerable one.

There is no doubt that some of these Conscientious Objectors who are imprisoned time after time are quite genuine in their convictions and ought to be excused from

Service, but nothing would induce me personally to take any
step which would bring me in conflict with the Tribunals.

I have suggested to the War Cabinet that there should
be a small round table conference called to consider the
whole matter, at which you should be present.

Before concluding his letter, Lord Derby turned to more
congenial matters:

With regard to Bobbety, it has been a real pleasure to
have him here, and I only wish I could keep him, but I am
certain in his own interests it is advisable that he should
be as much out of doors as possible. I have told him I
have written to Murray at Aldershot to ask him whether
he can be taken there as an extra ADC. He would then
have plenty of outdoor work, and at the same time be
employed on military duty.

Bobbety was, of course, the fourth marquess' son, Robert Gascoyne-
Cecil, who would in time succeed his father. After being invalided
home from France, he had spent some time serving as personal
military secretary to Lord Derby, the man who, in a matter of
weeks, would become Secretary of State for War.

Even from these few examples of the correspondence between
the Marquess of Salisbury and the Earl of Derby, we can see that,
in the middle years of the First World War, there were strong,
direct links between the War Office and the Central Tribunal.
Those links were both formal and deeply informal, and it is clear
that each man considered them ripe for exploitation.

For that reason, it is surely futile to speculate upon whether,
in Joseph Blackburn's case, a man from the military once
said something confidential at Queen Anne's Gate. That the
Thornton tribunal ever engaged in such speculation makes it
now seem hopelessly naive.

20378

42

Joseph will have known, as the train slowed down yet again, that the next station was still some way ahead. Through the window, for what must have been an hour, he had been watching field after field of maize and, above them, for all that time, an uneven blue line of mountains. He knew that when he stepped down onto the tracks he would feel sunlight and warmth and he would be surprised to find that he was sad.

Joseph thought of the mud and fog and corruption that was behind them all, and he knew that the next barked command would not be long in coming. Talk had broken out in the carriage among men who had passed the last hundred miles in silence. They would halt here, but any respite would be brief.

*

On 6th June 1917, Joseph Blackburn had been mobilised for military service and posted to the 4th Battalion of the Loyal North Lancashire Regiment. By then, he had stayed away from the Colours for a year longer than men who, under the Derby scheme, had shared his group. The following day, after being medically examined, Joseph was taken into the British Army. Having disappeared once again from the public record, he re-emerges on 29th October, when, after some basic training, he arrives in Folkestone and embarks for France and the war.

When the time came, Joseph went off to fight. Although there is nothing in the public facts of his life to suggest that he would have resisted mobilisation, we know that he was perfectly prepared to resort to law, or to Four Lane Ends at least. The fact that he didn't do so now, and didn't seek to defer his military service any longer, should not be overlooked.

It is likely, in fact, that Joseph had no grounds for exemption that he had not raised before. In those circumstances, the finding at Westminster that his involvement was not indispensable for the proper cultivation of his holding was devastating. It meant that ultimately, Thornton and Preston notwithstanding, any further claim he chose to make would be doomed to fail.

*

On 25th October 1917, a fortnight after Sir Everard Clare's splendid portrait was unveiled in Preston and four days before Joseph Blackburn crossed the English Channel, Cecil Heywood Brunner was killed in action. He was forty-five years of age.

Captain Brunner had been serving with the Royal Horse Artillery and Royal Field Artillery. He was the son of Joseph Brunner, who was himself the brother of John Fowler Leece Brunner, the Liberal Member of Parliament who sat on the Central Tribunal and had been one of the six men who dealt with Joseph's case. Cecil Brunner was therefore Sir John's nephew.

*

Joseph Blackburn disembarked in France on 30th October 1917, when he was taken from the Cauliflowers, transferred to the Queen's Own Royal West Kent Regiment and given the regimental number 20378. Three days later, he joined the regiment's 10th Battalion.

The 10th was one of a number of 'service' battalions of the Royal West Kents – those that had not existed before hostilities commenced but had been formed in the great surge of enthusiasm that followed Lord Kitchener's call to arms in

August 1914. The 20th of the King's Liverpool Regiment – which was commanded by Colonel Wilfred Ashley and, like Edward Falkner's irregulars, had been mustered in the city in a single day – was another such battalion.

The 10th Battalion had, in fact, been created in May 1915 at the request of the Army Council. At first, its men trained close to home, but in January 1916, they moved to Aldershot to be made ready for war. They were mobilised in May and then travelled to north-east France, where they quickly took up position close to the Belgian border.

In that year and the next, the men of the 10th Battalion were engaged in significant action on the Western Front. They took part in the Somme offensive, for example, notably at the Battle of Flers-Courcelette in September 1916, when the tanks that had been tried out in front of Hatfield House several months before were finally put to use. In June of 1917, the men were involved in the Battle of Messines; in August they were at the Third Battle of Ypres, notably in the Battle of Pilckem Ridge; and in September, they were engaged in fighting on the Menin Road Ridge.

This fighting inflicted heavy losses on the battalion, which, as another winter approached, was sorely in need of new recruits. By the time Joseph arrived, the 10th had been taken out of the front line and had arrived at Bray-Dunes, a seaside town that lies close to Dunkirk and contains France's northernmost point. Joseph was one of a number of men who quickly brought the battalion back to strength.

*

On 24th October 1917, Austro-Hungarian forces, supported for the first time by their German allies, launched the Battle of Caporetto in what is now north-west Slovenia. They hoped to strengthen a perceived weakness on their southern border and soon, they had routed the Italian forces and pushed the remnants back to defensive lines on the Piave River, close to Venice.

So swift and precise was the assault that the Italians suffered enormous losses. Almost all of the nation's artillery was lost, either destroyed or seized, and of its fighting force, ten thousand men were killed, thirty thousand were wounded and more than a quarter of a million were taken prisoner. There followed a process of reinforcement by the Allies that would see six French and five British infantry divisions move into the Veneto.

In early November, the 10th Battalion of the Royal West Kent Regiment moved the short distance from Bray-Dunes to Téteghem. The battalion had been in training for open warfare and it was in that small town that it received orders to entrain for north-east Italy. With the rest of his comrades, Joseph Blackburn began that journey on Tuesday 13th November 1917.

That was one day after Robert Graham Anderson was killed in action in Palestine. Lieutenant Anderson, who was serving with the 1st Battalion of the Royal Gloucestershire Hussars, was the son of Robert Anderson, Lord Derby's retainer and the manager of Knowsley Hall. He was twenty-seven years of age and had already gained recognition as a poet and a composer.

*

On 1st December 1917, Randle William Gascoyne-Cecil was killed in action during the Battle of Cambrai. He was twenty-eight years of age and, like his brother, Rupert, had gained the rank of lieutenant, this time in the Warwickshire Royal Horse Artillery. Lieutenant Gascoyne-Cecil was the son of Lord William Cecil, the Bishop of Exeter. Bishop William was a brother of Lord Salisbury, the member of the Central Tribunal who had taken the chair when Joseph Blackburn's case was considered in Westminster. Randle was therefore Lord Salisbury's nephew.

The death of Randle Gascoyne-Cecil, coming so close to that of Cecil Heywood Brunner, meant that in the space of little more than a month, two present or former members of the Central Tribunal had lost a nephew.

*

The train journey towards the Veneto was a slow and halting one, down the entire length of France and along the Italian Riviera, and it took almost five days to complete. It seems that the Royal West Kents received an enthusiastic reception from the Italians they encountered on the way, many of whom turned out with presents of tobacco, flowers and food.

Their train carried the men of the 10th Battalion, and also the 11th, to Verona and then due south to Isola della Scala. The men came together close to the city of Mantua, but almost immediately, they embarked on a one hundred-mile march to their destination – a point on a line that ran south-east from Vicenza.

A march of that kind was no small undertaking for men carrying equipment weighing as much as ninety pounds. They were hampered by inaccurate maps and uncomfortable billets and they were soon emptied of all the discipline and stamina they had carefully built up. They were also, however, fortified by the wine and fruit of the region, which were both cheap and abundant.

By the last week in November, the men of the 10th and 11th Battalions had reached the beginnings of the range Joseph had first seen from the train. It was there, close to Padua, that the British and Commonwealth forces were to be held in reserve. They would bolster morale within Italian ranks, but they would also ensure that the enemy did not enter Venice.

In February, there were brief skirmishes when patrols crossed the river and were quickly repelled, but otherwise, the Royal West Kents would see little in the way of serious fighting. A number of them would, however, succumb to sickness and Joseph Blackburn was among that number. He saw nothing of the skirmishing, for he had already been forced to leave his comrades and head back west. On 10th February 1918, Joseph was in Genoa, suffering from 'trench fever'.

*

What soldiers of the First World War knew as trench fever was also called 'five-day fever', 'shin bone fever' or, more properly, *febris quintana*. It is an illness whose symptoms – a high fever and a severe headache, eye pain and soreness of the muscles, especially in the legs – might appear suddenly, but which has often been incubating for up to a fortnight. Recovery can take a month and more and the illness is prone to relapse.

Trench fever is transmitted by body lice and, during the First World War, typically affected soldiers in Flanders and France, in the Balkans and Mesopotamia and also in Italy. In the last four years of the war, as many as a third of all British troops who reported sick were diagnosed with the illness. They included the writers J. R. R. Tolkien, A. A. Milne and C. S. Lewis.

That Joseph should have found himself in Genoa when he became unwell is not surprising. During the latter part of the Great War, that ancient city was a focal point for Allied forces, and for Commonwealth forces in particular, and it was home to a number of 'base' hospitals. These were military establishments of a kind that was considerably more common in France, where there were more than sixty, and also in Flanders. By the end of the war, however, they would also have spread to the Rhine.

Some distance removed from the front line – and so, theoretically at least, much less vulnerable to attack than the more exposed 'casualty clearing stations' – the base hospitals were often to be found in former hotels or factories and they were manned by troops from the Royal Army Medical Corps, assisted by volunteers from organisations such as the British Red Cross and the St John Ambulance.

*

Not long after Joseph was hospitalised, the 10th Battalion of the Royal West Kent Regiment was summoned back to the Western Front. It departed from a terminus close to Padua and travelled by train to concentrate in Picardy in northern France.

On 8th March 1918, Joseph Blackburn is recorded as suffering from trench fever once again, this time in the port city of Marseille, on France's Mediterranean coast. That location, too, is no surprise, for the city was also a focal point for Allied forces and, to the end of hostilities and even beyond, home to a number of base hospitals.

The bout of trench fever from which Joseph was suffering in Marseille in March 1918 is probably the same one that had afflicted him in Genoa in February, and it is likely that he remained hospitalised between those two dates. In fact, and as we shall see, Joseph was still laid up several months later.

*

On 21st March 1918, the German army launched its Spring Offensive, which aimed to outflank and so defeat British forces and to compel the French to seek an armistice. The offensive was timed for the brief interval after the surrender of Russia and the consequent freeing-up of almost fifty German divisions, but before the overwhelming resources the United States had finally agreed to commit to the Allied cause could be fully deployed.

The Kaiserschlacht, as it was also known, consisted of a

series of attacks along the Western Front and it saw the deepest advances by either antagonist since 1914. The British Army suffered particularly heavy losses, even from the first day, and within two days, large parts of it were in retreat. The men of the 10th Battalion of the Royal West Kents would feel the full force of this offensive.

On 23rd March, on the road from Bapaume to Cambrai – close to where Randle Cecil had died four months before – the battalion was involved in vicious fighting and suffered heavy casualties. It had missed an order to retreat that neighbouring forces had acted upon. As a result, the battalion's flanks were hideously exposed and it was soon overwhelmed not only by the enemy, but also by large numbers of wounded needing attention. The remnants of the battalion would surrender in large numbers and few of them would make it back to the Allied line.

Joseph Blackburn saw none of this and he took no part in the fighting on the Bapaume Road. He was somewhere else entirely that day, having dropped out of the public record once again. Joseph would never return to the 10th Battalion of the Royal West Kents.

*

On 11th April 1918, Arthur Walsh of the 4th Battalion of the South Lancashire Regiment was killed in action. Twenty-six years of age and the holder of the Military Cross, Captain Walsh was the son of Stephen Walsh, the coalminer turned Labour politician who was now a member of both the Cabinet and the Lancashire Appeal Tribunal.

43

Joseph Blackburn emerges once again on 29th May 1918, when, his records say, he was discharged to the base depot at Étaples in the very north of France. That is exactly two years after he would otherwise have gone into the Army, and the town is the last one in which we can know he was alive.

It is unclear whether, when Joseph arrived there, he was simply admitted to another hospital in succession to the ones he had occupied in Genoa and Marseille, or whether the fact that he was discharged meant that he was now considered fit to resume his military service. Étaples performed several important functions during the First World War and while it contained a number of medical facilities, it was also host to a large military camp. Once hostilities had ended, the town would be awarded the Croix de Guerre in recognition of all that it had endured.

There had been a British military presence in northern France since August 1914, when General John French and his Expeditionary Force arrived unexpectedly in Boulogne. The British, and the Allied military camps, would remain there for the duration and at Calais alone, in the summer of 1918, there were more than two thousand officers and ninety thousand men.

The base camp at Étaples had been established outside the town, which stands on the east bank of the River Canche close to the point where the sea begins. The area is part of a narrow strip that runs for seventy-five miles, south from Calais and beyond Boulogne, and has for at least a century been known as the Opal Coast. The land is flat and low-lying, it is bordered by sand dunes and woods, and in summer, it is covered in bluebells and daisies and in the mignonette that is a feature of local cuisine. There is little there to obstruct the wind, blowing in from the English Channel, and for much of the 19th century, Étaples was known as a place of windmills.

At the dawn of war, the civilian population numbered around five thousand, which made Étaples the rough equivalent at the time of the town of Thornton. The camp there was the largest the British Army had ever established overseas and it presented as a myriad of huts and tents, shimmering white and clean in the seaside sunlight.

Like other base camps in France, and especially in the north of the country, this one was served by a network of canals, railway lines and roads. It was therefore accessible from the battlefields of the north and the south – of Italy and Palestine as well as France and Belgium – and also from the ports along both sides of the English Channel. It was a base for British forces and also for those from the Empire.

Étaples was considered an ideal site for such a significant encampment. Despite its accessibility, and though the dull crump of artillery fire on the Front provided its own insistent rhythm, the town was thought to be remote from attack. Remote, that is, from attack by land or sea. The camp was a training base, a depot for supplies and a detention centre for errant personnel. It was also a place where the sick and wounded could be treated. The site was criss-crossed by roads, which, whether narrow or broad, were impressively straight. They had names such as Infantry Road and Scout Road, Gordon Road and Tipperary Road and, dividing the military camp from the polity of hospitals, Isolation Road.

In 1917, Étaples was home to around twenty hospitals, ministering to more than twenty thousand patients and extending north from the military camp for a distance of almost six kilometres. Of those, a significant number were base hospitals. There were eight such establishments at one time or another during the First World War and in May 1918, at least five of them were in operation. The military camp, meanwhile, was home to as many as a hundred thousand men, many of whom lived among the dunes that stretch for miles beyond the edge of the town. For the most part, those men were on their way to, or back to, the Front.

Troops who found themselves at Étaples would undergo intensive instruction in the use of a rifle, in fighting with bayonets and in gas warfare, and they had long sessions of marching at the double across the dunes. The camp was also home to The Bullring, a retraining ground away from the main drag, where troops who had returned from leave or convalescence were toughened up for the trenches. That will have been why Joseph Blackburn was sent there.

The camp was notorious for its brutality. Wilfred Owen and Siegfried Sassoon wrote disparagingly of it and it was said that wounded soldiers would rather return to the Front than remain there. Recently, the camp and the town had seen considerable unrest and disorder and a large number of men had found themselves facing a military charge. Three of them were sentenced to ten years' penal servitude and others were imprisoned for up to a year, while one man, Corporal Jesse Robert Short of the Northumberland Fusiliers, was condemned to death for attempted mutiny. Corporal Short probably fought on the first day of the Battle of the Somme. He was executed by firing squad on 4th October 1917, as the Marquess of Salisbury sat in the Central Tribunal for the very last time.

*

By the outbreak of the Great War, the name Étaples was already well-known, even across the Channel. The town was home to a veritable colony of artists, drawn from Britain, but also from the

Antipodes and Canada and from the United States. For almost half a century, an evanescent group of painters and printmakers had worked there and in surrounding villages, diligently recording the changing light, the sunrises and sunsets, the flowers and plants and the seasons.

One such was Alexander Young Jackson, a Canadian painter who came to live in the town in 1908, the year of Joseph Blackburn's marriage to Jessie Bennett, and who returned four years later. His works included impressionistic renderings of the sand dunes he found there and also of subjects such as *Autumn in Picardy*. Having entered military service, Mr Jackson was wounded on the Somme in the summer of 1916 and so found himself back in Étaples, receiving medical care at one of the hospitals there.

Another notable visitor to the town at around the same time was Nelson Dawson, the English artist and Arts and Crafts devotee, who was also a sailor and fisherman and a fine painter of marine scenes. Mr Dawson's greatest work might be the trowel and mallet used by Queen Victoria during her last public appearance, or the casket presented to President Woodrow Wilson on the eve of the Paris peace conference. It might, however, be the bronze and silver bath taps he created for Viscount Hambleden's riverside home.

For many such artists, the subject they found most fascinating was the working people of the town – its shrimpers, fisherfolk and market traders as well as the men and women who worked on the land. Walter Gay, an American painter, had been among the first to arrive and it is one of his works that is considered most emblematic of the colony and most redolent of the town that was its home. The painting is entitled *November, Étaples* and it dates from 1885, the year the future Lord Salisbury first entered Parliament. Done in lively shades of blue and green, it shows a woman in simple dress, leaning over a hoe and tending the many vegetables that grow outside her home. Those vegetables include several patches of cabbages.

*

Given its size and importance, the Étaples camp was always likely to attract the attention of the German military. That attention took several forms, but by far the most dramatic was a series of air raids that began in 1917 and reached its culmination the following spring. There were at least nine such raids, the most significant of which took place on 31st May. That was only two days after Joseph Blackburn had been discharged to the base depot at the camp and he will surely have been present for what happened there that night.

During the assault, Étaples and its inhabitants were bombed and also strafed by machine gun fire. There were many casualties – among military personnel, medics and patients alike – and the dead were eventually laid to rest in the cemetery that now lies next to the town in the place where the military camp once stood. That cemetery is, of course, one of those designed by Edwin Lutyens.

Among the hospitals at Étaples that were most grievously affected by the air raid was the one run by the St John Ambulance. In operation for nearly two years, the hospital was a cluster of wooden huts, providing two wards for officers and sixteen for other ranks, and its capacity had been increased by almost a half in recent weeks. On 31st May, one of the wards received a direct hit and was blown to pieces, while a further six wards were reduced to ruins and three were badly damaged. Five members of staff and eleven patients were killed outright that night, while five nurses are reported to have been among the wounded.

One of the St John nurses working there at the time of the raid was Dorothy Bateman Clare. She was the only child of Sir Harcourt Clare, the clerk both to Lancashire's county council and to its appeal tribunal. 'Dolly' Clare had been a nurse at least since the previous autumn, shortly after her father's portrait was unveiled in County Hall. We cannot know whether her path ever crossed with Joseph's, but what we do know is that at precisely the same time, on the turbulent, fractured night when May gave way to June, she and he were in precisely the same place.

44

On 6th June 1918, only a week after he had arrived at Étaples and only days after the air raid that devastated the military and medical bases there, Joseph Blackburn was posted back to the 10th Battalion of the Royal West Kent Regiment.

In Joseph's absence, the battalion had seen significant changes, including the arrival of many men of the 11th Battalion, which had now been disbanded. This change had an immediate effect on Joseph, for the following day, he was declared 'surplus to establishment'. That fate has befallen many soldiers, especially those whose fighting units have been incorporated into others. It was one that had befallen Winston Churchill almost two years before.

No longer required for the 10th Battalion, Joseph was therefore returned to the depot. It was from there that, on 23rd July, he was posted once again, this time to the 6th Battalion of the regiment, whose complement was somewhat less full.

During the early summer of 1918, the 6th Battalion had endured an arduous period of combat in trenches close to the town of Albert on the Somme. Although, in June, attempts were made to increase its depleted numbers, so many men were engaged on other duties that by the end of the month, its 'trench strength' was only two thirds of its nominal strength. Heavy losses incurred in early July only served to compound the problem and they reduced the battalion to less than five hundred men. A series of further drafts therefore followed and by the end of the month, its actual fighting strength had risen by nearly four hundred officers and men.

Joseph joined the 6th Battalion on 24th July 1918 and he

soon entered the field of battle once again. When he did so, it would be for the last time.

The 6th, like the 10th, was a service battalion of the Royal West Kent Regiment. Formed in August 1914 at Maidstone, it had trained in Essex before spending the winter billeted in Hythe. Early the following year, the battalion moved to Aldershot for final training and in June, it mobilised for war and went to France. By 23rd June 1915, the 6th had moved into Flanders and taken over a section of the front line. It was the section in which, until he became surplus and returned to civilian life, Lieutenant Colonel Winston Churchill was a commanding officer in the Royal Scots Fusiliers.

Thereafter, the 6th Battalion was heavily involved in fighting on the Western Front, most notably at the Battle of Loos. That battle, which took place in the autumn of 1915 and saw the first British use of poison, in the form of chlorine gas, was marked by enormous losses on both sides. The 6th also fought on the Somme in 1916 and at the Battles of Arras and Cambrai the following year, while in March 1918, during the German Spring Offensive, it was involved in the Battle of Bapaume.

A matter of days after joining the 6th Battalion, with thoughts of Étaples – to say nothing of Marseille and Genoa and of the bountiful, shimmering Veneto – doubtless receding fast, Joseph Blackburn was back in the fighting line.

In the dog days of summer, the Allies launched a sustained assault on the German forces that would ultimately prove decisive. What came to be known as the Hundred Days Offensive began on 8th August 1918 and saw the Fourth Army under General Sir Henry Rawlinson advance fully seven miles on the first day alone and inflict what the German General Ludendorff described as "the black day of the war for the German armies".

The 6th Battalion of the Royal West Kent Regiment played a full part in that advance, as part of its more defensive left flank. On 9th August, and in succeeding days, during what would come to be known as the Battle of Amiens, the battalion would help mount an overwhelming onslaught that destroyed German morale, saw an end to fighting in trenches and hastened the end of the war. At that point, however, there was much more fighting to be done and many more lives would be lost.

On 9th August, the men of the 6th were led by Lieutenant Colonel William Dawson, who went into battle on horseback. A second bar had recently been added to the Distinguished Service Order he received two years before and a third would come, posthumously, in March the following year. The fighting in which the men were engaged that day would see one of them, Sergeant T. J. Harris, posthumously awarded the Victoria Cross and three others earn the Military Cross. It would also see them gain over two thousand yards of ground, capture or destroy more than twenty enemy machine guns and take a substantial haul of prisoners. The fighting would come at a cost, however, with twenty-six men killed, another two missing and 157 wounded.

The men of the Royal West Kents were again engaged in the last week of August, as the Allies sought to consolidate their recent successes. In the space of a week, the 6th Battalion swept eastwards from Amiens, through the small towns of Méaulte, Carnoy and Hardecourt-aux-Bois, which lie close together on a line that follows the more undulating course of the Somme river to the south.

All we can deduce of Joseph Blackburn's movements in this period is what we know from those of his battalion. Of what happened next, however, we can be very sure. His desiccated, forgotten records tell us that on Saturday 24th August 1918, Joseph Septimus Blackburn died, killed in action in the fields of Picardy.

On that day, Joseph and his battalion were involved in heavy fighting outside Albert, somewhere between Amiens and Cambrai, immediately to the north of the Somme. On the evening of the previous day the battalion had assembled on farmland outside the town and at 1am it began to forge eastwards towards the village of Bécordel-Bécourt. Almost from the start, however, it encountered determined opposition. The ground in the area was broken, giving useful cover to enemy troops, and dense gunfire soon brought the initiative to a halt. Although, in the afternoon, a further assault was equally unsuccessful, the evening brought a change of fortune. Just before 8pm, the enemy was observed to be withdrawing from its positions and the men of the 6th were able to make a final, successful advance. By then, however, Joseph Blackburn had already fallen, on ground immediately to the north of what is now Albert-Picardy airport.

Joseph's name is inscribed on one of the panels that form the backdrop to the Vis-en-Artois cemetery. Standing next to the long, straight road between Arras and Cambrai, that memorial was designed not by Edwin Lutyens, but by John Reginald Truelove, an architect from northern England who happens to have shared with Joseph the year of his birth. The panels contain the names of nearly ten thousand British, Irish and South African soldiers who died in the three months before the Armistice, as the Great War drew towards its bitter, brittle, contested conclusion. For the most part, they are men who have no known grave.

*

On 27th August 1918, three days after the death of Joseph Blackburn, John Arthur Gascoyne-Cecil was also killed in action. He was the son of Lord William Cecil, the Bishop of Exeter, and, therefore, the nephew of Lord Salisbury. Captain Cecil served, like his deceased brother, Randle, in the Royal Horse Artillery and Royal Field Artillery. At the time of his death, he was twenty-five years of age and had recently been awarded the Military Cross. He is buried in the Bucquoy Road Cemetery, near the town of Ficheux. It, too, was designed by Edwin Lutyens.

The three sons of Bishop William who died during the First World War – John, Rupert and Randle – are commemorated together on a stained glass window in St Etheldreda's Church in Hatfield, Hertfordshire. The church stands close to Hatfield House, at the heart of the parish of which William Cecil was for a long time rector.

Only a week after Joseph Blackburn's death, Lady Clara, the wife of Sir Harcourt Clare, died suddenly at the couple's home by the River Ribble. Their daughter was present at her mother's death as she had been staying at Bank Hall since her return from Étaples. Dolly Clare had recently left the St John Ambulance, her last day of service having been 1st June. That was the day after the German bombers had come so awfully in the night.

Little more than a fortnight later, the Blackburn family suffered another tragic loss. On Sunday 15th September 1918, Thomas Blackburn, Joseph's cousin – the son of his uncle, James – was killed in action. A private in the 5th Battalion of the King's Own Royal Lancaster Regiment, he was twenty-one years of age.

Unlike Joseph, and if only in death, Private Blackburn would eventually be returned home to Thornton, where he now lies buried in the churchyard of Christ Church. Thomas' grave is close to that of George Kings, the man whose case the Thornton tribunal considered alongside Joseph Blackburn's on 9th January 1917, and who died just two months after the exemption he was awarded that day was taken away by the appeal tribunal in Preston. Driver Kings' headstone bears the inscription *Smile on my evening hour*, which is the refrain of Charlotte Elliott's celebrated hymn, *The Sabbath day has reached its close*:

And, oh, when life's short course shall end,
And death's dark shades around impend,
My God, my everlasting Friend,
Smile on my evening hour.

The name *Joseph S Blackburn* appears on the Thornton war memorial, alongside that of Thomas Blackburn and those of eighty other men of the town who died in the First World War. Unveiled on 11th November 1923, the replacement for a temporary one put up four years before, the Thornton memorial is a tall, tapered column supporting a bronze sculpture of a bare-headed soldier shown in a mourning pose. The column was created by a local mason, Mr W. L. Cookson, and the sculpture was the work of Albert Tofts, whose similar works adorn other memorials in places such as Oldham, Ipswich, Cardiff, Leamington and Birmingham.

The memorial stands in a neat garden on one of the corners created by the intersecting roads of Four Lane Ends. Part-fringed by tall trees, the garden affords a view at least of the uppermost red sails of Marsh Mill, if not of the whitened mill itself. In the leafless months of the year, and especially around Armistice Day, it can also be seen from the council offices there.

AFTERWARDS

45

The hubbub, he realised, had been kept within the building, and when he heard it, as he approached what he thought must be the chamber, it will have come as a surprise. The staircase was like none he had seen, its uppermost steps peppered with men who seemed to know just what was expected. How could they be so sure? His chest fluttered, which made him more anxious. What was he thinking, coming here like this? He began to count the times he had been above ground floor. There was a clock, saying he was too early, and as he looked for somewhere to wait, a lean man in a long, sombre coat threatened to cross his path.

"After you."

"No, after you." His eyes found the man's. "I insist."

*

I don't think Joseph Blackburn ever met the fourth Marquess of Salisbury or, for that matter, Lord Cavendish or the seventeenth Earl of Derby. They lived somewhere else entirely, in places that were large but still, somehow, managed to remain hidden from view. I don't think Joseph met Sir Algernon Firth either, or James Openshaw or Max Muspratt.

He came from people who shared their given names as if they were farm tools, or noble titles, and lived where what isn't sky is often sea. It is a low-lying, treeless place of handy creeks and usable minerals and it was there that they spent their lives, within sight of the great impermeable windmill close to Four Lane Ends. But Marsh Mill was only one of many that dotted the Fylde and it was in another such land – flat, green and blue and uninterrupted – that Joseph spent almost his last days.

The trades Joseph's relatives followed had not taken them very far. They were old trades, close to the soil, or very new ones on the railways or in chemicals, and they were carried on in Thornton and in the fields and marshes nearby. Not for those people the heat or the famine or the pomp of the Raj, or the rewards or terrors of Abyssinia, Egypt or the Antipodes.

I don't think anyone among the Blackburns or the Bennetts was dined by von Ribbentrop or dubbed anything by *The Times*; did good works among the wretched of the East End; wrote about John Singer Sargent; mustered a thousand men in a single day, or hour; became boxing champion of the Army; patronised Lear or played host to Sheridan; freed the slaves or handsomely compensated their erstwhile owners; married a prince of Lichtenstein or the child of a knight of the stage; or won a Nobel Prize or looked into venereal disease. There may have been times when, leaning on his hoe, Joseph wondered how people got to do all that.

Eventually, Joseph Blackburn would leave his garden and enter the world beyond the Bowland fells, and while he might not have done so willingly, he did so nonetheless. With the people he met there, Joseph at least shared the time of his birth, at the something close to the height of Victorian England. That didn't, however, bring him the benefits it brought to many of them.

The deeds of the people Joseph met are not hard to find. They are celebrated in the nation's theatres and law courts and on the walls of its cathedrals, mess rooms and places of government, and they are certainly celebrated in the nation's libraries. Many of those people wrote tirelessly about their own lives, or the lives of the people they knew or were related to or hoped to impress, or about the subjects that interested them and of which they had made a calling and for which they had gained renown. Not for them the dried-out file served up on the municipal trolley.

The people Joseph Blackburn met beyond the Fylde coast were, it turns out, connected to each other in a myriad of ways. They had strong ties of family and kinship and of education, religion, politics and profession. Many of them were linked by the doctrine of collective responsibility or by a particular elaborate handshake, and they will have had some, perhaps less overt, obligations their other links entailed.

There was, for example, a filigree of commercial links – covering chemicals and the land, but also covering cotton, coffee, rum, rubber, guano, tea and flax – and it is plain that their interests often made those people the masters of lives besides their own. They were also linked by their military careers, which were invariably ones they, like their forebears, had chosen to pursue. In a time of war, in a country well used to fighting it, that is perhaps to be expected. In a judicial setting, however, it makes one wonder whether the interests of the Army were sometimes put before those of men. I think they were certainly put before the interests of justice. These people had something in common with Weeton's duplicitous piping minstrel.

And we can see them sharing with each other not just their titles, decorations, appointments and memberships, but also their clubs and sumptuous homes and their parliamentary candidacies and, inevitably, seats and ultimately their ministerial portfolios. They also shared their judgeships and their membership of the Privy Council, and some even found themselves sharing their debts.

Those people wished, seemed impelled even, to serve their nation and its empire and if they were sometimes given to speechifying, they also knew about government and how it worked at the highest level. They were used to being listened to and, if it should come to that, obeyed, and they had a faith in public administration that was plainly shared with the men who put themselves in the hands of the tribunals rather than simply refuse to fight. As in the time of Abbot Paslew, the momentary rebellions in parts of the north must have come as a profound shock.

Bereavement, too, connected them. None of the members of the Central Tribunal who dealt with Joseph Blackburn's claim appears to have lost a child in the First World War. At least five of the six, however, lost a cousin or nephew. Four children of Lord Salisbury's siblings would be dead by the time the fighting was done and both he and Sir Francis Gore would see another nephew wounded in action. Of those five members, four had already experienced a fatality by the time Joseph's case was heard and Lord Salisbury had also seen his own son invalided home. It would not be surprising if that inexorable toll came to influence the members' approach to their judicial work. The same is true, of course, of members of the Lancashire Appeal Tribunal, including Stephen Walsh, although it did not prevent that tribunal finding in Joseph's favour. The same will also be true of the local tribunal at Four Lane Ends.

Other links are more recondite. Not surprisingly, perhaps, King George V casts a long shadow over the life of Joseph Blackburn. Here, we have encountered the king's long-time aide-de-camp and the official photographer at his coronation; we have encountered his prize-winning biographer and, in Robert Blatchford, the man who turned down the chance to be his tutor; and we have encountered one of the few men to make a portrait of him, the man who painted his consort and two men who will have watched them both lay the foundation stones of New Delhi. We have also encountered at least one of the men whose wedding we know the king attended, and a man after whose health he once stopped his glittering cavalcade to enquire.

A similar shadow is cast by the Earl of Derby, the man under whose brief, underwhelming scheme Joseph attested his willingness to enter military service. The earl had played host to the new king and queen at Knowsley Hall and the splendid performance they watched there had also served to honour his own son. Like other members of the Lancashire tribunal, Lord Derby had been Lord Mayor of Liverpool and the man who managed his estate sat on the part of the tribunal that covered the city itself. And Lord Derby's assistant during part of the Great War was Lord Salisbury's son and heir.

Perhaps the earl's most numerous, if not his strongest, links were with Colonel Wilfred Ashley. The man who helped him found the Comrades of the Great War and commanded one of the battalions he had raised with such expedition sat in Parliament for the constituency in which Joseph Blackburn lived. It was the same constituency the earl's father had represented two decades before and its incumbent would be replaced in a subsequent seat by the earl's own honoured son.

Lord Salisbury, too, figures prominently in this story. It was his speech during the debate on the second Military Service Bill that was interrupted by Lord Derby. The earl would support the marquess on that occasion and their later disagreement, about conscientious objectors, would not be allowed to damage their close personal ties. But Lord Salisbury's connections went further than that. He was related by marriage to his Central Tribunal colleague Sir Francis Gore and also to Lord Richard Cavendish, who combined his judicial role in Westminster with one in Preston. That link cannot, of course, account for the fact that Joseph lost his case at Queen Anne's Gate only after he had won it at County Hall. And there was at least one other such matrimonial link – between Sir John Brunner of the Central Tribunal and Max Muspratt of the appeal tribunal: two men who, in 1917 at least, were surely also commercial rivals.

In both Lancashire and Westminster, the men who considered Joseph Blackburn's case were educated at Harrow or Eton and at Cambridge University or Oxford University. At Queen Anne's Gate, in fact, fully half of them were Oxford men. They included Sir Robert Carlyle and Sir George Talbot.

Sir George's father, furthermore, represented the university in the House of Commons for more than thirty years and he was succeeded by Lord Salisbury's youngest sibling – his brother, Lord Hugh Cecil – who was the sitting member when Joseph's case came up. Lord Hugh, too, was an Oxford man, while of Cambridge men there were Sir John Brunner and Lord Richard Cavendish. The same is true of the inspector sent to quell the rebellion at Four Lane Ends, of the man who spoke for the military at the local tribunal held there and of Joseph Blackburn's own Member of Parliament, Colonel Ashley.

The two tribunals were also joined by political ties. A large number of their members were, or had been, Members of Parliament and the politics that linked them were Conservative – or Unionist or Liberal Unionist – in nature. Occasionally, those politics were Liberal, although it is noticeable that many Liberals became somewhat less so as the years rolled by. And what sometimes connected the tribunal men was an inclination towards Adolf Hitler.

For many of the politicians who sat in the tribunals the year 1906 had marked a watershed in their careers. That was true where they favoured Labour, for it was in the general election held then that the party won its first seats. It was also true of Richard Cavendish, the Liberal who lost his seat to a Conservative, while for other tribunalists, the year would mark the beginning of their time in the House of Commons. They included John Brunner, James O'Grady and Stephen Walsh, but also George Younger and George Barnes, each of whom would hold his seat for the best part of two decades. They also included Colonel Ashley, who would represent one constituency or another well into the 1920s.

Labour politics in fact linked only a minority of the men we have seen here, but they included Stephen Walsh and George Barnes. At that time, both men were also ministers in the coalition government of David Lloyd George – Mr Walsh at the Local Government Board and Mr Barnes at the Ministry of Pensions. The same was true of Lord Derby, who was the Secretary of State for War, and of Lord Robert Cecil, another of Lord Salisbury's brothers, who was a minister in the Foreign Office and Minister of Blockade.

Among men who were considered representatives of labour, it is striking how many fell into disagreement with the movement's official party. Some of them seem to have been opposed to the whole notion of socialism, while for others their apparent left-wing sympathies were combined with fierce patriotism and with energetic support not only for the Great War but also for the cause of military recruiting. Their story is matched outside Parliament by that of Robert Blatchford, Allen Clarke's close friend, who would himself turn decisively rightwards in later years and who, for now, argued fiercely for war and for the cause of conscription.

In the cases of Mr Walsh and Mr Barnes, and also of James O'Grady and Robert Tootill, their patriotism also found expression in close links to the British Workers' League. Those men, whose role was a judicial one and required them to decide whether civilians should be compelled to fight, had subscribed to the notion that, according to the creed of the league, it was *every citizen's duty to defend the life of the State*. Whether in Preston or Westminster, when the sound of the fife came shrilling through the tribunal room, that must have left them precious little room for manoeuvre.

*

Joseph Blackburn, on the other hand, left almost no public trace. He is not to be found in the National Photographic Record and no sombre portrait of him now glowers from the wall of a chamber in some former spinning town. Joseph's thirty-odd years of life were not dignified by the red despatch box, and they are not the subject of fulsome reminiscence in the pages of the Edwardian theatrical press.

Apart from his military service appeal – which was, in any case, conducted at arm's length – I know of only one occasion when Joseph might have intruded upon the elite world of his day. That was in the early summer of 1918, in the encampment at Étaples, where he spent the last days before his return to the Front and Dolly Clare ended her St John's nursing career.

We shouldn't, however, dismiss Joseph's appeal. We cannot know what would have happened to him if he had never made the trip to Four Lane Ends, or if the plain facts of his life had never been bandied about in Preston or at Queen Anne's Gate. But we can be sure that it was the failure of his appeal that made it possible for Joseph to be sent to the Army and so to his death. Paradoxically, and perhaps distastefully, it was Joseph's death that would gain for him the only public commemoration he ever received.

46

What happened that May day in Queen Anne's Gate is far from clear.

I cannot be sure whether, when members of the Central Tribunal considered Joseph Blackburn's case, someone else was present to speak for the military. And if there was someone else, I don't know whether it was Mr Seymour Lloyd or even Captain Dixey, Major Booth or Mr Pym Williamson.

It is tempting to imagine the as yet un-knighted and un-hyphenated temporary lieutenant colonel taking his place before the assembled knights of the realm, whose ranks he would in a matter of weeks join; leafing through documents lately, and confidentially, shared with him; and, with the blinds half-dipped against the central London glare, leaning into the table-talk of Lord Salisbury and his colleagues.

But whether or not a military representative was present, the result of the Westminster hearing is plain for all to see.

In deciding that the size of a patch of land says nothing, necessarily, about the number of men required to cultivate it, and that each case must be decided upon its own facts, the tribunal was simply following a course that had been set already and that has been followed by sensible judicial bodies both before and since. In sending the case to Westminster for that question to be determined, however, the county appeal tribunal was surely itself at fault. The Central Tribunal was never going to commit itself in that regard.

If the case had not reached Queen Anne's Gate, the exemption the Thornton tribunal granted in January 1917 would have remained undisturbed and Joseph Blackburn would have remained at home at least until April. Paradoxically, the appeal that would ultimately send Joseph to his death at first had the effect of postponing his military service for a further two months. What would have happened to him then, without the intervention of Lord Salisbury and his colleagues, we simply cannot know. Given the approach of the local tribunals, however, and certainly of the one at Thornton, it is likely that if Joseph had claimed a third exemption from military service, he would have been given it.

The Preston tribunal can hardly have imagined, however, that when it came to consider Joseph's case, the Westminster one would take into account new information that had not been shown to the man himself. That is the main mischief here.

As a question of fact, it is difficult to believe that a horticultural holding with the characteristics the Thornton tribunal found Joseph's to have, and with the dimensions he said it had, could have been maintained in the way he maintained it if his attention was usually elsewhere.

The Central Tribunal decided, however, that it was in a position to make findings of fact, even though that task was more usually performed by inferior tribunals that had been able to hear oral evidence from live witnesses. The Thornton tribunal had been able to do that in Joseph's case, even if the Preston one had not, yet that did not discourage Lord Salisbury and the rest. In acting as they did, those men not only breached the practice of appellate tribunals through the centuries, and certainly in the present day. They also breached their tribunal's own self-denying ordinance, which had been laid down only a few months before.

What I do know is that the local tribunal believed that a military representative had been present in Queen Anne's Gate and it suspected that what he said persuaded the Central Tribunal to send Joseph Blackburn to the Front. Councillor Dewhurst and his colleagues were so firm in that belief that they were willing to lay their judicial work aside for three months.

It seems that the Central Tribunal had intelligence it could not have gained from the papers sent by Mr Bowman or Sir Harcourt Clare. How else could it have concluded that Joseph spent most of his time hawking his wares; a suggestion that would be treated with something approaching derision at Four Lane Ends? As we shall see, however, it is plain that the intelligence never found its way to Rose Cottage.

The Westminster tribunal also failed in Joseph's case to do what it had done in a large number of other cases, and what it had committed itself to doing wherever necessary. It did not pursue the suggestion that, as a hawker, he was only part-time engaged in his garden. The tribunal might have pursued that suggestion with Joseph himself and, beyond him and through others, it might have done so in Thornton and even at County Hall. It was a suggestion about which the agricultural representative might also have had something useful to say, but although Mr Walsh had recently been restored to health, it seems he did not hear from Mr Gibbon.

Why, in any case, was the time Joseph spent as a hawker not included in the time he was deemed to spend in market gardening? Surely the first activity is a necessary part of the second. If it were otherwise, how would Joseph ever dispose of his produce and gain reward for his labour? The Westminster tribunal concluded that his hawking should not count because it included fruit he had bought and not grown, but how, save from what Joseph himself said at Four Lane Ends, could it have known that? And if the tribunal was aware of the evidence he had given, why did it accept that which related to the time he spent hawking but reject the unequivocal statement, which even a local newspaper reported, that he spent twice as long working his patch?

Even if Joseph was not engaged full-time on the land,

why couldn't he have been required to perform other work of national importance or join the Government Rejects as the price of remaining exempt from military service? That was an indulgence the Central Tribunal had afforded other men, including those working in market gardens, and there is nothing in the tribunal's brief reasons to explain why it could not have been afforded to Joseph. In the more demanding jurisprudential environment of the present day, that is a defect that would be considered fatal. Lord Salisbury's decision, let's make no bones about it, would itself have been set aside.

It is striking, and also frustrating, that many men were granted similar indulgences and that even where they followed a very different calling, they were sometimes exempted from service on condition that they spent at least some time on the land. We do not know how much time Joseph Blackburn spent in his market garden; that was an issue upon which the different tribunals reached very different conclusions. Whatever the time, however, it was surely more than a hairdresser, a cab proprietor or a mason could spare as a condition of his being allowed to remain at home.

On occasions, Lord Salisbury was heard to deplore the taking of men from the land and the lies by which that end might have been achieved. On other occasions, in common, at the time of their wedding, with his own son and daughter-in-law – and also in common with Sir Harcourt Clare – he said things that suggested he favoured the periphery over the centre. For all that, however, those were for him purely abstract concerns. They were not ones upon which Lord Salisbury chose to act, even when he was given what now seems the perfect opportunity to do so.

47

I would find it hard to say what sort of a book this is. It certainly isn't a biography: it says far too little about Joseph Blackburn, its nominal subject, for that.

Save for his dimensions, I know nothing about how Joseph looked. I don't know the colour of his hair, if he had hair, and though I might suspect as much of a man approaching his middle years at the end of the Edwardian age, I don't know that he had a moustache. In official England, moustaches – whether the 'paintbrush' favoured by Lord Salisbury, the 'soup-strainer' of Sir Algernon Firth and Lord Derby or the striking 'handlebar' worn by Sir John Brunner – were almost de rigueur. More or less the only men here without a moustache were Sir Robert Carlyle and Sir Harcourt Clare.

Neither do I know what Rose Cottage, now gone, looked like. Was Joseph's entire world contained there or did he, on occasions, raise his eyes beyond Raikes Road? Was Marsh Mill the only one he knew or had he seen the big white tower at Little Marton that would later be dedicated to Allen Clarke? Had Joseph, perhaps by bicycle, ever ventured out to salt-rich Preesall or the rummy, certainly haunted creek at Skippool, from where his grandparents came? Had he ever, before he was dragooned into doing so, crossed the Ribble or the Lune or even the Wyre?

I imagine flowers in the cottage and I can't resist seeing some cheerful Staffordshire pottery as well, but was there anything to read there apart from seed catalogues? (Do I offend his memory by even asking the question?) Did Joseph take *Teddy Ashton's Northern Weekly* and, a man of the land, was he aware of *The Effects of the Factory System*, to say nothing of the generous, freeing works of Edward Carpenter?

And that, sadly, is only the beginning of my ignorance. I cannot tell how Joseph lived his life in Thornton; whether, for example, he drank in the Gardeners' Arms or the Bay Horse or visited the avowedly abstinent Rechabites in their prospect tent every fourth Monday. I know, from the forms he filled in, that Joseph was C of E, but whether he was a regular at Christ Church I cannot say. And if he ever took music lessons, I don't know whether they were given by Miss Tonge or Miss Park, LLCM.

My ignorance of Joseph extends to his beliefs. I don't know whether he was to be seen in the premises of the Co-operative Society or the habitation of the Primrose League, whether he voted for or against Colonel Wilfred Ashley in the general elections of 1910 and whether he favoured Mr Balfour or Mr Asquith or, indeed, the Labour party that had briefly been led by George Barnes. He might even have been a Liberal Unionist and so – curiously, uncomfortably – aligned with the Cecils.

I don't in fact know whether Joseph Blackburn had any politics at all, or whether he was even given the opportunity to vote. He had been too young for the general election of 1906 and it is possible that he was still ineligible four years later. Although the franchise was by then enjoyed by men over twenty-one, that was only where they held land or paid rent to the value of £10. Was Joseph such a man? Did he have any part in choosing those who would send others to war?

Even after the franchise was extended, forty per cent of adult males were still without the vote. That remained the case until December 1918, when the property qualification was abolished, and by then, Joseph was dead. His wife, Jessie, a woman who had reached her thirtieth birthday, will have been able to vote for the first time in the general election held then. But whether she did so, and if so for whom, I simply do not know.

This book, then, contains nothing but a skein of Joseph Blackburn and it says more about the men, and occasionally women, he encountered. Any shape I have given him is formed by the edges of the people surrounding him and, in my reading, his life is characterised by the events that came at its end.

*

Neither is this a military history of any kind.

The book mentions some of the events of the First World War, of course, and it rehearses the doings – and the heroism and the loss – of a number of combatants, both more and less celebrated. There is also the usual talk of service battalions and trench fever, of the tank that was royally put through its paces outside Hatfield House and of General John French and the BEF and the equestrian Colonel Dawson. And there is the familiar tenebrous litany of places where men had no choice but to give up the ghost – Sorrel Wood, Ypres, the Menin Road.

But none of those things is explored here at any length and none is properly explained. I might lack the knowledge or the energy for that task and I certainly lack the inclination. I have no desire to press men into serving my story as if they were unsuspecting farmhands in the back room of the Eagle and Child. Every man here had another and a better life to live, both before and beyond the Colours.

Those things, furthermore, did not constitute Joseph Blackburn. He wasn't the khaki armband he was given to wear just in case someone felt like forcing a white feather into his hand, nor was he regimental number 204824 or 20378. He wasn't the mud and fog of the Western Front, nor even the sunlight and fruit of the Veneto. He wasn't Bray-Dunes or Téteghem or the military hospitals at Genoa and Marseille. He wasn't the severely depleted trench strength of the 10th Battalion of the Royal West Kents and he certainly wasn't the 2s 9d paid to him in Poulton on that sodden day during one of the worst winters in history.

Joseph was not the Final Advance in Picardy, though he

gave everything he had in that cause. I won't permit him to be that, nor the Battle of Caporetto, the Kaiserschlacht or the Spring Offensive. Joseph was none of those things. I know next to nothing about him, but I know that much. And his life wasn't someone else's to give away.

What Joseph was is easy to state. I might not be able to summon an image of his face, but I know that he was Rose Cottage and Raikes Road. He was the flat, sandy plain of the Fylde coast, the salt on the breeze and the sharp eastwards bend in the Wyre. Most of all, Joseph Blackburn was a man, his own man, and a husband and father. He was a son, a brother and a cousin, an uncle and a nephew and a grandson. Joseph was Jessie and Thomas Junior and little Elizabeth; he was his parents, Thomas Blackburn and Elizabeth Bailey; and he was his grandparents, John Blackburn and Mary Anne Walmsley and John Bailey and Mary Hull. They loved him who knew him well. Private Joseph Blackburn was only to those that didn't know him.

*

Nor is this a warrior's tale. Aside from his two campaign medals, which many men were given, Joseph gained no battle honours. Neither did he conscientiously, and gallantly, object to service or find himself blindfolded on some desolate market cross in the grey light of dawn. He resembles none of our burnished archetypes.

Even if he did so reluctantly, Joseph Blackburn did finally go to the Colours and in his end, at least, he achieved the dignity that, while certainly his due, is also and rightly accorded to many thousands of his generation. In his military service, too, Joseph was unremarkable.

Joseph Blackburn does, however, deserve to be called a soldier just as much as any other man who has taken up arms. What he endured on the Somme, in the base hospitals and in the brutal forcing-ground of Étaples ensures that. Above all, his end – in heat, dust and confusion in the dog days of summer – ensures that. But the few facts we know about him tell us plainly that in 1915, and in 1916 and 1917 as well, Joseph wished neither to be part of the British Army nor to go to war.

*

So, is this book a legal history? It is full of claims, of course, and of men being expected to act judicially, or at least quasi-judicially, and it has its fair share of hearings and submissions and of representatives – especially military representatives – vowing to go to appeal. Yet the book cites almost no Acts of Parliament, nor other legislation, and the provisions and decisions that are mentioned are quickly left behind. More or less the only law cited here is what applied in Joseph Blackburn's case, but as we have seen, it was the facts of the case that made the difference to him.

Here, there is no slowly evolving jurisprudence and we see no venerable principles being developed case by painstaking case. The only pattern visible – aside from the dense, sickening one of too-young death – is formed by the strikes the local tribunals embarked upon but then abandoned. There is little in the work of those tribunals or their superiors to suggest that the judicial understanding of the Military Service Acts ever progressed very far.

That said, the book might not be without its value. It seeks to describe a particular legal process and to explain how that process was brought to bear in a particular case. It is there that any claim to legal history will have to rest. For all that the process occupied a number of busy men day in, day out for more than three years, it is now as good as lost.

This book shows that ultimately, Joseph Blackburn's life was shaped by the law and those who were supposed to apply it just as much as by high politics and the military. It was Lord Salisbury, and not just Lord Derby, who sent Joseph to war.

48

Was there, in the work done at Queen Anne's Gate, anything to resemble work done today?

We no longer find it necessary to decide whether civilians should be forced to go to war, military demands being satisfied by the numbers of young men, and women, who are seemingly spoiling for a fight. There is, however, much for modern-day tribunals to do and those tribunals have never been so numerous. There are dozens of them, all arranged into neat 'chambers', and they adjudicate upon such things as employment disputes, tax and property matters and entitlement to welfare benefits.

As the term suggests, judicial tribunals are presided over by judges. Those judges must be lawyers and they must possess knowledge not just of the law they apply, but of the world in which their decisions will have to take hold. Lord Salisbury, and Lord Sydenham before him and Viscount Hambleden afterwards, did not meet the first condition and it is questionable whether they or their colleagues ever met the second.

Many modern tribunals also include lay members and those members are often in the majority. But if a tribunal's non-lawyers are often highly qualified professionals in their own right – medical doctors, for example, or social workers or accountants – some are still drawn from the ranks of the great and good. Often, important decisions – about disability support or psychiatric detention or educational provision – continue to be made by people similar to those who sat in judgement of Joseph Blackburn. Though maybe not as great as the one that separated Joseph from the fourth Marquess of Salisbury, the gulf between members and appellants in modern-day tribunals can still be impossibly large.

For the most part, tribunals now have more time to consider their cases than was available to military service tribunals a century ago. But that time is by no means luxurious and hearings about rent support or benefits sanctions can still be allocated as little as twenty minutes. Although Joseph's claim had only a quarter of that time at Four Lane Ends, it probably had rather fuller consideration at Queen Anne's Gate. It is unlikely, however, that the case ever received more than twenty minutes at a single session or that it occupied the time of all three tribunals, including the county appeal tribunal, for as much as an hour. Given what was at stake in Thornton, Preston and Westminster – nothing less than whether a man should have to put himself in harm's way – that is regrettable.

In fact, the work of judicial tribunals is still done hurriedly and, too often, in a perfunctory manner. Now, as before, the tribunals can make their decisions on the basis of evidence that is incomplete and of questioning that is superficial, unfocused and shot through with poorly disguised bias.

In many modern tribunals, legal representation is rare and becoming rarer. In that, those tribunals closely resemble their equivalents of a century ago and they all too often fall into the same solicitous attitude towards the few appellants who do come with lawyers that the Central Tribunal displayed in its dealings with Mr Martin.

The possibilities of appeal were as great under the Military Service Acts as they are now. In each case, an error at the first stage might be corrected on appeal and an error at that second stage might be corrected at a third. In theory, at least, there should now be less chance of an error being made at any of those stages and, for disappointed appellants, a greater chance of success at the last two. As the Upper Tribunal continues to demonstrate, however, the enlargement of administrative law and the growth of a professionalised tribunals judiciary have done little to reduce the appetite of appellate judges for wearisome self-indulgence.

In one key respect, however, the judicial tribunals of the modern day differ considerably from their counterparts at the beginning of the last century – they must explain themselves far more thoroughly than the Central Tribunal did, and was able to get away with doing, in the case of Joseph Blackburn.

*

I cannot say that it was Joseph's humble background that caused his case to be dismissed.

The Westminster tribunal, and also the appeal tribunal in Preston, included as members men with equally humble backgrounds. They were weavers, cabinetmakers, blast furnace men and miners. Or rather, they had been those things. By the time the men came to sit on military service appeals, their circumstances were a good deal less humble. The men had risen to positions of influence and the war work for which they were now selected confirmed that they were considered part of the elite.

Those men were, in any case, in a minority. For the most part, military service tribunals – certainly beyond the local level – were composed of the usual representatives of landed interests, of manufacturing industry, of the professions and, in so far as it is a discrete group, of conservative politics. In Queen Anne's Gate, it was those men, and not a single one-time weaver or miner, who dealt with Joseph Blackburn's case.

But that isn't a sufficient explanation for the decision that sent Joseph to war.

We have here seen a number of the men of the Central Tribunal act thoughtfully and generously and we know that they often came trailing the very finest of good works. It was largely thanks to Viscount Hambleden, for example, that

King's College Hospital was built, and his colleague, Sir Robert Carlyle, was lauded for his efforts in a time of great famine. Lord Salisbury demonstrated, in May 1916 at least, that he was keen to protect men from being deceived into becoming soldiers, while Sir Algernon Firth gave up a house to the wounded of the war, erected an impressive memorial, endowed a pathology institute and built not one, but two model communities. John Brunner was concerned for the lot of blind piano tuners and he was the inheritor of an impressive family tradition of capitalistic philanthropy; one that had seen public buildings put up across Cheshire, professors appointed in Liverpool and a handsome bridge erected not just across the Mersey but across the Manchester Ship Canal too. More broadly, it is intriguing that in the Ribble Valley, a little archipelago of asylums grew up where Sir James Travis-Clegg had made his home.

In any case, and whatever the background of its members, the Central Tribunal found itself dealing with many men whose backgrounds were at least as humble as those of Joseph Blackburn and it did not seem concerned that some of those men, at least, would be kept out of the war. I cannot discern in the work of the tribunal any hint of actual bias.

That said, it was not beyond the Westminster men to act in what, to modern eyes at least, is a startlingly harsh manner. On at least three occasions, for example – on successive days in October 1917 and again the following May – the tribunal adjourned proceedings so that a particular course could be taken to free a man for military service. That course was to have the man's relative – his father, his wife or his brother – admitted to an asylum. There is nothing in any of the cases to suggest that inpatient care is truly what was required, and had it not been for the perceived demands of the war, it is likely that the men's relatives would have continued to be cared for where they were loved and known. One of the men came from Lancashire and another worked the land on his own account, while two of the decisions were made by Sir John Brunner and the other was made by Sir Algernon Firth and Sir Robert Carlyle.

*

At its highest, then, and whatever the composition of the Central Tribunal or the sometime harshness of its actions, my claim is simply this: Joseph Blackburn was a man of whom too little account was taken. At moments that seem significant, and at the hands of the more celebrated, the better favoured or the simply more assertive, men like him are apt to be overlooked and their interests to be too lightly set aside. I suspect that was often so during wartime and I have seen for myself that it was so in this case.

I know that isn't a grand conclusion, but I am satisfied it is one I can reach on the evidence available.

That might not, however, be a bad thing, for an unremarkable outcome is surely consistent with the rest of this book and with what I have said about the man who is the book's subject.

Even though my conclusion isn't grand, I am satisfied that it is warranted. The tribunal might have treated some humble men well, but in denying Joseph Blackburn knowledge of what had been said about him, it treated him very badly indeed. The result, however indirectly, was that Joseph lost the only life he had, and that was not an unremarkable thing.

Joseph's case stands in marked contrast to that of Mr Martin. The Westminster tribunal was never more solicitous of a claimant's welfare, and of his good opinion, than when it was confronted by a professional man and the lawyers he had himself engaged. That said, in its dealings with the solicitor from East Suffolk, the tribunal did no more than adhere to rules it had set for itself. It was in its treatment of Joseph Blackburn that the tribunal broke those rules.

Joseph's appearances in the book are few and brief, but

they are not without their colour or their consequences. There might be rather more about business at Four Lane Ends and in Queen Anne's Gate – about exemptions granted and withheld and about war cemeteries and decorous portraits – but Joseph Blackburn, what he wanted and was made to endure, is still the core of the tale told here. For all their apparent triviality, we cannot lose sight of the windmills, or the bicycle trips, or the glass coffin or, even as we remember the Cauliflowers, of the cabbages.

Maybe, therefore, this book is about Joseph Blackburn after all. Maybe the deeds and misdeeds of the great and good are of much less importance. Maybe the book doesn't need to be a calling to account; maybe it's just an account, plain and simple.

49

There followed the wretched bureaucracy of official death. In time, Joseph's wife, Jessie, would receive at Rose Cottage a number of buff-coloured envelopes, containing, for example, details of the weekly pension she, and Elizabeth and young Joseph, would be paid.

In time, too, Jessie Blackburn would be sent the medals awarded to Joseph after his death – the British War Medal and the Victory Medal. Both are common. The first was given to all officers and men of the British and Empire forces who served for at least twenty-eight days during the Great War or who had died during active service, while the second was received by all those who had entered a theatre of war. Colloquially, and perhaps unkindly, the medals were together known as the 'Mutt and Jeff pair', after two popular, if risible, American cartoon characters of the period.

Jessie would also in time receive the bronze memorial plaque, sometimes called the 'Dead Man's Penny', that was issued to the next of kin of all British and Empire service personnel who died as a consequence of the war. It will have come with a commemorative scroll, sent in the name of King George V.

One of the first packages Jessie Blackburn received was from No. 2 Infantry Records Office on Staines Road in Hounslow, Middlesex. The package was sent out on 29th January 1919 and its receipt acknowledged two days later. It contained some of Joseph's personal effects, which were listed as follows:

2 wallets
1 big case

1 big holder
1 Cap Badge
Small flag
Notebook

According to the businesslike, perhaps curt note sent with it, the package also contained *Mirror (Broken)* and also *Photos* and, lastly, *Lock of hair.*

50

The records that survive from Queen Anne's Gate contain the following brief, typewritten memorandum, inserted into the papers at what must have seemed an appropriate place:

> *The Central Tribunal decided on 12 September 1917 that if at any stage a new fact is alleged by one side so material that it would probably affect their decision of the case, the other side should be given an opportunity of answering the allegation.*

The memorandum fills the top half of a single sheet of paper. It bears no date of its own and no other marking that would even hint at its author or its purpose. The meeting it mentions took place around six weeks after the Thornton tribunal wrote to the Westminster one, protesting about the handling of Joseph Blackburn's case.

The minutes tell us nothing about the way the Thornton letter was received in Westminster. We have seen, however, that in the weeks and months that followed, the Central Tribunal emphatically changed its approach, especially in relation to allegations made by military representatives. The September memorandum reveals that the change was the result of a positive decision, and there is no other case than Joseph's to explain why that decision was made.

The day mentioned in the memorandum – Wednesday 12th September 1917 – is the one after the case of Mr Tulloch was considered in Queen Anne's Gate. It was in that case, of course, that the Central Tribunal decided to refer a military representative's additional comments to the man concerned. The tribunal did so then for the first time since the Thornton tribunal gave notice of its strike.

The members of the Central Tribunal who came together in Westminster that day included Lord Richard Cavendish and Sir Osmond Williams. They were joined by Lord Salisbury, Sir John Brunner, Sir Algernon Firth, Sir Francis Gore and Mr Talbot, who were five sixths of the panel that had considered Joseph Blackburn's case. (Only Sir Robert Carlyle was missing.)

I am satisfied that the memorandum which followed the hearing of Joseph's case was written because of what had happened in the interim – at Four Lane Ends, in Thornton on the Fylde coast.

*

There is, I suppose, something noble in recognising and acknowledging an error one has made, and the September memorandum of the Central Tribunal should be looked upon in that light. It is, rather, in their response to that error that the entitled, doubtless diligent men in Queen Anne's Gate came up short.

Having drafted their memorandum, those men appear neither to have recognised its implications nor to have attempted to undo what they had done.

The Great War slouched towards its final year, Lord Salisbury was succeeded by Lord Hambleden and Sir Harcourt Clare saw his impressive portrait unveiled in County Hall. Joseph Blackburn, meanwhile, began his last inexorable journey, away from and then back to the hell of the Western Front, finally disappearing from public view in the sand dunes, near the sea.

Despite all of that, however, despite the significant error that had been made in his case, no official voice was ever raised again and no one, certainly, was heard to call Joseph home.

Sources

The prologue is taken from a report in the *Blackpool Herald* on 29th June 1917, as is the transcript of the session at which the Thornton tribunal decided to strike. Captain Dixey's "pettish" comments also come from that newspaper, on 10th July 1917, as do the extracts from the tribunal's first decision about Joseph Blackburn, on 12th January 1917. The discussion of the 'allotment question', meanwhile, appeared in the *Blackpool Gazette & News* the same day and the resumption of the tribunal's activities was reported in the *Blackpool and Fylde Observer* on 18th August 1917.

Details of the lives of Joseph Blackburn and members of his family are taken from census returns and from birth, marriage and death records available at the General Register Office. Joseph's military service records, meanwhile, may be found in The National Archives (Microfilm Publication WO363/20378 and /204824), as may the records of his nephew, Robert Blackburn, and of Thomas Hume Dunlop (/4812 and /36374 respectively).

The minute book and letter book of the Thornton tribunal are kept at the Lancashire Archives in Preston and extracts from them are published here by permission of Lancashire County Council. The session at which Joseph received his first exemption may be found at UDTh 2/12/25-27 and the one at which he received his second exemption at /48-51. The tribunal's letter of protest, meanwhile, may be found at UDTh 3/23/293 and 294. The records of the Clayton-le-Moors local tribunal are also kept in Preston (UDCL 53/1/1 et seq.), as are the remnants of the Lancashire Appeal Tribunal (TA/1).

The minutes of the Central Tribunal are also held at The National Archives in Kew. The session at which the tribunal considered Joseph's case may be found at MH 47/2/1 (on the thirty-eighth page) and the September memorandum is at MH 47/2/2. The tribunal's decision as to its procedure, meanwhile, is at MH/47/1/1.

The Great War diary of the 6th Battalion of the Royal West Kent Regiment is kept at the Kent History and Library Centre in Maidstone (reference WKR/B6/A1); while what happened to the men of that regiment may be read in its official history (Captain C. T. Atkinson, 1924, *The Queen's Own Royal West Kent Regiment 1914–1919*, The Naval & Military Press – see, in particular, Chapters 22, 25 and 27).

The letters of the fourth Lord Salisbury are held at Hatfield House. Those concerning his attempts to find work are at s(4) 77/11, /32, /41, /42 and /44, and his correspondence with Lord Derby about conscientious objectors is at 77/122, /146 and /179, at 78/148 and 78/149 and at 80/109b. The letter from Lady Barlow is at 77/90, the one from Virgil Boys at /92 and the one about Bobbety's wedding at 76/123. The letters are quoted with the permission of the Marquess of Salisbury.

What the marquess said in Parliament on 22nd May 1916 may be found in Hansard (HL Deb 22nd May 1916, vol. 22, cc6-68) and Mr Brunner's question about blind piano tuners is also there (HC Deb 13th March 1917, vol. 91, col 901-2).

In so far as it might be relevant, publication of the public sector information referred to here is licensed under Open Government Licence v2.0.

Information about William Elias' inquiry in Salford comes from editions of the *Manchester Evening News* for 17th, 18th and 26th June 1914. His interventions into the debates about the detention of children, about hospital accommodation for sick children and about the compulsory bathing of workhouse inmates were reported in the *Liverpool Echo* of 5th November

1915, the *Manchester Evening News* of 18th June 1914 and the *Rochdale Observer* of 16th May 1914 respectively. Mr Elias' culinary advice, meanwhile, can be found in the *Burnley News* of 12th January 1916, the *Yorkshire Post* of 26th January that year and the *Liverpool Echo* of 23rd March 1917. And further reports of the man's doings may be found in the *Burnley News* of 24th October 1914, the *Lancashire Daily Post* of 9th October 1917 and the *Rochdale Observer* of 15th August 1914, 27th May 1916 and 13th January 1917.

Sir Harcourt Clare's gracious speech was reported in the *Lancashire Daily Post* of 11th October 1917 and Viscount Hambleden's lovely bath tap is in the collection of the Victoria and Albert Museum (CIRC 191 to N-1963).

The work of the local tribunals has been considered in some detail by James McDermott in his *British Military Service Tribunals 1916–1918* (2011, Manchester University Press), while the lot of conscientious objectors is the subject of *We Will Not Fight...* by Will Ellsworth-Jones (2008, Aurum Press) and of *Blindfold and Alone* by Cathryn Corns and John Hughes-Wilson (2005, Cassell).